MLA Handbook for Writers of Research Papers

Fifth Edition

Joseph Gibaldi

THE MODERN LANGUAGE ASSOCIATION
OF AMERICA
New York   1999

The Modern Language Association publishes two books on its documentation style: the *MLA Handbook for Writers of Research Papers* (for high school and undergraduate students) and the *MLA Style Manual and Guide to Scholarly Publishing* (for graduate students, scholars, and professional writers). These volumes provide the most accurate and complete instructions on MLA style. If updates of the information in this handbook become necessary, they will be posted at the MLA's Web site (www.mla.org).

For information about obtaining permission to reprint material from
MLA book publications, send your request by mail (see address below),
e-mail (permissions@mla.org), or fax (646 458-0030).

Library of Congress Cataloging-in-Publication Data

Gibaldi, Joseph, 1942–
    MLA handbook for writers of research papers / Joseph Gibaldi. — 5th ed.
        p.   cm.
    Includes bibliographical references and index.
    ISBN 0-87352-975-8 (paper)
    1. Report writing—Handbooks, manuals, etc.   2. Research—Handbooks,
manuals, etc.   I. Modern Language Association of America.   II. Title.
LB2369.G53   1999
808'.027—dc21   99-18319

Fifth printing 2002

Book design by Charlotte Staub. Set in Melior and Prestige Elite. Printed on
recycled, acid-free paper

Published by The Modern Language Association of America
26 Broadway, New York, New York 10004-1789
www.mla.org

Contents

Foreword

The *MLA Handbook for Writers of Research Papers* is designed to introduce you to the customs of a community of writers who greatly value scrupulous scholarship and the careful documentation, or recording, of research. Read from beginning to end, the *MLA Handbook* provides a comprehensive picture of how research papers are created. Once you are familiar with the contents, you can use the book as a reference tool. Chapter 1 suggests some of the educational and intellectual purposes of research and describes the first steps in a scholarly project: choosing a topic; using a library and the Internet; evaluating electronic sources; producing a working bibliography, notes, outlines, and drafts; and avoiding plagiarism. Chapter 2 gives practical advice on such matters as spelling, punctuation, and the presentation of names, numbers, titles of works, and quotations. This chapter is meant to help you craft writing that is clear, consistent, and stylistically authoritative. Chapter 3 gives guidelines on the physical format of the paper. The next two chapters cover the MLA's system, or style, of documenting print and electronic sources: chapter 4 explains how to list sources at the end of a paper, while chapter 5 shows how to cite them in the text of a paper. Chapter 6 describes abbreviations that are useful in documentation and in certain other contexts. Appendix A lists notable reference works in specialized fields; appendix B presents some systems of documentation other than the MLA's. Finally, there are sample pages of a research paper that illustrate MLA style.

Learning the rules the *MLA Handbook* outlines will help you become a writer whose work deserves serious consideration. Similarly, your study of these rules can make you a more discerning reader: knowing how an author is supposed to use sources is essential to judging a text's reliability.

If you are consulting this book for the first time, you may be surprised by its focus on the details of preparing a piece of writing. This concern with details grows out of a respect for the responsibilities writers have to readers—and to other writers. The general practices the *MLA Handbook* describes are followed by writers of studies and reports that serve the needs of many different readers, in government, business, industry, the professions, the academy, and the media.

Because research has the power to affect opinions and actions, responsible writers compose their work with great care. They specify when they refer to another author's ideas, facts, and words, whether they want to agree with, object to, analyze, or interpret the source. This kind of documentation tends to discourage the circulation of error, by inviting readers to determine for themselves whether a reference to another text presents a reasonable account of what that text says.

The *MLA Handbook* was developed by the Modern Language Association of America (MLA), an organization of teachers and scholars founded in 1883, when the modern languages were just beginning to gain a place in the college curriculum alongside the classical languages—ancient Greek and Latin. The MLA now has over thirty thousand members and supports a variety of publications and activities designed to strengthen teaching and scholarship in languages and literature. One of the association's best-known publications, the *MLA Handbook* has been widely used by generations of students at colleges and universities throughout the United States and in other countries. The documentation style the book outlines is preferred by a substantial majority of scholarly journals in languages and literature.

The *MLA Handbook* originated nearly fifty years ago. Convinced that commonly agreed-on rules for documenting quotations, facts, opinions, and paraphrases would simplify the task of preparing a manuscript for publication, William Riley Parker, the MLA executive director, compiled and published the "MLA Style Sheet" in 1951 in the association's journal, *PMLA*. The "Style Sheet" gained almost immediate acceptance among MLA members and scholarly publishers both because Parker codified uniform practices among journal editors and university presses and because he encouraged consensus on matters about which there was less agreement. The "Style Sheet" continued to respond to the changing needs of scholars, editors, and publishers and, in time, also addressed the needs of undergraduate students, becoming in 1977 the *MLA Handbook for Writers of Research Papers*. Over the years Walter S. Achtert, John Hurt Fisher, and Joseph Gibaldi contributed to the publication.

The second edition of the *MLA Handbook*, which appeared in 1984, introduced the current simplified set of rules for documentation that allow citations to be placed in the text within parentheses. Although the third edition, produced in 1988, covered some aspects of electronic publication, its treatment of these developments was quickly outdated. The fourth edition suffered a similar fate. Updated in 1995 before the World Wide Web came into broad use, it too required revision only a few years after it appeared. The book you hold, the fifth edition, not only encompasses recent technological changes but also includes guidelines for doing research on the Internet and for evaluating the reliability of Web sites.

You happen to be learning the ways of writers, scholars, libraries, and publishers at a time when preserving the vital legacy of print presents a growing challenge. Librarians and scholars are particularly concerned about preserving the "brittle" books and other documents published or written on the inexpensive acidic paper that began to be used in the mid–nineteenth century. If you have ever tried to save newspaper articles or if you enjoy browsing in secondhand bookstores, you have probably noticed how paper yellows and crumbles with age. Unless steps are taken to preserve the paper of books and periodicals or to reproduce their contents, these documents will be lost forever.

Large-scale photographing of brittle materials has been under way for some time, and the future study of them will be possible primarily through the use of photographs or electronic formats derived from photographs. Resources are insufficient, however, to guarantee the survival of all materials published or written on acidic paper from 1850 to the present, and many documents will disappear before your generation can consult them.

Preserving electronic records also presents problems. Recently librarians, scholars, foundation executives, heads of government agencies, and members of Congress have begun to grapple with the difficulties associated with preserving electronic communications and publications. You may have had the common experience of trying to retrieve a stored electronic document only to discover that it was unreadable because of changes in your computer hardware or software or because the disk containing the document was damaged. On a vastly greater scale, the same obstacles confront the effort to maintain the diverse electronic records a literate society produces and consults each day. The magnitude of this task, like that of preserving the print legacy, raises major financial, logistic, and public policy questions and may exceed the resources currently available for the work.

Adapting scholarly practices to electronic media is another historic challenge facing writers, publishers, scholars, and librarians as our society moves from a six-hundred-year-old print era to an electronic era. One important question debated by the members of the two MLA committees that oversaw the creation of the fourth and fifth editions of the handbook concerns how much information readers need in a citation of an electronic work to be able to find the source. A reader who wishes to locate a book can take a few pieces of information—such as the author's name and the title—to a library or bookstore in this country and in many others and readily determine whether the volume is available. Publication practices, copyright laws, and the organization of libraries provide an infrastructure that makes locating print publications a relatively simple matter. Consequently, references to print sources can be brief. Because no comparable infrastructure yet exists for electronic publications, citations of them must provide more information than references to print sources normally contain.

A second question the two MLA committees discussed concerns the ease with which electronic communications and texts can be changed. This feature of electronic texts is an important strength of the new technology, but it poses problems for the documentation of research. By the time a reader tries to locate an electronic text referred to by an author, the text may have changed and the cited version may no longer exist or may be difficult to find. Sometimes the changes are planned and meant to enhance the publication. Consider, for example, the *MLA International Bibliography*. The association issues this reference work in print, as a CD-ROM, and online. The print volume is published annually, and each installment stands as a permanent record of the books and articles identified when it went to press. The CD-ROM version, however, is updated four times a year, and so the listings change quarterly; the online version is updated even more frequently—ten times a year. (Updating includes adding new entries and correcting errors in existing items.) Therefore, a student who consults an electronic version of the bibliography at different times in the year can end up with different lists of sources for a research assignment.

Regular additions to an electronic database do not pose a substantial problem as long as the user of the database understands that it will change. Greater problems arise from alterations that a writer or a reader cannot anticipate. An electronic document may be modified unpredictably, by its author or other interested parties.

The MLA committees that oversaw the creation of the fourth and fifth editions debated the value of ensuring that readers can get back to the texts a writer read and cited. Some committee members assumed that electronic documents would not—and need not—remain stable. Why, these specialists asked, shouldn't an improved version of a text be substituted for an earlier version whenever improvements are recognized? The other members of the committee replied, Who would determine what constitutes an improvement, and how could readers assess the effects of a change on the substance or wording of a text? After considerable discussion, committee members agreed that electronic texts will and probably should change but that readers must be able to get back to the original texts (or "archival copies") a writer consulted and cited. Ways must be found to archive electronic texts reliably at specific times in their history. A minimal standard is for electronic documents to be dated. In electronic research as in print research, only the ability of readers to verify an author's use of a source can discourage the circulation of error. How this important goal will be achieved remains to be seen.

The fifth edition of the *MLA Handbook* covers the new media while continuing to supply authoritative guidelines on traditional publications. As you will see, the rules for citing electronic material that the MLA committees established are not presented as definitive, and they will surely change as the technology and practices governing electronic communication evolve.

Because the MLA is a membership association, all its projects are communal efforts. The collaborative work on the *MLA Handbook* is particularly far-reaching; the various editions have benefited for over forty years from the contributions of MLA committees and staff members, editors, scholars, librarians, teachers, and students. Overseeing the development of this edition were the members of two *MLA Handbook* committees: Wayne C. Booth, Marshall J. Brown, Wendy Chun, Anne Ruggles Gere, Joel D. Goldfield, James L. Harner, Susan Kallenbach, John W. Kronik, Ian Lancashire, and Cynthia L. Selfe. They brought to their work wisdom and experience, a respect for old and new technologies, and a strong commitment to the students who will use this book. The views of the members of the MLA Committee on Computers and Emerging Technologies in Teaching and Research also helped shape the revision.

A number of MLA staff members aided in the planning, writing, and design of this edition of the handbook. Joseph Gibaldi, director of book acquisitions and development, did the lion's share of the revision, working with Martha Noel Evans, director of the MLA book publication program. Members of the MLA editorial department, headed by Judy Goulding, made several specific contributions. Elizabeth Holland enlarged and improved the section on punctuation for the fourth edition, Eric Wirth was the principal copyeditor, and Judith Altreuter coordinated the book's design.

Of central importance in the development of the section on library research were the following librarians, who generously supplied information about resources and services in college and university libraries: Mary Beth Aust-Keefer, Paul Burnham, William Calhoon, Nancy Carter, Paul Doty, Kathryn Franco, Ellen Gilbert, Francisca Goldsmith, Susan Hockey, Robert Hohl, Kay Klayman, Naomi Lederer, Rosemary Little, Mary Sue Livingston, S. David Mash, Carol McAllister, James McPhee, Jill Miller, Elaine Misko, Ann Okerson, Val Ontell, Rona Ostrow, Catherine Palmer, Sarah Philips, John Price-Wilkins, Sharon Propas, Anne Marie Secord, Linda Sharp, Victoria Swinney, Susan Szasz, Linda TerHaar, Virginia Tiefel, Alan Wallace, Helene Williams, and James Wyatt.

The MLA also owes special thanks to library staff members at Fairleigh Dickinson University, Florham-Madison; the University of Findlay; Kean College; the New York Public Library; New York University; the University of North Carolina, Chapel Hill; Northern Illinois University; and Union County College. Finally, I acknowledge the contributions of the many teachers who have assigned the *MLA Handbook* to students and who sent suggestions for improvements that we incorporated in this edition.

As you learn to guide your research by the rules outlined in the *MLA Handbook*, you will take your place in a community of writers who are sure to influence the development of new rules. In time, you too may identify ways of improving future editions of this book.

Phyllis Franklin
Executive Director
Modern Language Association

1 Research and Writing

1.1. THE RESEARCH PAPER AS A FORM OF EXPLORATION

During your school career you have probably written many personal essays that presented your thoughts, feelings, and opinions and that did not refer to any other source of information or ideas. Some subjects and assignments, however, require us to go beyond our personal knowledge and experience. We undertake research when we wish to explore an idea, probe an issue, solve a problem, or make an argument that compels us to turn to outside help. We then seek out, investigate, and use materials beyond our personal resources. The findings and conclusions of such an inquiry appear in the research paper. The term *research paper* describes a presentation of student research that may be in a printed, an electronic, or a multimedia format.

The research paper is generally based on primary research, secondary research, or a combination of the two. Primary research is the study of a subject through firsthand observation and investigation, such as analyzing a literary or historical text, a film, or a performance; conducting a survey or an interview; or carrying out a laboratory experiment. Primary sources include statistical data, historical documents, and works of literature or art. Secondary research is the examination of studies that other researchers have made of a subject. Examples of secondary sources are books and articles about political issues, historical events, scientific debates, or literary works.

Most academic papers depend at least partly on secondary research. No matter what your subject of study, learning to investigate, review, and productively use information, ideas, and opinions of other researchers will play a major role in your development as a student. The sorts of activities that constitute a research paper—identifying, locating, assessing, and assimilating others' research and then developing and expressing your own ideas clearly and persuasively—are at the center of the educational experience.

These skills are by no means just academic. Like the research papers you write in school, many reports and proposals required in business, government, and other professions rely on secondary research. Learning how to write a research paper, then, can help prepare you for assignments in your professional career. It is difficult to think of any profession that would not require you to consult sources of information about a specific subject, to combine this information with your ideas, and to present your thoughts, findings, and conclusions effectively.

Research increases your knowledge and understanding of a subject. Sometimes research will confirm your ideas and opinions; sometimes it will challenge and modify them. But almost always it will help to shape your thinking. Unless your instructor specifically directs you otherwise, a research paper should not merely review publications and extract a series of quotations from them. Rather, you should look for sources that provide new information, that helpfully survey the various positions already taken on a specific subject, that lend authority to your viewpoint, that expand or nuance your ideas, that offer methods or modes of thought you can apply to new data or subjects, or that furnish negative examples against which you wish to argue. As you use and scrupulously acknowledge sources, however, always remember that the main purpose of doing research is not to summarize the work of others but to assimilate and to build on it and to arrive at your own understanding of the subject.

A book like this cannot present all the profitable ways of doing research. Because this handbook emphasizes the mechanics of preparing effective papers, it may give you the mistaken impression that the process of researching and writing a research paper follows a fixed pattern. The truth is that different paths can and do lead to successful research papers. Some researchers may pursue a more or less standard sequence of steps, but others may find themselves working less sequentially. In addition, certain projects lend themselves to a standard approach, whereas others may call for different strategies. Keeping in mind that researchers and projects differ, this book discusses activities that nearly all writers of research papers perform, such as selecting a suitable topic, conducting research, compiling a working bibliography, taking notes, outlining, and preparing the paper.

If you are writing your first research paper, you may feel overwhelmed by the many tasks discussed here. This handbook is designed to help you learn to manage a complex process efficiently. As you follow the book's advice on how to locate and document sources, how to format your paper, and so forth, you may be tempted to see doing a paper as a mechanical exercise. Actually, a research paper is an adventure, an intellectual adventure rather like solving a mystery: it is a form of exploration that leads to discoveries that are new—at least to you if not to others. The mechanics of the research paper, important though they are, should never override the intellectual challenge of pursuing a question that interests *you*. This quest or search should guide your research and your writing. Even though you are just learning how to prepare a research paper, you may still experience some of the excitement of pursuing and developing ideas that is one of the great satisfactions of research and scholarship.

1.2. THE RESEARCH PAPER AS A FORM OF WRITING

A research paper is a form of written communication. Like other kinds of nonfiction writing—letters, memos, reports, essays, articles, books—it should present information and ideas clearly and effectively. You should not let the mechanics of gathering source materials, taking notes, and documenting sources make you forget to apply the knowledge and skills you have acquired through previous writing experiences.

This handbook is not about expository writing. (See 1.12 for a selected list of useful books on composition, usage, language, and style.) It is, instead, a guide for the preparation of research papers. No set of conventions for preparing a manuscript can replace lively and intelligent writing, however, and no amount of research and documentation can compensate for a poor presentation of ideas. Although you must fully document the facts and opinions you draw from your research, the documentation should only support your statements and provide concise information about the sources cited; it should not overshadow your own ideas or distract the reader from them.

1.3. SELECTING A TOPIC

Your instructor may let you choose what to write about in your paper or may assign a topic. Even if the topic is assigned, you will probably need to decide which specific idea to explore or which approach to use. Selecting an appropriate topic is seldom a simple matter. Even after you discover a subject that attracts your interest, you may well find yourself revising your choice, modifying your approach, or changing topics altogether after you have begun research.

Remember the time allotted to you and the expected length of the research paper. "International politics in the modern age" would obviously be too broad a subject for a ten-page term paper. You may prefer to begin with a fairly general topic and then to refine it, by thought and research, into a more specific one that can be fully explored. Try to narrow your topic by focusing on an aspect of the subject or an approach to it. A student initially interested in writing on Shakespeare's poetic imagery, for instance, might decide, after careful thought and reading, to focus on the blood imagery in *Macbeth*; the topic "violence in the media" could likewise be narrowed to "the effects of cartoon violence on preschool children." When you begin to focus on a topic, you should consult library materials and other information resources to see whether enough work has been done on the subject to permit adequate research and whether the pertinent source materials are readily accessible (see 1.4).

In general, then, give yourself plenty of time to think through and rethink your choice of a topic. Look for a subject or an issue that will continue to engage you throughout research and writing. Preliminary reading is essential in evaluating topics. Consult some general reference works, such as encyclopedias, as well as books and articles in the areas you are considering. Before settling on a final topic, make sure you understand the amount and depth of research required and the type of paper expected. If necessary, your instructor can clarify the assignment or help you choose a topic.

1.4. CONDUCTING RESEARCH

1.4.1. The Modern Academic Library

Since most of your research papers will draw on the published work of experts, you should become thoroughly acquainted with the libraries available to you. The modern academic library typically offers researchers both print and electronic resources, like bibliographic and full-text databases, as well as computer services, such as word processing, high-quality printers, and access to the Internet.

Many libraries have programs of orientation and instruction to meet the needs of all students, from beginning researchers to graduate students. Ask about introductory pamphlets or handbooks, guided tours, lectures, and courses on using the library. Be sure to take full advantage of the services your library provides.

Nearly all public and academic libraries have desks staffed by professional reference librarians who can tell you about available instructional programs and help you locate sources. Consulting a librarian at key points in your research may save you considerable time and effort. Often librarians also prepare and hand out informative bulletins that describe library resources and services.

1.4.2. The Central Information System

A typical academic library provides an online central information system to serve students and faculty members engaged in research. The system ordinarily includes the library's catalog of holdings (books, serials, electronic publications, audiovisual materials, and so forth; see 1.4.4); incorporates a number of bibliographic databases, such as *National Newspaper Index*, *Readers' Guide to Periodical Literature*, *Business Periodicals Index*, *Humanities Index*, *Social Sciences Index*, and *General Science Index*, and other kinds of reference works like those discussed in the next section; and often permits access to other electronic resources, including the full texts of sources, available at the school or over the Internet (see 1.4.6 on using the Internet for research). A central information system might also be part of a network linking the catalogs of a number of libraries. For instance, the system in your school might permit you to search the holdings of local public libraries or of other schools. If your library is part of a network such as the Online Computer Library Center (OCLC) or the Research Libraries Information Network (RLIN), you may be able to locate sources recorded in the catalogs of thousands of other libraries.

You can often use the central information system even if you are not physically in the library. There may be connections with the library at various locations on the campus. With a personal computer and a modem, you might also be able to access information in the system from locations on and off the campus.

1.4.3. Reference Works

A useful way to begin a research project is to consult relevant reference works. Some reference works, like indexes and bibliographies, provide data about research materials; others, like encyclopedias, dictionaries, and biographical sources, give basic information about subjects. This section provides a brief introduction to the range of general and specialized reference works you should know about, many of which are available in both print and electronic forms. For a more comprehensive listing by subject area, see appendix A.

a. Types of Reference Works

Indexes. Indexes guide you to material in newspapers, magazines, and journals as well as to writings in book collections. *The New York Times Index* lists news stories and feature articles in the *New York Times*. *National Newspaper Index* covers the *Christian Science Monitor*, *Los Angeles Times*, *New York Times*, *Wall Street Journal*, and *Washington Post*. *Canadian News Index* provides citations to the major newspapers in Canada. *Readers' Guide to Periodical Literature* indexes the contents of popular magazines. *Essay and General Literature Index* lists essays and articles published in books. Most subject areas have their own specialized indexes, such as *Art Index, Business Periodicals Index, Education Index, General Science Index, Humanities Index, Index to Legal Periodicals, Philosopher's Index,* and *Social Sciences Index.*

Bibliographies. Bibliographies are lists of related publications and other materials. Serial bibliographies in specific disciplines include *Bibliography of Agriculture, Bibliography and Index of Geology,* and *MLA International Bibliography* (for the field of language and literature). *Bibliographic Index* contains citations to bibliographies that are published as books or pamphlets, as parts of books, or in periodicals. (For sample citations from a bibliography, see 1.4.3c.)

Collections of abstracts. Abstracts are summaries of journal articles and other literature. Collections of abstracts include *Biological Abstracts, Chemical Abstracts, Historical Abstracts, Linguistics and Language Behavior Abstracts, Physics Abstracts, Psychological Abstracts,* and *Sociological Abstracts.* Summaries of doctoral dissertations are available in *Dissertation Abstracts International.*

Guides to research. There are guides intended to direct you to the most important sources of information and scholarship in the area you are researching. Whereas indexes, bibliographies, and collections of abstracts tend to strive for comprehensiveness and objectivity in presenting information, guides to research are usually selective and evaluative. Some research guides cover entire fields, such as James L. Harner's *Literary Research Guide* (3rd ed. [New York: MLA, 1998]);

other similar works have titles like *A Guide to the Literature of Art History*, *A Guide to the Literature of Pharmacy and the Pharmaceutical Sciences*, and *Philosophy: A Guide to the Reference Literature*. Some guides to research are devoted to specific subjects (e.g., *The English Romantic Poets: A Review of Research and Criticism*). To learn of any guides that might be useful to your project, consult the latest edition of the American Library Association's *Guide to Reference Books* or your instructor or a librarian.

Dictionaries. Dictionaries are alphabetically arranged works that provide information, usually in concise form, about words or topics. Two of the most authoritative dictionaries of words are *Webster's Third New International Dictionary of the English Language* and, especially for the history of a word's meanings and usages, *The Oxford English Dictionary*. Major fields of study have specialized dictionaries, such as *A Dictionary of Botany*, *Computer Dictionary*, *Black's Law Dictionary*, *Dorland's Illustrated Medical Dictionary*, *The New Grove Dictionary of Music and Musicians*, *A Dictionary of Philosophy*, *The Interpreter's Dictionary of the Bible*, and *A Dictionary of the Social Sciences*.

Encyclopedias. Encyclopedias are works, usually alphabetically arranged, that give introductory information about subjects. Popular general encyclopedias are *Academic American Encyclopedia*, *The Encyclopedia Americana*, and *The New Encyclopaedia Britannica*. Specialized encyclopedias include *Encyclopedia of World Art*, *Encyclopedia of Economics*, *The Film Encyclopedia*, *An Encyclopedia of World History*, *The New Princeton Encyclopedia of Poetry and Poetics*, *Encyclopedia of Psychology*, and *McGraw-Hill Encyclopedia of Science and Technology*.

Biographical sources. Information on living persons is collected in *Current Biography*, *The International Who's Who*, and *Who's Who in America*. Sources for persons no longer living are *American National Biography* (for the United States), *Dictionary of Canadian Biography*, *Dictionary of National Biography* (for Great Britain), and *Webster's New Biographical Dictionary*.

Yearbooks. Yearbooks present information about specific years in the past. Examples are *The Americana Annual*, *Britannica Book of the Year*, and *The Europa Yearbook*.

Atlases. Atlases are collections of maps. *The National Atlas of the United States of America* is the official atlas of the United States; *The Times Atlas of the World* covers regions and nations of the entire world.

Gazetteers. Gazetteers provide geographic information. Examples are *The Columbia Gazetteer of the World* and *Webster's New Geographical Dictionary.*

Statistical data sources. Collections of statistics are often published by governmental agencies. Such works include the following annual publications: *Statistical Abstract of the United States,* issued by the United States Bureau of the Census, and *Statistical Yearbook* and *Demographic Yearbook,* both published by the United Nations.

b. Publication Forms of Reference Works: Print and Electronic

Your library probably has reference works in both print and electronic forms. Print works may be located in a reference room. General reference books, like dictionaries, encyclopedias, biographical sources, yearbooks, atlases, and gazetteers, may all be shelved together in one place, while specialized reference books may be grouped according to subject area—biology, business, literature, psychology, and so forth. The volumes of reference works published annually—indexes, bibliographies, and abstracts collections—are probably lined up in chronological order.

Many reference works are available in electronic form, as databases. The most widely used databases at present are available online or on CD-ROM.

An online database is stored in a computer. The researcher accesses information in an online database by means of a computer terminal. Searching the database can be done in the library and may also be possible outside the library through a personal computer and a modem. Some databases are available on the Internet (see 1.4.6). Searching online databases may entail paying a fee. If your library provides access to online databases, consult a librarian for further information.

A CD-ROM database is stored on a small disc. The researcher uses a standard personal computer to access information in the CD-ROM database; there is no need of a telecommunication connection. The disc is usually preinstalled in a computer in the library and, like print publications, is available for public use free of charge. Some libraries make selected CD-ROM databases available as part of the central information system. Databases are also stored on other media, such as DVDs, discs that can hold much more information than CD-ROMs.

Online and CD-ROM databases have a number of advantages over print versions of reference works. Much more information is generally available in a database. Whereas the print version of an annual bibliography covers research and scholarship for only one year, the electronic version of the work typically covers several years. Let us say, then, that you want to find out what was written on a subject during the last five years. With the print version of an annual bibliography, you would need to consult five volumes—in effect, conduct five searches—to identify what you want. With the electronic version, you would need to do just one search.

In addition, information is usually more current in electronic formats. The printed volume of an annual reference work is published once a year. A CD-ROM version of the same work is commonly updated and issued to subscribers several times a year. An online database is normally an ongoing, continually updated project and is, therefore, the most up-to-date of the three forms.

In using printed sources, moreover, you need to copy the information you wish. Electronic databases generally allow you to print out or download information. You can transfer downloaded data from your computer diskette to your research paper without the risk of introducing errors through copying by hand. Since database compilers sometimes make errors, however, you need to verify the information derived from a database (author's name, title, etc.) against the source. Most important of all, you can search electronic versions of a reference work in many more ways than you can the printed version (see 1.4.3c).

c. Searching a Reference Database

Every field of study has standard reference works. One such work is the *MLA International Bibliography*. The printed library edition of this work is published annually, in two clothbound books. The first contains listings in five areas: literature in English, literature in other languages, linguistics, general literature and related topics, and folklore. The second book provides a subject index to the first.

Like other such reference works, the *MLA International Bibliography* is available online and on CD-ROM. Using these electronic editions involves searching techniques common to most databases. The following description suggests ways in which you might search this bibliography using the CD-ROM version available, as of this writing, from SilverPlatter Information, Inc. The SilverPlatter disc contains all citations published in annual volumes of the bibliography from 1963 to the present. Therefore, while an annual print volume of the *MLA International Bibliography* lists around fifty thousand titles, the CD-ROM version offers information on more than a million titles.

The standard ways of searching this database and similar ones are through author, title, and subject. For example, if you want to know what studies by Toni Morrison or Deborah Tannen have been published in the fields covered by this bibliography, you can enter the author's name. Or if you know only the title of a work—like "Black Matter(s)" or *Talking Voices*—you can call forth complete bibliographic information about it from the database. If you remember only part of the title (e.g., "city"), you can request a listing of all titles containing that term.

In addition, since every work added to this bibliography is accompanied by a descriptor, or index term, you can also search the database by subject. Thus, if you ask for studies that discuss, for instance, "detective fiction," the system will search through its files and present you with all titles that have "detective fiction" as a descriptor.

Databases like the SilverPlatter CD-ROM version of the *MLA International Bibliography* also permit you to expand or narrow your searches usefully. While you are trying to decide on a topic, you may want to do expanded searches to get a broad sense of possibilities. The index and thesaurus of this database can be particularly helpful when you are developing a suitable research topic. If you have a vague notion to write on detective fiction, you can find related subjects by taking a look at the bibliography's index, a list of the terms used to describe the works in the database. Here you will encounter not only "detective fiction" but also "detective drama," "detective film," "detective magazines," "detective novel," and "detective story," among others. The thesaurus is a more extensive and detailed list, which includes, for example, synonyms for and other terms related to the index descriptors. Consulting it will yield additional terms that might suggest a specific topic, such as "American detective fiction," "English detective novel," "French detective," "hard-boiled detective fiction," and "woman detective."

Also useful for expanded searches is this database's truncation feature. By using a truncated or shortened term—for example, a word root—followed by an asterisk, you can retrieve all variants of it. If you wish, for instance, to do a paper on feminism but cannot decide what aspect to focus on, you can enter as a search term "femini*" and receive records on, among others, "feminine," "femininity," "feminist literary theory and criticism," "feminist movement," and "feminist writers."

The database also permits searching according to Boolean logic—

named after the nineteenth-century British mathematician and logician George Boole. In this kind of searching, you customize your search request with the operators *and*, *or*, and *not*. For example, you can use the Boolean operator *or* to expand your search. Entering "Arthur Conan Doyle *or* Sherlock Holmes" will furnish more titles than either "Arthur Conan Doyle" or "Sherlock Holmes" by itself would. Moreover, if you want to perform narrower searches, the Boolean operators *not* and *and* can limit the field of titles accessed. If you are interested in finding studies on, say, versions of the story of Othello other than Shakespeare's, enter "Othello *not* Shakespeare." Or if you would like to identify studies that compare Shakespeare's play with *Otello*, Verdi's operatic adaptation of it, keying "Othello *and* Otello" rather than just "Othello" will result in a shorter, more focused list of sources.

The *MLA International Bibliography* in its SilverPlatter CD-ROM version offers other ways to restrict your search. It allows you to retrieve titles from a single publication source—for instance, articles on *Othello* that have appeared in *Shakespeare Quarterly* since 1963. The database also allows you to limit your search according to language of publication (e.g., Japanese, Spanish), publication type (e.g., book, journal article), and publication year. You can obtain a list, for example, of books on Goethe's *Faust* that were written in German and published in 1995 or later.

This brief discussion far from exhausts the searching possibilities provided by this database and similar ones. SilverPlatter supplies a typical user's manual that extensively describes the features of the database as well as the codes and procedures for accessing information from it. Typically, too, the database allows you to print out and download information. It also gives you a choice of how to view, print, or download data. You may prefer to select the complete record, which includes information on title, author, source, international standard numbers, language of publication, publication type, publication year, descriptors, update code, and accession number (see fig. 1). Or you can select a shortened citation that gives only title, author, source, and accession number (see fig. 2).

The advantage of the short form is that it saves time and space while providing the information necessary both for locating the material and for creating a preliminary entry for your works-cited list. You can easily convert the bibliographic data in figure 2 to MLA documentation style (see ch. 4):

Tannen, Deborah. "Repetition in Conversation: Toward a
Poetics of Talk." <u>Language</u> 63 (1987): 574-605.

```
TI: Repetition in Conversation: Toward a
Poetics of Talk

AU: Tannen,-Deborah

SO: Language:-Journal-of-the-Linguistic-
Society-of-America, Pittsburgh, PA
(Language). 1987 Sept., 63:3, 574-605.

IS: ISSN 0023-8260

LA: English

PT: journal-article

PY: 1987

DE: English-language-Modern; pragmatics-;
repetition-; in conversation-; relationship
to poetic-language

UD: 8701

AN: 87-3-6464
```

Fig. 1. A complete citation from a bibliographic database.

```
TI: Repetition in Conversation: Toward a
Poetics of Talk

AU: Tannen,-Deborah

SO: Language:-Journal-of-the-Linguistic-
Society-of-America, Pittsburgh, PA
(Language). 1987 Sept., 63:3, 574-605.

AN: 87-3-6464
```

Fig. 2. A shortened citation from a bibliographic database.

1.4.4. The Online Catalog of Library Holdings

An important part of a library's central information system is the online catalog of holdings (e.g., books, journals, electronic publications, audio-visual materials). You search the catalog by typing information and commands on the keyboard of a computer terminal; the terminal's monitor displays the results of the search. There is no standard system for online catalogs. Systems differ, for example, in how users access information and in what appears on the screen. Online catalog systems also vary considerably in the assistance they provide. Most offer on-screen help. Check to see if all the library's holdings are included in the online catalog; in some libraries only recent acquisitions are, and older works are listed in a card catalog or some other form of catalog (see 1.4.4c).

a. Searching an Online Catalog

When using an online catalog, you can locate a work in a number of ways. The most common are by author, by title, and by subject. If you enter the author's full name, the screen displays a list of all the works the library has by that author. Entering the title produces a list of all works the library has with that title. If you have no author or title in mind, you can enter a subject to produce a list of works about it. (To find out the subjects by which the catalog is organized, see *Library of Congress Subject Headings* or the list your library follows.)

The online catalog can help you locate works even if you lack some of the information you would ordinarily use for the search. If you know only the beginning of a book title—for example, only *Advertising, Competition*, instead of *Advertising, Competition, and Public Policy: A Simulation Study*—you can enter what you know, and the screen will display all titles that begin with those words. If you know only an author's last name, you can obtain a list of all authors with that last name.

The computer-stored catalog also helps you to initiate more sophisticated searches, such as by keyword or subject. You can, for example, call up a list of all works that contain the word "competition" somewhere in their titles. A subject search using "competition" will produce the titles of all works whose subject descriptions include the word. In addition, some online catalogs allow you to limit your search in various ways. You may ask for titles published during a certain range of years (e.g., 1995 to the present) or titles located only in one specific part of your library (e.g., the main collection). You may be able, too, to limit your search to specific media (e.g., books, serials, electronic publications, archives, manuscripts, musical scores, films, video or sound recordings). This feature will let you find out, say, if your library has any video recordings about mythology or the Civil War.

Some online catalogs permit searching according to Boolean logic. For instance, suppose you are interested in studies on the relation between nutrition and cancer. A search using "nutrition" alone or "cancer" alone would yield a list of all works having anything to do with the subject of the search, and you would have to pick out the items dealing with the two subjects together. In contrast, a Boolean search using "nutrition *and* cancer" excludes all works not about both subjects. Likewise, if you would like to see which authors besides Goethe wrote about the Faust theme, you can enter "Faust *not* Goethe." In addition to narrowing lists of titles, Boolean searching is useful for expanding them. For example, if you wish to research solar heating, you might enter "solar *or* sun *and* heating," which will produce more titles than would just "solar *and* heating." (On using Boolean logic in searching a reference database, see 1.4.3c.)

When you access a title, the screen shows something like the example in figure 3. The top lines of the screen image contain the author's name and date of birth (Geherin, David, 1943–), the full title of the book (*The American Private Eye: The Image in Fiction*), and complete publication information (the book was published by the Frederick Ungar Publishing Company in New York City in 1985). Then follows the call number, the designation by which the book is shelved in the library. The next section tells you that the library possesses one copy of the work, which is located on an open shelf (the "stack"), and that the copy is in the library and not on loan to anyone else. The following lines describe the physical characteristics of the book (it has 11 pages of front matter—material before the main text— and 228 pages of text and measures 22 centimeters in height), indicate that it contains an index and a bibliography, show the subject entries under which the book is cataloged, and give the Library of Congress catalog card number, the International Standard Book Numbers for the cloth and paperback versions of the book, and the Research Libraries Information Network identification number.

```
AUTHOR: Geherin, David, 1943-

TITLE: The American Private Eye: The Image in
Fiction

IMPRINT: New York: F. Ungar Pub. Co., 1985

CALL NUMBER: PS374.D4 G39 1985

LOCATION               COPY                Status

  Stack                 #1           In Library

PHYSICAL FEATURES: xi, 228 p.: 22cm.

NOTES: Includes index * Bibliography: p. 211-
21.

SUBJECTS: Detective and mystery stories,
American--History and criticism * Detectives
in literature * American fiction--20th
century--History and criticism.

LC CARD: 84015251

ISBN: 0804422435 * 0804461848 (pbk.)

RLIN ID NO.: 85-B34382
```

Fig. 3. An entry from an online catalog.

b. Information Needed for Research and Writing

For the purposes of researching and writing your paper, you normally will not use most of the information that appears in the catalog entry. You need to know the call number, of course, to locate the work in the library (see 1.4.4d); and, for your paper's works-cited list, you also need to know the author, title, and full publication information (see ch. 4 on information needed for compiling the list of works cited). Following is the entry in the works-cited list for the title given above:

```
Geherin, David. The American Private Eye: The Image in
     Fiction. New York: Ungar, 1985.
```

Transcribe this information carefully. Some online catalog systems give the option of printing out or downloading onto computer diskettes the bibliographic data displayed on the screen. This feature not only saves you the time and effort of copying the information but also eliminates the possibility of transcription errors. You should, of course, verify the information you derive from the catalog against the source itself; errors sometimes occur during cataloging.

c. The Card Catalog and Other Forms of Catalogs

Your library's catalog of holdings may exist, in whole or in part, in some other form besides online. For example, a version of the online catalog may be available on a CD-ROM. Sometimes libraries list only recent works online and catalog older works with printed files on microfilm or microfiche, in bound books, or on cards kept in drawers. If your library keeps a print catalog as well as an online catalog, be sure to consult each, for titles in one may not be in the other.

In some libraries, the main catalog is primarily in the form of cards. Books in a card catalog are usually listed by author, title, and subject. Although author cards, title cards, and subject cards may be arranged alphabetically in a single catalog, many card catalogs are divided into two sections (author and title cards in one, subject cards in the other) or, more rarely, into three sections (one each for authors, titles, and subjects). Finally, your library may have special catalogs for publications other than books, such as serials or periodicals (e.g., newspapers, magazines, scholarly journals) or audiovisual materials.

d. Location of Library Materials

The call numbers in your library probably follow one of two systems of classification: the Dewey decimal system or the Library of Congress system. Learning your library's system will help you not only to find works but also to know their contents from their call numbers.

The Dewey decimal system classifies books under ten major headings:

000	General works
100	Philosophy and psychology
200	Religion
300	Social sciences
400	Language
500	Natural sciences and mathematics
600	Technology and applied sciences
700	Fine arts
800	Literature
900	Geography and history

The Library of Congress system divides books into twenty major groups:

A	General works
B	Philosophy, psychology, and religion
C	General history
D	World history
E–F	American history
G	Geography and anthropology
H	Social sciences
J	Political science
K	Law
L	Education
M	Music
N	Fine arts
P	Language and literature
Q	Science
R	Medicine
S	Agriculture
T	Technology
U	Military science
V	Naval science
Z	Bibliography and library science

Library holdings are kept either on open shelves, to which the public has direct access, or in closed stacks. To obtain a work in closed stacks, you usually have to present a call slip to a library staff member, who will locate the book for you. Regardless of the classification system used, all libraries keep some books separate from the main collection. If a work is kept in a special area, the main catalog should indicate the location. For example, the word *Reserved* in a catalog entry indicates a work required in a course and stored in a special section, at the instructor's request, so that the work stays available for students in the course. A work shelved in the reference section, designated by an *R* or *Ref*, must also remain in the library. Some libraries have additional special collections, such as rare books or government documents, that are kept separate from the main collection.

Libraries also commonly set aside specific areas for various types of materials—current periodicals, pamphlets, and nonprint materials, like CD-ROMs, films, and audio and video recordings. Consult the library directory or a librarian for locations.

1.4.5. Other Library Resources and Services

Besides knowing about these print and nonprint materials, you should become familiar with microforms, which are also usually kept in a special section of the library. *Microform* designates printed matter greatly reduced in size by microphotography; common types are microfilm, microfiche, and microcard. Libraries use microforms to store such materials as back copies of periodicals (newspapers, magazines, scholarly journals), the library card catalog for older books not yet on the central online catalog, and rare books. To use microforms, you need a special reader to magnify them. Library staff members are usually on hand to assist researchers in locating microform materials and operating the readers.

Most libraries offer interlibrary loans. If your library does not have the materials you need, ask whether it can borrow them from another library. To find out which libraries own your title, consult such databases as the Online Computer Library Center (OCLC) or the Research Libraries Information Network (RLIN), if they are available to you. Or you can consult such print sources as *National Union Catalog*, for book holdings at other libraries, or *Union List of Serials* and *New Serial Titles*, for periodicals. Most libraries have agreements for the exchange of research materials on a regional, statewide, or national basis.

Photocopying machines are common in libraries. Some schools have electronic-resources centers in the library as well. Such centers provide computers and high-quality printers for student use, with a variety of software applications for tasks such as word processing, spreadsheet analysis, database management, desktop publishing, drawing, and drafting. Some schools even have facilities for photographic, audio, and video production.

Computer terminals are typically located at various sites in the library to give direct access to the central catalog and other databases, either online or on CD-ROM. Your library may also provide access to computer services, like Dialog or Dow Jones News Retrieval Service, or to the Internet.

1.4.6. Internet Sources

a. Range of Sources

Researchers regularly use facts and ideas from Internet sources to complement those derived from traditional print sources. The Internet is a vast international computer network originally developed in 1969 to facilitate the work of scientists and engineers at universities, laboratories, and such government agencies as the National Aeronautics and Space Administration (NASA). Widely used today in many phases of life, the Internet makes it possible to communicate electronically with individuals and groups, to read the files of other linked computers, and to transfer files between computers. The popular Internet service known as the World Wide Web provides hypertextual links between and within electronic sites. Through the Web, a researcher can read and transfer material from library catalogs and millions of other useful sites, created by professional organizations (e.g., American Chemical Society, American Philosophical Association), government agencies (e.g., Library of Congress, Bureau of the Census), commercial enterprises (e.g., publishers of encyclopedias, news organizations), educational entities (e.g., universities, libraries, academic departments, research centers, scholarly projects), and individual scholars and researchers. These sites provide not only information sources but also the full texts of documents—such as historical papers, literary and religious works, and articles in electronic periodicals (e.g., journals, magazines, newspapers)—and audiovisual materials (e.g., photographs, paintings, sound and video recordings).

b. Searching for Internet Sources

Even those who are familiar with the World Wide Web find that using it to do research requires practice and training the way using a library does. Therefore, whenever possible, follow the guidance of an instructor or a librarian in selecting Internet sites for research. Your library may provide access to important online sources that were likely selected after careful evaluation and consultation. Some of these sources may be available only through library subscription. A librarian might also be able to advise you about other useful sites. Similarly, many instructors are knowledgeable about Internet resources in their fields. An instructor might direct you to specific sites or to a "metapage" or "gateway" that provides links to other sites.

One gateway site is *Voice of the Shuttle: Web Page for Humanities Research*, created at the University of California, Santa Barbara. The home page of this site offers a menu of subjects within the humanities—anthropology, archaeology, architecture, history, literature, and so forth. Selecting "media studies," for example, gives you a list of specific fields (e.g., journalism, television, film and video, popular music). The choice of "media history and theory" presents links to numerous resources in this area: professional organizations, bibliographies, chronologies, journals, articles and papers, course descriptions, and other related sites, including some created and maintained by scholars in media studies.

Some gateway sites are refereed (see 1.6 on refereed publications). *Argos*, for example, developed at the University of Evansville, is currently a "peer-reviewed, limited-area search engine" designed for student, teachers, and scholars of the "ancient and medieval worlds." An editorial board of specialists reviews and approves each site before it is included in this search engine. A list of these "associate sites"— such as *Byzantium: Byzantine Studies on the Internet, Diotima: Materials for the Study of Women and Gender in the Ancient World*, and *Exploring World Cultures*—appears on the home page of *Argos*.

If you are working without professional guidance, use the search tools created to help locate Internet materials. Common ways to conduct searches with these tools are by subject and by keyword. Some search tools, such as *Yahoo!*, offer hierarchically arranged subject directories through which you can navigate until you find specific topics you wish to explore. Thus, if you click on the subject "humanities," you might receive a list of such categories as classics, critical theory, history, literature, medical humanities, philosophy, and theology. The selection "medical humanities" would lead you to "biomedical ethics," which would prompt another set of subtopics (abortion issues, animal testing, cloning, euthanasia, genetic engineering), and so forth. Your eventual choice of a specific subject (e.g., "human cloning") would yield a listing of documents and files devoted to the subject.

If you know at the outset the exact topic you wish to research, you can perform a keyword search, which produces a listing of files containing the word or words you specify. To avoid long lists containing many irrelevant sites, be as specific as possible in your commands— thus, "human cloning" will yield a shorter, more unified list than "cloning" alone would. Most search tools offer instructions on how to phrase search requests for the best results. You can often use Boolean and other operators to make searches precise (see 1.4.3c on Boolean logic).

Whenever you discover what seems a useful document or site, be sure to add it to your bookmark list. In so doing, you can easily return to the source for further information or clarification. If you cannot use a bookmark—perhaps because you share a computer—keep a precise record of the network address, or uniform resource locator (URL). In any event, you may want to keep a log of all sites you visit, whether or not you initially bookmark them, since a site you originally passed over may seem more useful later. In addition, always make note of the date or dates on which you consult a source. The date of access is important because the material could be revised between different visits to the site. The URL and the date of access are items of information you will need for your working bibliography and your list of works cited.

Whereas most instructors permit and many encourage using Internet sources, few consider a search of the World Wide Web alone adequate research for a paper; most require that other materials, including print publications, be sought. Similarly, e-mail discussion lists and online "chat rooms" are helpful for sharing ideas but, except for rare occasions, are not deemed acceptable resources for research papers. (See 1.6 on evaluating source materials.)

1.5. COMPILING A WORKING BIBLIOGRAPHY

As you discover information and opinions on your topic, you should keep track of sources that you may use for your paper. A record of such sources is called a working bibliography. Your preliminary reading will probably provide the first titles for this list. Other titles will emerge when you consult reference works and the library's central catalog and when you explore the Internet. If you read carefully through the bibliography and notes of each work you consult, more often than not you will discover additional important sources. Your working bibliography will frequently change during your research as you add new titles and eliminate those that do not prove useful and as you probe and emphasize some aspects of your subject in preference to others. The working bibliography will eventually evolve into the list of works cited that appears at the end of the research paper.

A computer is particularly useful for compiling the working bibliography. Create a computer file for this purpose, and enter full information about sources into the file as you proceed with your research. Whenever you wish to add new works to the list, to remove works you no longer think helpful, or to correct entries already stored, you retrieve the file, make the changes, and save the revised file for future use. As you research, you can arrange and rearrange your sources however you wish (e.g., in alphabetical order, in chronological order by date of publication, in order of relevance to your topic); you can also divide sources into groups (e.g., those already consulted and those not yet consulted, those most useful and those less so). At any point, you can print the file to review it or to use it for research. Since bibliography files are essential to researching and writing the paper, be certain to save these files and to keep copies of them on paper and on a backup disk.

When you add sources to your working bibliography, be sure you enter all the publication information needed for the works-cited list. The information to be recorded depends on the kind of source used. Following are typical examples of citations for a book, an article in a scholarly journal, a newspaper or magazine article, and an Internet source. The sources you encounter might require more information. See chapter 4 for complete guidelines on compiling the works-cited list of the research paper.

BOOK (see 4.6)

1. Author's full name (last name first)
2. Full title (including any subtitle)
3. Edition (if the book is a second or later edition)
4. Number of the volume and the total number of volumes (if the book is a multivolume work)
5. City of publication
6. Shortened form of the publisher's name (see 6.5)
7. Year of publication

Budden, Julian. The Operas of Verdi. Rev. ed. 3 vols.
    Oxford: Clarendon, 1992.

ARTICLE IN A SCHOLARLY JOURNAL (see 4.7.1–4)

1. Author's name
2. Title of the article
3. Title of the journal

4. Volume number
5. Year of publication
6. Inclusive page numbers of the article (i.e., the number of the page on which the article begins, a hyphen, and the number of the page on which the article ends)

```
Vartanov, Anri. "Television as Spectacle and Myth."
    Journal of Communication 41 (1991): 162-71.
```

NEWSPAPER OR MAGAZINE ARTICLE (see 4.7.5–6)

1. Author's name
2. Title of the article
3. Title of the periodical
4. Date of publication
5. Inclusive page numbers of the article

```
Shea, Christopher. "The Limits of Free Speech."
    Chronicle of Higher Education 1 Dec. 1993: A37-38.
```

INTERNET SOURCE (see 4.9.1–4)

1. Author's name
2. Title of the document
3. Title of the scholarly project, database, periodical, or professional or personal site
4. Name of the editor of the scholarly project or database
5. Date of electronic publication or last update
6. Name of the institution or organization sponsoring or associated with the site
7. Date when you accessed the source
8. Network address, or URL

```
Oakley, John H. "The Achilles Painter." The Perseus
    Project. Ed. Gregory Crane. Mar. 1997. Tufts U. 14
    May 1998 <http://www.perseus.tufts.edu/Secondary/
    Painter_Essays/Achilles_toc.html>.
```

Besides the data needed for the works-cited list, it is useful to add other information to items in the working bibliography. For example, if you derive a source from a bibliographic work, record where you found the reference, in case you need to recheck it. Always also note the library call number, the network address (URL), or other identifying information required to locate each work.

The following entry in a working bibliography contains not only all the facts needed for the final bibliography (author's name, full title, and relevant publication information) but also information useful for research: the origin of the reference (the electronic database of the *MLA International Bibliography*) and the call number (PS374.D4 G39).

```
Geherin, David. The American Private Eye: The Image in
    Fiction. New York: Ungar, 1985. [MLA Bib.; PS374.D4
    G39]
```

You will delete reference origins and call numbers when you convert your working bibliography into the list of works cited.

Whenever you consult a source, carefully verify the publication facts against your records—even if you have printed out or downloaded the data. Add any missing information that you will need for the works-cited list, and correct any part of your records that does not match the data obtained from the work. Recording and verifying all the information about your sources when you first consult them will spare you many last-minute problems and frustrations.

Eventually, you will transform your working bibliography into a works-cited list. If your working bibliography is in a computer file, edit the entries to remove unnecessary information (e.g., origin of reference, call number), and arrange them alphabetically by author. When you have finished the final draft of your paper, transfer the edited bibliography file to the end of the file containing the paper.

If compiled with care and attention, the working bibliography will be invaluable to you throughout the preparation of your paper. It will, on the one hand, function as an efficient tool for finding and acquiring information and ideas and, on the other, provide all the data you will need for your list of works cited.

1.6. EVALUATING SOURCES

Researchers need to evaluate the quality of any work before using and citing it. Students writing their first research papers often find it difficult to evaluate sources. Not all sources are equally reliable or of equal quality. In reading and evaluating potential sources, you should not assume that something is truthful or trustworthy just because it appears in print or on the Internet. Some material may be based on incorrect or outdated information or on poor logic, and the author's knowledge or view of the subject may be too limited. Weigh what you read against your own knowledge and intelligence as well as against other treatments of the subject.

In evaluating a book, you might consult *Book Review Index* and *Book Review Digest* to see how the book was received by experts in the field of study. If you are working with historical documents or literary texts that exist in various versions, make certain you use reliable editions. For example, versions of Shakespeare's plays published during his lifetime and shortly after his death sometimes differ drastically. The task of a modern scholarly editor is to compare, analyze, and evaluate these variations and produce an edition that is as historically authoritative as possible. Therefore, if you want to use, say, an electronic text of a Shakespeare play, look for one that, at a minimum, clearly states who the editor of the text is and when the electronic edition was published or identifies the printed source that was the basis for the electronic version.

Assessing Internet resources is a particular challenge. Whereas the print publications that researchers depend on are generally issued by reputable publishers, like university presses, that accept accountability for the quality and reliability of the works they distribute, relatively few electronic publications currently have comparable authority.

Most scholarly journals and academic book publishers are committed to a policy of consultant review—commonly referred to by scholars as "peer review." This means that the publishers seek the advice of expert readers, or referees, before considering a manuscript for publication. Each consultant reads the work and sends the publisher a report evaluating the manuscript and, in general, either recommending or not recommending it for publication. Readers comment on such matters as the importance of the subject, the originality and soundness of the argument, the accuracy of the facts, and the currency of the research. At most scholarly journals and presses, moreover, there is also an editorial board that similarly reviews the manuscript, along with the readers' reports, before deciding on whether to publish the work. Thus a manuscript submitted to a refereed publication must undergo rigorous scrutiny before it is published. Some Internet publications conduct this kind of evaluation, but most do not. Many online materials are self-published without any outside review.

Researchers need to be concerned about the authority, accuracy, and currency of all sources they use. Following are some criteria to keep in mind when evaluating sources. If you have doubts about a source, your instructor or a librarian can probably help you.

1.6.1. Authorship and Authority

When we consult a printed book or article, we expect to find prominently displayed the name of the author and the name of the publisher of the work. Whenever you consult a source, print or electronic, make sure that the author of the document or the person or group responsible for the publication or site is identified. Once you establish authorship, consider the authoritativeness of the work. Publications sometimes indicate an author's credentials in the field by including relevant biographical information (e.g., professional title or affiliation, list of publications or other accomplishments) or a link to a home page. (You can also search the Internet and other sources to find information about an author.)

Take note, too, of the entire work or site even if you are interested only in a particular document within it. In a journal or at a Web site, look for a statement of mission or purpose as well as for evidence that the document underwent consultant review (e.g., the listing of an editorial board, for a journal, or of a moderator, for a discussion group).

Just as the name of the publisher is normally evident in print publications, the name of the sponsoring organization of an Internet site should be given, preferably with access to information about the organization. To determine the kind of organization from which a Web site emanates, note the last part of the domain name (e.g., the *.org* in "www.mla.org"). This suffix identifies where the source originates from—for example, a commercial enterprise (*.com*), an educational institution (*.edu*), a government agency (*.gov*), or a not-for-profit organization (*.org*). There is no guarantee, of course, that material from, say, an *.edu* site is always reliable; such a site probably includes students' unsupervised personal pages as well as scholarly projects. Nonetheless, knowing the organization involved might help you evaluate potential usefulness or shortcomings. For instance, many sites ending in *.com* offer helpful information, but some are no more than advertisements, such as a book company's lavish praise for books that it publishes.

1.6.2. Accuracy and Verifiability

If you are evaluating scholarly material, check to see that the work's sources are indicated, so that its information can be verified. The sources probably appear in a list of works cited. The titles in the list might also tell you something about the breadth of the author's knowledge of the subject and about any possible bias. The author of a Web publication might supply hypertextual links to the sources. Note, too, if the document or site gives an e-mail address or otherwise tells how you can ask the author or sponsoring organization for further information or clarification.

1.6.3. Currency

The publication date of a print source suggests how current the author's scholarship is. Although online documents and sites have the potential for continual updating, many remain in their original states and, depending on the subject, may be out-of-date. When considering any resource, be sure at least one date is assigned to it. Several dates are sometimes listed for an electronic publication. For example, if a document on the Internet had a previous print existence, there could be the date of print publication as well as the date of electronic publication. In addition, there might be the date when the material was last revised or updated. Ideally, a document should record all dates of publication and revision. Finally, scrutinizing the works cited in the text also reveals the currency of its scholarship.

1.7. TAKING NOTES

When you determine that material is reliable and useful, you will want to take notes on it. Although everyone agrees that note-taking is essential to research, probably no two researchers use exactly the same methods. Some prefer to take notes by hand on index cards or sheets of paper. Using a computer might save you time and should improve the accuracy with which you transcribe material, including quotations, from your sources into the text of your paper. However you take notes, set down first the author's full name and the complete title of the source—enough information to enable you to locate the source easily in your working bibliography.

There are, generally speaking, three methods of note-taking: summary, paraphrase, and quotation. Summarize if you want to record only the general idea of large amounts of material. If you require detailed notes on specific sentences and passages but do not need the exact wording, you may wish to paraphrase—that is, to restate the material in your own words. But when you believe that some sentence or passage in its original wording might make an effective addition to your paper, transcribe that material exactly as it appears, word for word, comma for comma. Whenever you quote verbatim from a work, be sure to use quotation marks scrupulously in your notes to distinguish the quotation from summary and paraphrase. Using electronic materials calls for special vigilance. If you download a text and integrate quotations from it into your paper, check to see that you have placed quotation marks around words taken from the source.

In summarizing, paraphrasing, or quoting, keep an accurate record of the pages or other numbered sections (e.g., numbered paragraphs in an electronic text) that you use. When a quotation continues to another page or section, carefully note where the page or section break occurs, since only a small portion of what you transcribe may ultimately find its way into your paper.

Using a word processor to store notes is handy, but while you are doing research, you may find yourself in a situation—for example, working in the library—where you do not have access to a computer. Then you will need to write your notes by hand and transfer them into a computer later.

Strategies of storing and retrieving notes vary. For a short paper for which you have taken few notes, you may place all notes in a single file and draw material from it whenever you want. For a longer paper that makes use of numerous sources, you may create a new file for each source. (See 1.10 for using note files during writing.)

Another strategy is to write out summaries and paraphrases of the source by hand and to enter into computer files only quotations, which you can electronically copy into your text as you write. At the least, this strategy will eliminate the time and effort and, more important, the possibility of error involved in transcribing quoted words more than once. Of course, when you download quotations from a database to your computer disk, you never transcribe them at all. Finally, since note files are essential to your paper, be certain to save them on your working disk and to keep copies of them both on paper and on a backup disk.

In taking notes, seek to steer a middle course between recording too much and recording too little. In other words, try to be both thorough and concise. Above all, strive for accuracy, not only in copying words for direct quotation but also in summarizing and paraphrasing authors' ideas. Careful note-taking will help you avoid the problem of plagiarism.

1.8. PLAGIARISM

You probably have heard the charge of plagiarism used in disputes within the publishing and recording industries. You may also have had classroom discussions about academic plagiarism. Derived from the Latin word *plagiarius* ("kidnapper"), *plagiarism* refers to a form of cheating that has been defined as "the false assumption of authorship: the wrongful act of taking the product of another person's mind, and presenting it as one's own" (Alexander Lindey, *Plagiarism and Originality* [New York: Harper, 1952] 2). To use another person's ideas or expressions in your writing without acknowledging the source is to plagiarize. Plagiarism, then, constitutes intellectual theft. Strictly speaking, it is a moral and ethical offense rather than a legal one, since most instances of plagiarism fall outside the scope of copyright infringement, a legal offense (see below). Nonetheless, plagiarism often carries severe penalties, ranging from failure in a course to expulsion from school.

Plagiarism in student writing is often unintentional, as when an elementary school pupil, assigned to do a report on a certain topic, goes home and copies down, word for word, everything on the subject in an encyclopedia. Unfortunately, some students continue to use such "research methods" in high school and even in college without realizing that these practices constitute plagiarism. At all times during research and writing, guard against the possibility of inadvertent plagiarism by keeping careful notes that distinguish between your own musings and thoughts and the material you gather from others. Forms of plagiarism include the failure to give appropriate acknowledgment when repeating another's wording or particularly apt phrase, when paraphrasing another's argument, or when presenting another's line of thinking.

You may certainly use other persons' words and thoughts in your research paper, but the borrowed material must not seem your creation. Suppose, for example, that you want to use the material in the following passage, which appears on page 625 of an essay by Wendy Martin in the book *Columbia Literary History of the United States*.

> Some of Dickinson's most powerful poems express her firmly held conviction that life cannot be fully comprehended without an understanding of death.

If you write the following sentence without any documentation, you have committed plagiarism:

```
Emily Dickinson strongly believed that we cannot
understand life fully unless we also comprehend death.
```

But you may present the material if you cite your source.

```
As Wendy Martin has suggested, Emily Dickinson strongly
believed that we cannot understand life fully unless we
also comprehend death (625).
```

The source is indicated, in accordance with MLA style, by the name of the author and by a page reference in parentheses. The name refers the reader to the corresponding entry in the works-cited list, which appears at the end of the paper.

```
Martin, Wendy. "Emily Dickinson." Columbia Literary
     History of the United States. Emory Elliott, gen.
     ed. New York: Columbia UP, 1988. 609-26.
```

Two more examples follow:

ORIGINAL SOURCE

Everyone uses the word *language* and everybody these days talks about *culture* [. . .]. "Languaculture" is a reminder, I hope, of the *necessary* connection between its two parts [. . .]. (Michael Agar, *Language Shock: Understanding the Culture of Conversation* [New York: Morrow, 1994] 60)

PLAGIARISM

```
At the intersection of language and culture lies a
concept that we might call "languaculture."
```

ORIGINAL SOURCE

Humanity faces a quantum leap forward. It faces the deepest social upheaval and creative restructuring of all time. Without clearly recognizing it, we are engaged in building a remarkable civilization from the ground up. This is the meaning of the Third Wave.

Until now the human race has undergone two great waves of change, each one largely obliterating earlier cultures or civilizations and replacing them with ways of life inconceivable to those who came before. The First Wave of change—the agricultural revolution—took thousands of years to play itself out. The Second Wave—the rise of industrial civilization—took a mere hundred years. Today history is even more accelerative, and it is likely that the Third Wave will sweep across history and complete itself in a few decades. (Alvin Toffler, *The Third Wave* [1980; New York: Bantam, 1981] 10)

PLAGIARISM

There have been two revolutionary periods of change in history: the agricultural revolution and the industrial revolution. The agricultural revolution determined the course of history for thousands of years; the industrial civilization lasted about a century. We are now on the threshold of a new period of revolutionary change, but this one may last for only a few decades.

In the first example, the student borrowed a specific term ("languaculture") without acknowledgment; in the second example, the student presented another's line of thinking without giving credit. The students could have avoided the charge of plagiarism by rewording slightly and inserting appropriate parenthetical documentation.

At the intersection of language and culture lies a concept that Michael Agar has called "languaculture" (60).

According to Alvin Toffler, there have been two revolutionary periods of change in history: the agricultural revolution and the industrial revolution.

> The agricultural revolution determined the course of
> history for thousands of years; the industrial
> civilization lasted about a century. We are now on the
> threshold of a new period of revolutionary change, but
> this one may last for only a few decades (10).

In each revision, the author's name refers the reader to the full description of the work in the works-cited list at the end of the paper, and the parenthetical documentation identifies the location of the borrowed material in the work.

> Agar, Michael. Language Shock: Understanding the Culture
>   of Conversation. New York: Morrow, 1994.
> Toffler, Alvin. The Third Wave. 1980. New York: Bantam,
>   1981.

In writing your research paper, then, you should document everything that you borrow—not only direct quotations and paraphrases but also information and ideas. Of course, common sense as well as ethics should determine what you document. For example, you rarely need to give sources for familiar proverbs ("You can't judge a book by its cover"), well-known quotations ("We shall overcome"), or common knowledge ("George Washington was the first president of the United States"). But you must indicate the source of any appropriated material that readers might otherwise mistake for your own. If you have any doubt about whether or not you are committing plagiarism, cite your source or sources.

Two issues related to plagiarism do not deal with outside sources. The first occurs when a student submits in a course a paper done for a previous course. Although obviously not the same as stealing someone else's ideas, this practice nonetheless qualifies as a kind of self-plagiarism and constitutes another form of cheating. If you want to rework a paper that you prepared for another course, ask your current instructor for permission to do so.

The other issue concerns collaborative work, such as a group project you carry out with other students. Joint participation in research and writing is common and, in fact, encouraged in many courses and in many professions, and it does not constitute plagiarism provided that credit is given for all contributions. One way to give credit, if roles were clearly demarcated or were unequal, is to state exactly who did what. Another way, especially if roles and contributions were merged and truly shared, is to acknowledge all concerned equally. Ask your instructor for advice if you are not certain how to acknowledge collaboration.

A final related issue concerns copyright infringement. Because of the omnipresence of the Internet and the ease with which it is possible to download and duplicate Internet publications, many people think online materials are free to be reproduced and distributed at will. The truth is that most materials on the Internet, like most printed works, are protected by copyright law. Read carefully any special instructions or restrictions specified in the document or at the site. Whereas summaries, paraphrases, and brief quotations in research papers are normally permissible with appropriate acknowledgment, reproducing and distributing an entire copyrighted document or significant portions of it without obtaining permission from the author or publisher to do so is an infringement of copyright law and a legal offense, even if the violator acknowledges the source. For a detailed discussion of copyright and other legal issues related to publishing, see chapter 2 of the *MLA Style Manual and Guide to Scholarly Publishing* (New York: MLA, 1998).

1.9. OUTLINING

1.9.1. Working Outline

Some writers like to work from an outline; others do not. For research papers, outlining can be a particularly useful intermediate activity between research and writing. In fact, some instructors require each student to hand in an outline with the final draft. Others require a draft outline earlier, asking the student to submit not only a topic for the paper but also a tentative list of subtopics for research. They then suggest that this working outline be continually revised—items dropped, added, modified—as the research progresses.

You may find a series of outlines helpful, whether or not your instructor requires them, especially if you are a beginning writer of research papers. An outline will help you to get an overall view of your paper and, perhaps more important, to figure out how each section of the paper relates to the others. Thus, developing an outline can help you to see the logical progression of your argument.

Word processing is useful for preparing a working outline, which may well pass through many and sometimes quite different versions. Word-processing programs commonly have an outlining feature that offers several formats with automatic numbering and lettering. It is probably best to create a different computer file for each version of an outline. For example, assign the first version a label like "outline1," and save the file when it is finished. When you are ready to revise the outline, create a new file for the second version ("outline2"), copy the first-draft file into the new file, and revise. If you become dissatisfied with the way the second or a subsequent one is progressing, you can discard it, return to an earlier draft, which is stored untouched on the disk, and begin revising in another direction. Printing out each new version will let you compare it more easily with other versions.

A working outline will make it easier to keep track of all important aspects of your subject and to focus your research on relevant topics. Continual revision of the working outline, moreover, will encourage you to change your thinking and your approach as new information modifies your understanding of the subject.

1.9.2. Thesis Statement

As you get closer to writing, you can begin to shape the information you have at hand into a unified, coherent whole by framing a thesis statement for your paper: a single sentence that formulates both your topic and your point of view. In a sense, the thesis statement is your answer to the central question or problem you have raised. Writing this statement will enable you to see where you are heading and to remain on a productive path as you plan and write. Try out different possibilities until you find a statement that seems right for your purpose. Moreover, since the experience of writing may well alter your original plans, do not hesitate to revise the thesis statement as you write the paper. Word processing, through its storage and retrieval capabilities, can help you build effectively on previous drafts of a thesis statement.

Two factors are important to the shaping of a thesis statement—your purpose and your audience:

- What purpose will you try to achieve in the paper? Do you want to describe something, explain something, argue for a certain point of view, or persuade your reader to think or do something?

- What audience are you writing for? Is your reader a specialist on the subject? someone likely to agree or disagree with you? someone likely to be interested or uninterested in the subject?

The answers to these questions should to a large extent give your research the appropriate slant or point of view not just in your thesis statement but also in the final outline and the paper itself.

Many instructors require students to submit thesis statements for approval some two or three weeks before the paper is due. If you have difficulty writing one, talk with your instructor about the research you have done and about what you want to say; given this information, your instructor can probably help you frame an appropriate thesis statement.

The following sample is a thesis statement for section 1.4 of this book.

Students who wish to write successful research papers must know as much as possible about the modern academic library—its central information system, reference works, online catalog of holdings, and other resources and services—and must be knowledgeable about finding useful Internet sources.

1.9.3. Final Outline

After you have a satisfactory thesis statement, you can transform your working outline into a final one. This step will help you organize your ideas and the accumulated research into a logical, fluent, and effective paper. Again, many instructors request that final outlines be submitted with papers.

Start by carefully reviewing all your notes to see how strongly they will support the various points in the working outline. Next, read over your working outline *critically* and delete everything that is irrelevant to the thesis statement or that might weaken your argument.

Eliminating material is often painful since you might have a natural desire to use everything you have collected and to impress your readers (especially teacher readers) with all the work you have done and with all you now know on the subject. But you should resist these temptations, for the inclusion of irrelevant or repetitive material will detract from the effectiveness of your paper. Keep your thesis statement and your audience in mind. Include only the ideas and information that will help you accomplish what you have set out to do and that will lead your readers to care about your investigation, your presentation, and your conclusions.

As you continue to read, reread, and think about the ideas and information you have decided to use, you will begin to see new connections between items, and patterns of organization will suggest themselves. Bring related material together under general headings, and arrange these sections so that one logically connects with another. Then order the subjects under each heading so that they, too, proceed logically. Finally, plan an effective introduction and a conclusion appropriate to the sequence you have worked out.

Common organizing principles are chronology (useful for historical discussions—e.g., how the Mexican War developed); cause and effect (e.g., what consequences a scientific discovery will have); process (e.g., how a politician got elected); and logic, deductive or inductive. A deductive line of argument moves from the general to the specific (e.g., from the problem of violence in the United States to violence involving handguns), while an inductive one moves from the specific to the general (e.g., from violence involving handguns to the problem of violence in the United States).

As you choose an organizational plan, keep in mind the method or methods you will use in developing your paper. For example, do you plan to define, classify, or analyze something? to use descriptive details or give examples? to compare or contrast one thing with another? to argue for a certain point of view? The procedures you intend to adopt will influence the way you arrange your material, and they should be evident in your outline.

It is also a good idea to indicate in the outline, specifically and precisely, the quotations and reference sources you will use. All this planning will take a good deal of time and thought, and you may well make several preliminary outlines before arriving at the one you will follow. But the time and thought will be well spent. The more planning you do, the easier and more efficient the writing will be.

If the final outline is only for your use, its form will have little importance. If it is to be submitted, your instructor will probably discuss the various forms of outline—for example, the topic outline (which uses only short phrases throughout) and the sentence outline—and tell you which to use. Whatever the form, maintain it consistently.

The descending parts of an outline are normally labeled in the following order:

I.
   A.
      1.
         a.
           (1)
             (a)
             (b)
           (2)
         b.
      2.
   B.
II.

Logic requires that there be a *II* to complement a *I*, a *B* to complement an *A*, and so forth.

The following sample is a topic outline of section 1.4 of this book.

Conducting Research

I. The modern academic library
   A. Range of available resources
      1. Print publications
      2. Electronic resources (e.g., bibliographic and full-text databases)
      3. Computer services (e.g., word processing, printers, access to Internet)
   B. Programs of orientation and instruction
      1. Pamphlets, handbooks, other materials distributed by the library
      2. Orientation tours, lectures, courses
   C. Professional reference librarians
II. The central information system
   A. Library's catalog of holdings
   B. Bibliographic reference databases
   C. Other electronic resources
   D. Links to other library catalogs
   E. On-campus and off-campus access to system
III. Reference works
   A. Types of reference works
      1. Indexes
      2. Bibliographies
      3. Collections of abstracts

      4. Guides to research
      5. Dictionaries
      6. Encyclopedias
      7. Biographical sources
      8. Yearbooks
      9. Atlases
    10. Gazetteers
    11. Statistical data sources
  B. Publication forms of reference works
      1. Print
      2. Electronic (online databases, CD-ROM databases)
  C. Searching a reference database (example: *MLA International Bibliography*)
IV. The online catalog of library holdings
  A. Definition and description
  B. Searching the online catalog
      1. Searching by author, title, subject, keywords
      2. Limiting the search
      3. Using Boolean logic
      4. Information accessed from the online catalog
  C. Information needed for research and writing
  D. Card catalog and other catalogs
  E. Location of library materials
      1. Classification systems (Dewey decimal system, Library of Congress system)
      2. Main collection (open shelves, closed stacks)
      3. Special sections (reserved books; reference works; special collections; periodicals, nonprint materials, etc.)
V. Other library resources and services
  A. Microforms: microfilm, microfiche, microcard
  B. Interlibrary loans
  C. Photocopying
  D. Electronic-resources centers
  E. Access to databases, computer services, Internet
VI. Internet sources
  A. Range of sources
      1. Definition of Internet
      2. Types of useful sites
      3. Resources available (information sources, full texts, audiovisual materials)
  B. Searching for sources

1. Professional guidance (librarians, instructors)
2. Gateway sites and search tools
3. Searches by subject and by keyword
4. Recording URL and date of access

If you have stored your notes in your computer, a helpful intermediate activity between outlining and writing is to incorporate your notes into your outline. Using this strategy, you should create a separate file for each major topic of your outline and shift relevant material, in appropriate order, from note files into the various topic files. Then, as you write, you can call up the topic files one by one and blend material from them into the text of the paper. Be sure to save and to back up your outline files.

1.10. WRITING DRAFTS

Do not expect your first draft to be the finished product. The successful research paper is usually the culmination of a series of drafts. Habits, capacities, and practices of writers differ widely. Some individuals write more slowly and come close to a final draft the first time through. Others prefer to work in stages and expect to undertake several drafts. In any case, review and rewriting are always necessary. Plan ahead and leave plenty of time for revision.

You might start off by trying to set down all your ideas in the order in which you want them to appear. Do not be concerned if the writing in the first draft is hasty and fairly rough. Attempt to stay focused by following your outline closely. Revise the outline, of course, whenever new ideas occur to you and it no longer works. After you complete a rough draft, read it over and try to refine it.

In revising, you may add, eliminate, and rearrange material. If a section in the first draft seems unclear or sketchy, you may have to expand it by writing another sentence or two or even a new paragraph. Similarly, to improve the fluency and coherence of the paper, you may need to add transitions between sentences and paragraphs or to define connections or contrasts. Delete any material that is irrelevant, unimportant, repetitive, or dull and dispensable. If the presentation of ideas seems illogical or confusing, you may find that you can clarify by rearranging phrases, clauses, sentences, or paragraphs.

In later drafts you should concern yourself with the more mechani-

cal kinds of revision. For example, strive for more precise and economical wording. Try, in addition, to vary your sentence patterns as
well as your choice of words. Finally, correct all technical errors,
using a standard writing guide to check punctuation, grammar, and
usage and consulting a standard dictionary for the spelling and meaning of words. Your last draft, carefully proofread and corrected, is the
text of your research paper.

If you do not own a computer, see whether your school has personal
computers available for student use. With a word processor, you can
store a first draft—or just a portion of one—and later retrieve and
revise it. If you create a different file for each draft, you can return to a
preceding draft whenever you wish.

Word processing makes it easy to insert words into, or delete words
from, your text and to shift a word or a block of words from one part of
the text to another. Moreover, you can produce a printed version of a
revision without having to retype the whole new draft. Word processing can also help you center titles, format pages, and perform other
such mechanical tasks. For example, the global revision feature of
word processing permits you to search for and automatically change
text. Thus, if you realize you misspelled the same word several times
in your draft, you can correct all the misspellings with a single
command.

Word processing similarly allows for more efficient transitions
between the various activities related to the research paper. After
developing an outline, for instance, you can copy it into a new file,
where the outline can serve as the basis for your writing of the text. Or
if you created a file of notes for each major topic in your outline (see
1.9.3), you can copy into the text file each topic file in sequence as you
write. If your paper will be short and you have taken few notes, you
may choose to copy the entire note file into the text file. Using this
approach, you can scroll up and down the file and transfer what you
want into the text of the paper. If your paper will be longer and you
have created a separate file for each of numerous sources, you can
readily transfer material (e.g., an effective quotation) from a note file to
the text file. You might find it easier to print out all your notes before
writing the paper and to decide in advance which ones you want to
use in the text. In this way, when you retrieve note files, you will
know exactly what parts you are seeking. Another way to proceed is to
use split screens or multiple windows to read note files as you write
the paper. When you have completed your final draft, you can simply
add the file containing the works-cited list to the end of the paper.

With practice and planning, then, as you write your paper you can use a word processor strategically to draw on outline, note, and bibliography files that you created earlier in the project.

Word processing has certain limitations. Since no more than a fixed number of lines of text are visible on a computer screen, you may find it difficult to get a sense of your whole project. Some writers like to print out text regularly to see better how the writing is developing from paragraph to paragraph and from page to page. Use spelling and usage checkers cautiously, for they are only as effective as the dictionaries they contain. On the one hand, a spelling checker will call your attention to words that are correctly spelled if they are not in its dictionary. On the other, it will not point out misspellings that match words in the dictionary—for example, *their* used for *there* or *its* for *it's*.

Finally, in working on a computer file, you run the risk of losing it, through a technical mistake, equipment failure, or a power outage. Be sure to save your work frequently (after writing a page or so), not just when you finish with it or leave the computer. It is also a good idea to keep a paper copy of text you write and to create a backup disk in case something happens to the disk you are using to prepare the paper. Most important of all, leave yourself ample time to cope with any technical problems that may arise.

1.11. LANGUAGE AND STYLE

Effective writing depends as much on clarity and readability as on content. The organization and development of your ideas, the unity and coherence of your presentation, and your command of sentence structure, grammar, and diction are all important considerations, as are the mechanics of writing—capitalization, spelling, punctuation, and so on. The key to successful communication is using the right language for the audience you are addressing. In all writing, the challenge is to find the words, phrases, clauses, sentences, and paragraphs that express your thoughts and ideas precisely and that make them interesting to others.

Because good scholarship requires objectivity, careful writers of research papers avoid language that implies unsubstantiated or irrelevant generalizations about such personal qualities as age, economic class, ethnicity, sexual orientation, political or religious beliefs, race, or sex. Discussions about this subject have generally focused on wording that could be labeled sexist. For example, many writers no longer use *he*, *him*, or *his* to express a meaning that includes women or girls: "If a young artist is not confident, he can quickly become discouraged." The use of *she*, *her*, and *hers* to refer to a person who may be of either sex can also be distracting and momentarily confusing. Both usages can often be avoided through a revision that recasts the sentence into the plural or that eliminates the pronoun: "If young artists are not confident, they can quickly become discouraged" or "A young artist who is not confident can quickly become discouraged." Another technique is to make the discussion refer to a person who is identified, so that there is a reason to use a specific singular pronoun. *They*, *them*, *their*, and *theirs* cannot logically be applied to a single person, and *he or she* and *her or him* are cumbersome alternatives to be used sparingly. Many authors now also avoid terms that unnecessarily integrate a person's sex with a job or role. For instance, *anchorman*, *policeman*, *stewardess*, and *poetess* are commonly replaced with *anchor*, *police officer*, *flight attendant*, and *poet*. For advice on current practices, consult your instructor or one of the guides to nonsexist language listed in 1.12.

1.12. GUIDES TO WRITING

A good dictionary is an essential tool for all writers. Your instructor will probably recommend a standard American dictionary such as *The American Heritage College Dictionary*, *Merriam-Webster's Collegiate Dictionary*, or *Random House Webster's College Dictionary*. Because dictionaries vary in matters like word division and spelling preference, you should, to maintain consistency, use the same one throughout your paper.

You should also keep on hand at least one reliable guide to writing. A selected list of writing guides appears below, classified under four headings. Your instructor can help you choose among these titles.

Handbooks of Composition

Baker, Sheridan. *The Practical Stylist*. 8th ed. New York: Longman-Addison, 1998.
Beene, Lynn, and William Vande Kopple. *The Riverside Handbook*. Boston: Houghton, 1992.

Corbett, Edward P. J., and Sheryl L. Finkle. *The Little English Handbook: Choices and Conventions*. 8th ed. New York: Longman-Addison, 1997.

Crews, Frederick. *The Random House Handbook*. 6th ed. New York: McGraw, 1992.

Fowler, H. Ramsey, and Jane E. Aaron. *The Little, Brown Handbook*. 7th ed. New York: Longman-Addison, 1998.

Hacker, Diana. *The Bedford Handbook for Writers*. 5th ed. Boston: Bedford–St. Martin's, 1998.

Hairston, Maxine C., and John J. Rusziewicz. *The Scott, Foresman Handbook for Writers*. 4th ed. New York: Longman-Addison, 1996.

Heffernan, James A. W., and John E. Lincoln. *Writing: A College Handbook*. 4th ed. New York: Norton, 1994.

Hodges, John C., et al. *Harbrace College Handbook*. 13th ed. New York: Harcourt, 1998.

Kirszner, Laurie G., and Stephen R. Mandell. *The Holt Handbook*. 4th ed. New York: Harcourt, 1998.

Kramer, Melinda G., Glenn Leggett, and C. David Mead. *Prentice Hall Handbook for Writers*. 12th ed. Englewood Cliffs: Prentice, 1994.

Lunsford, Andrea, and Robert Connors. *The St. Martin's Handbook*. 3rd ed. New York: St. Martin's, 1995.

Marius, Richard, and Harvey S. Wiener. *The McGraw-Hill College Handbook*. 4th ed. New York: McGraw, 1994.

Mulderig, Gerald P. *The Heath Handbook*. 13th ed. Boston: Houghton, 1995.

Rosen, Leonard J., and Laurence Behrens. *The Allyn and Bacon Handbook*. 3rd ed. Boston: Allyn, 1997.

Troyka, Lynn Quitman. *Simon and Schuster Handbook for Writers*. 4th ed. Englewood Cliffs: Prentice, 1995.

Watkins, Floyd C., and William B. Dillingham. *Practical English Handbook*. 9th ed. Boston: Houghton, 1992.

Dictionaries of Usage

Bernstein, Theodore. *The Careful Writer: A Modern Guide to English Usage*. New York: Atheneum, 1965.

Bryant, Margaret M. *Current American Usage: How Americans Say It and Write It*. New York: Funk, 1962.

Copperud, Roy H. *American Usage and Style: The Consensus*. New York: Van Nostrand, 1980.

Evans, Bergen, and Cornelia Evans. *A Dictionary of Contemporary American Usage*. New York: Random, 1957.

Follett, Wilson. *Modern American Usage: A Guide.* Ed. Jacques Barzun. New York: Hill, 1966.

———. *Modern American Usage: A Guide.* Rev. Erik Wensberg. Rev. ed. New York: Hill-Farrar, 1998.

Fowler, H[enry] W. *A Dictionary of Modern English Usage.* Ed. Ernest Gowers. 2nd ed. New York: Oxford UP, 1965.

———. *The New Fowler's Modern English Usage.* Ed. R. W. Burchfield. 3rd ed. Oxford: Clarendon, 1996.

Garner, Bryan A. *A Dictionary of Modern American Usage.* New York: Oxford UP, 1998.

Mager, Nathan H., and Sylvia K. Mager. *Prentice Hall Encyclopedic Dictionary of English Usage.* 2nd ed. Englewood Cliffs: Prentice, 1992.

Morris, William, and Mary Morris. *Harper Dictionary of Contemporary Usage.* 2nd ed. New York: Harper, 1985.

Nicholson, Margaret. *A Dictionary of American-English Usage Based on Fowler's* Modern English Usage. New York: Oxford UP, 1957.

Waite, Maurice, Edmund S. Weiner, and Andrew Delahunty. *The Oxford Dictionary and Usage Guide to the English Language.* New York: Oxford UP, 1995.

Weiner, Edmund S., and Andrew Delahunty. *The Oxford Guide to English Usage.* 2nd ed. New York: Oxford UP, 1994.

Wilson, Kenneth G. *The Columbia Guide to Standard American English.* New York: Columbia UP, 1993.

Guides to Nonsexist Language

American Psychological Association. "Guidelines to Reduce Bias in Language." *Publication Manual of the American Psychological Association.* 4th ed. Washington: Amer. Psychological Assn., 1994. 46–60.

Frank, Francine Wattman, and Paula A. Treichler, with others. *Language, Gender, and Professional Writing: Theoretical Approaches and Guidelines for Nonsexist Usage.* New York: MLA, 1989.

International Association of Business Communication. *Without Bias: A Guidebook for Nondiscriminatory Communication.* Ed. J. E. Pickens, P. W. Rao, and L. C. Roberts. 2nd ed. New York: Wiley, 1982.

Maggio, Rosalie. *The Dictionary of Bias-Free Usage: A Guide to Nondiscriminatory Language.* Phoenix: Oryx, 1991.

———. *The Nonsexist Word Finder: A Dictionary of Gender-Free Usage.* Phoenix: Oryx, 1987.

———. *Talking about People: A Guide to Fair and Accurate Language.* Phoenix: Oryx, 1997.

Miller, Casey, and Kate Swift. *The Handbook of Nonsexist Writing.* 2nd ed. New York: Harper, 1988.

Schwartz, Marilyn, and the Task Force of the Association of American University Presses. *Guidelines for Bias-Free Writing.* Bloomington: Indiana UP, 1995.

Sorrels, Bobbye D. *The Nonsexist Communicator: Solving the Problems of Gender and Awkwardness in Modern English.* Englewood Cliffs: Prentice, 1983.

Warren, Virginia L. "Guidelines for the Nonsexist Use of Language." *American Philosophical Association Proceedings* 59 (1986): 471–84.

Books on Style

Barzun, Jacques. *Simple and Direct: A Rhetoric for Writers.* Rev. ed. New York: Harper, 1984.

Beardsley, Monroe C. *Thinking Straight: Principles of Reasoning for Readers and Writers.* 4th ed. Englewood Cliffs: Prentice, 1975.

Cook, Claire Kehrwald. *Line by Line: How to Edit Your Own Writing.* Boston: Houghton, 1985.

Eastman, Richard M. *Style: Writing and Reading as the Discovery of Outlook.* 3rd ed. New York: Oxford UP, 1984.

Elbow, Peter. *Writing without Teachers.* 2nd ed. New York: Oxford UP, 1998.

———. *Writing with Power: Techniques for Mastering the Writing Process.* New York: Oxford UP, 1981.

Gibson, Walker. *Tough, Sweet, and Stuffy: An Essay on Modern American Prose Styles.* Bloomington: Indiana UP, 1966.

Gowers, Ernest. *The Complete Plain Words.* Ed. Sidney Greenbaum and Janet Whitcut. Rev. ed. Boston: Godine, 1990.

Lanham, Richard A. *Style: An Anti-textbook.* New Haven: Yale UP, 1974.

Smith, Charles K. *Styles and Structures: Alternative Approaches to College Writing.* New York: Norton, 1974.

Strunk, William, Jr., and E. B. White. *The Elements of Style.* 3rd ed. New York: Macmillan, 1979.

Williams, Joseph M. *Style: Ten Lessons in Clarity and Grace.* 5th ed. New York: Longman-Addison, 1996.

———. *Style: Toward Clarity and Grace.* Chicago: U of Chicago P, 1990.

2 The Mechanics of Writing

Although the scope of this book precludes a detailed discussion of grammar, usage, style, and related aspects of writing, this chapter addresses mechanical questions that you will likely encounter in writing research papers.

1. Spelling
2. Punctuation
3. Italics (underlining)
4. Names of persons
5. Numbers
6. Titles of works in the research paper
7. Quotations
8. Capitalization and personal names in languages other than English

2.1. SPELLING

2.1.1. Consistency

Spelling, including hyphenation, should be consistent throughout the research paper—except in quotations, which must retain the spelling of the original, whether correct or incorrect. You can best ensure consistency by always adopting the spelling that your dictionary gives first in any entry with variant spellings. (See 1.12 for titles of standard dictionaries.)

2.1.2. Word Division

To save time and avoid possible errors, do not divide words at the ends of lines. If a word you are about to type on a typewriter will not fit on the line, you may leave the line short and begin the word on the next line. The "word-wrap" feature of word-processing programs performs this operation automatically. If you choose to divide a word, consult your dictionary about where the break should occur.

2.1.3. Plurals

The plurals of English words are generally formed by adding the suffix -*s* or -*es* (*laws, taxes*), with several exceptions (e.g., *children, halves, mice, sons-in-law, bison*). The tendency in American English is to form the plurals of words naturalized from other languages in the standard manner. The plurals *librettos* and *formulas* are therefore now more common in American English than *libretti* and *formulae*. But some adopted words, like *alumni* and *phenomena*, retain the original plurals. Consult a dictionary for guidance. If the dictionary gives more than one plural form for a word (*appendixes, appendices*), use the first listed. (See 2.2.7 for plurals of letters and for possessive forms of plurals.)

2.1.4. Foreign Words

If you quote material in a foreign language, you must reproduce all accents and other marks exactly as they appear in the original (*école, pietà, tête, leçon, Fähre, año*). If you need marks that are not available on your word processor or typewriter, write them in by hand. On the use of foreign words in an English text, see 2.3.2; on capitalization and personal names in languages other than English, see 2.8.

2.2. PUNCTUATION

2.2.1. The Purpose of Punctuation

The primary purpose of punctuation is to ensure the clarity and readability of writing. Punctuation clarifies sentence structure, separating some words and grouping others. It adds meaning to written words and guides the understanding of readers as they move through sentences. The rules set forth here cover many of the situations you will encounter in writing research papers. For the punctuation of quotations in your text, see 2.7. For the punctuation of parenthetical references and bibliographies, see chapters 4 and 5. See also the individual listings in the index for specific punctuation marks.

2.2.2. Commas

a. Use a comma before a coordinating conjunction (*and, but, for, nor, or, yet,* or *so*) joining independent clauses in a sentence.

```
Congress passed the bill, and the president signed it
into law.
```

```
The poem is ironic, for the poet's meaning contrasts
with her words.
```

```
Take along a tape recorder, or you risk misquoting your
interviewee.
```

```
Other wars were longer, but few were as costly in human
lives.
```

b. Use commas to separate words, phrases, and clauses in a series.

WORDS

```
Boccaccio's tales have inspired plays, films, operas,
and paintings.
```

PHRASES

```
Alfred the Great established a system of fortified
towns, reorganized the military forces, and built a
fleet of warships.
```

CLAUSES

```
In the Great Depression, millions lost their jobs,
businesses failed, and charitable institutions closed
their doors.
```

But use semicolons when items in a series have internal commas.

```
Pollsters focused their efforts on Columbus, Ohio; Des
Moines, Iowa; and Saint Louis, Missouri.
```

c. Use a comma between coordinate adjectives—that is, adjectives that separately modify the same noun.

Critics praise the novel's unaffected, unadorned style. (The adjectives *unaffected* and *unadorned* each modify *style*.)

The new regime imposed harsh, repressive laws. (The adjectives *harsh* and *repressive* each modify *laws*.)

But note:

Most of the characters are average city dwellers. (The adjective *average* modifies *city dwellers*.)

A famous photo shows Marianne Moore in a black tricornered hat. (The adjective *black* modifies *tricornered hat*.)

d. Use commas to set off a parenthetical comment, or an aside, if it is brief and closely related to the rest of the sentence. (For punctuation of longer, more intrusive, or more complex parenthetical elements, see 2.2.5.)

The Tudors, for example, ruled for over a century.

The vernacular, after all, was the language of everyday life.

Tonight's performance, I'm sorry to say, has been canceled.

e. Use commas to set off a nonrestrictive modifier—that is, a modifier that is not essential to the meaning of the sentence. A nonrestrictive modifier, unlike a restrictive one, could be dropped without changing the main sense of the sentence. Modifiers in the following three categories are either nonrestrictive or restrictive. (For the use of parentheses and dashes around complex nonrestrictive modifiers, see 2.2.5b.)

Words in apposition

NONRESTRICTIVE

The color of the costume, blue, acquires symbolic meaning in the story.

The theme song of the campaign, "Happy Days Are Here Again," is indelibly associated with the Great Depression.

Isabel Allende, the Chilean novelist, will appear at the arts forum tonight.

RESTRICTIVE

The color blue acquires symbolic meaning in the story.

The campaign song "Happy Days Are Here Again" is indelibly associated with the Great Depression.

The Chilean novelist Isabel Allende will appear at the arts forum tonight.

Clauses that begin with *who*, *whom*, *whose*, *which*, and *that*

NONRESTRICTIVE

Scientists, who must observe standards of objectivity in their work, can contribute usefully to public-policy debates.

The Italian sonnet, which is exemplified in Petrarch's Canzoniere, developed into the English sonnet.

RESTRICTIVE

Scientists who receive the Nobel Prize sometimes contribute usefully to public-policy debates.

The sonnet that is exemplified in Petrarch's Canzoniere developed into the English sonnet.

Note that some writers prefer to use *which* to introduce nonrestrictive clauses and *that* to introduce restrictive clauses.

Adverbial phrases and clauses

NONRESTRICTIVE

The novel takes place in China, where many languages are spoken.

The ending is sad, as the narrator hinted it would be.

RESTRICTIVE

The novel takes place in a land where many languages are spoken.

The ending is as the narrator hinted it would be.

f. Use a comma after a long introductory phrase or clause.

PHRASE

After years of anxiety over the family's finances, Linda Loman looks forward to the day the mortgage will be paid off.

CLAUSE

Although she was virtually unknown in her day, scholars have come to recognize the originality of her work.

g. Use commas to set off alternative or contrasting phrases.

The king remains a tragic figure, however appalling his actions.

A determined, even obsessed, taxi driver tells of his ambitions.

It is Julio, not his mother, who sets the plot in motion.

But note:

Several cooperative but autonomous republics were formed. (The conjunction *but* links *cooperative* and *autonomous*, making a comma inappropriate.)

h. Do not use a comma between subject and verb.

Many of the characters who dominate the early chapters and then disappear [no comma] are portraits of the author's friends.

i. Do not use a comma between verb and object.

The agent reported to the headquarters staff [no comma]
that the documents had been traced to an underground
garage.

j. Do not use a comma between the parts of a compound subject,
compound object, or compound verb.

COMPOUND SUBJECT

A dozen wooden chairs [no comma] and a window that admits
a shaft of light complete the stage setting.

COMPOUND OBJECT

Ptolemy devised a system of astronomy accepted until the
sixteenth century [no comma] and a scientific approach to
the study of geography.

COMPOUND VERB

He composed several successful symphonies [no comma] but
won the most fame for his witticisms.

k. Do not use a comma between two parallel subordinate elements.

Nona thought of the crew members, who worked from dawn to
dusk [no comma] but whose lives seemed free and joyful.

She broadens her analysis by exploring the tragic
elements of the play [no comma] and by integrating the
hunting motif with the themes of death and resurrection.

The farmhouse stood on top of a hill [no comma] and just
beyond the Silver Creek bridge.

l. Use a comma in a date whose order is month, day, and year. If such
a date comes in the middle of a sentence, include a comma after the year.

Martin Luther King, Jr., was born on January 15, 1929,
and died on April 4, 1968.

But commas are not used with dates whose order is day, month,
and year.

```
Martin Luther King, Jr., was born on 15 January 1929 and
died on 4 April 1968.
```

m. Do not use a comma between a month and a year or between a season and a year.

```
The events of July 1789 are as familiar to the French as
those of July 1776 are to Americans.
```

```
I passed my oral exams in spring 1999.
```

See 2.7.7 for commas with quotations.

2.2.3. Semicolons

a. Use a semicolon between independent clauses not linked by a conjunction.

```
The coat is tattered beyond repair; still, Akaky hopes
the tailor can mend it.
```

b. Use semicolons between items in a series when the items contain commas.

```
Present at the symposium were Henri Guillaume, the art
critic; Sam Brown, the Daily Tribune reporter; and Maria
Rosa, the conceptual artist.
```

2.2.4. Colons

The colon is used between two parts of a sentence when the first part creates a sense of anticipation about what follows in the second. Leave only one space after a colon, not two.

a. Use a colon to introduce a list, an elaboration of what was just said, or the formal expression of a rule or principle.

LIST

The reading list includes three Latin American novels: The Death of Artemio Cruz, One Hundred Years of Solitude, and The Green House.

ELABORATION

The plot is founded on deception: the three main characters have secret identities.

RULE OR PRINCIPLE

Many books would be briefer if their authors followed the logical principle known as Occam's razor: Explanations should not be multiplied unnecessarily. (A rule or principle after a colon should begin with a capital letter.)

But a verb or preposition that performs the same introductory function as a colon makes the colon unnecessary.

The novels on the reading list include The Death of Artemio Cruz, One Hundred Years of Solitude, and The Green House. (The verb *include* performs the introductory function.)

The reading list includes such novels as The Death of Artemio Cruz, One Hundred Years of Solitude, and The Green House. (The preposition *as* performs the introductory function.)

b. Use a colon to introduce a quotation that is independent from the structure of the main sentence.

In The Awakening, Mme Ratignolle exhorts Robert Lebrun to stop flirting with Edna: "She is not one of us; she is not like us."

A quotation that is integral to the sentence structure is generally preceded by no punctuation or, if a verb of saying (*says, exclaims, notes, writes*) introduces the quotation, by a comma. A colon is used after a verb of saying, however, if the verb introduces certain kinds of formal literary quotations, such as long quotations set off from the main text (see 2.7.2–4, 2.7.7).

2.2.5. Dashes and Parentheses

Dashes make a sharper break in the continuity of the sentence than commas do, and parentheses make a still sharper one. To indicate a dash in typing, use two hyphens, with no space before, between, or after. (Some word processors have a dash, and you may use it instead of hyphens.) Your writing will be smoother and more readable if you use dashes and parentheses sparingly. Limit the number of dashes in a sentence to two paired dashes or one unpaired dash.

a. Use dashes or parentheses to enclose a sentence element that interrupts the train of thought.

```
Soaring in a balloon--inventors first performed this
feat in 1783--is a way to recapture the wonder that
early aviators must have felt.

The "hero" of the play (the townspeople see him as
heroic, but he is the focus of the author's satire)
introduces himself as a veteran of the war.
```

b. Use dashes or parentheses to set off a parenthetical element that contains a comma and that might be misread if set off with commas.

```
The colors of the costume--blue, scarlet, and yellow--
acquire symbolic meaning in the story.

The Italian sonnet (which is exemplified in Petrarch's
Canzoniere, along with other kinds of poems) developed
into the English sonnet.
```

c. Use a dash to introduce words that summarize a preceding series.

```
Ruthlessness and acute sensitivity, greed and
compassion--the main character's contradictory qualities
prevent any simple interpretation of the film.
```

A dash may also be used instead of a colon to introduce a list or an elaboration of what was just said (see 2.2.4a).

2.2.6. Hyphens

Compound words of all types—nouns, verbs, adjectives, and so on—are written as separate words (*hard drive, hard labor*), with hyphens (*hard-and-fast, hard-boiled*), and as single words (*hardcover, hardheaded*). The dictionary shows how to write many compounds. A compound not in the dictionary should usually be written as separate words unless a hyphen is needed to prevent readers from misunderstanding the relation between the words. Following are some rules to help you decide whether you need a hyphen in compounds and other terms that may not appear in the dictionary.

a. Use a hyphen in a compound adjective beginning with an adverb such as *better, best, ill, lower, little,* or *well* when the adjective precedes a noun.

```
better-prepared ambassador
best-known work
ill-informed reporter
lower-priced tickets
well-dressed announcer
```

But do not use a hyphen when the compound adjective comes after the noun it modifies.

```
The ambassador was better prepared than the other
delegates.
```

b. Do not use a hyphen in a compound adjective beginning with an adverb ending in *-ly* or with *too, very,* or *much.*

```
thoughtfully presented thesis
very contrived plot
too hasty judgment
much maligned performer
```

c. Use a hyphen in a compound adjective ending with the present participle (e.g., *loving*) or the past participle (e.g., *inspired*) of a verb when the adjective precedes a noun.

```
sports-loving throng
fear-inspired loyalty
hate-filled speech
```

d. Use a hyphen in a compound adjective formed by a number and a noun when the adjective precedes a noun.

```
twelfth-floor apartment
second-semester courses
early-thirteenth-century architecture
```

e. Use hyphens in other compound adjectives before nouns to prevent misreading.

```
continuing-education program
```
(The hyphen indicates that the term refers to a program of continuing education and not to an education program that is continuing.)

```
Portuguese-language student
```
(The hyphen makes it clear that the term refers to a student who is studying Portuguese and not to a language student who is Portuguese.)

f. Do not use hyphens in familiar unhyphenated compound terms, such as *social security*, *high school*, *liberal arts*, and *show business*, when they appear before nouns as modifiers.

```
social security tax
high school reunion
liberal arts curriculum
show business debut
```

g. Use hyphens to join coequal nouns.

```
writer-critic
scholar-athlete
author-chef
```

But do not use a hyphen in a pair of nouns in which the first noun modifies the second.

```
father figure
opera lover
```

h. In general, do not use hyphens after prefixes (e.g., *anti-, co-, multi-, non-, over-, post-, pre-, re-, semi-, sub-, un-, under-*).

`antiwar`	`overpay`	`semiretired`
`coworker`	`postwar`	`subsatellite`
`multinational`	`prescheduled`	`unambiguous`
`nonjudgmental`	`reinvigorate`	`underrepresented`

But sometimes a hyphen is called for after a prefix:

`post-Victorian` (Use a hyphen before a capital letter.)

`re-cover` (The hyphen distinguishes this verb, meaning "cover again,"
from *recover*, meaning "get back.")

`anti-icing` (Without the hyphen, the doubled vowel would make the
term hard to recognize.)

2.2.7. Apostrophes

A principal function of apostrophes is to indicate possession. They are also used to form contractions (*can't, wouldn't*), which are rarely acceptable in research papers, and the plurals of the letters of the alphabet (*p's and q's, three A's*).

a. To form the possessive of a singular noun, add an apostrophe and an *s*.

`the zebra's stripes`

`a poem's meter`

`the dean's list`

b. To form the possessive of a plural noun ending in *s*, add only an apostrophe.

`photographers' props`

`firefighters' trucks`

`tourists' luggage`

c. To form the possessive of an irregular plural noun not ending in *s*, add an apostrophe and an *s*.

```
children's entertainment
the media's role
women's studies
```

d. To form the possessive of nouns in a series, add a single apostrophe and an *s* if the ownership is shared.

```
Palmer and Colton's book on European history
Fred, Lucinda, and Nan's house
```

But if the ownership is separate, place an apostrophe and an *s* after each noun.

```
Fred's, Lucinda's, and Nan's coats
```

e. To form the possessive of any singular proper noun, add an apostrophe and an *s*.

```
Venus's beauty
Dickens's reputation
Descartes's philosophy
Marx's precepts
```

f. To form the possessive of a plural proper noun, add only an apostrophe.

```
the Vanderbilts' estate
the Dickenses' economic woes
```

g. Do not use an apostrophe to form the plural of an abbreviation or a number.

```
PhDs                    1990s
MAs                     fours
VCRs                    SAT score in the 1400s
IRAs
```

On using apostrophes to abbreviate dates, see 2.5.5.

2.2.8. Quotation Marks

a. Place quotation marks around a word or phrase given in a special sense or purposefully misused.

```
A silver dome concealed the robot's "brain."
```

```
Their "friend" brought about their downfall.
```

If introduced unnecessarily, this device can make writing heavy-handed. Quotation marks are not needed after *so-called*.

```
Their so-called friend brought about their downfall.
```

b. Use quotation marks for a translation of a foreign word or phrase.

```
Et ux., a legal abbreviation for the Latin et uxor, means
"and wife."
```

```
The first idiomatic Spanish expression I learned was
irse todo en humo ("to go up in smoke").
```

You may use single quotation marks for a translation that follows the original directly, without intervening words or punctuation.

```
The word text derives from the Latin verb texere 'to
weave.'
```

On quotation marks with titles, see 2.6.3–4. On quotation marks with quotations and with translations of quotations, see 2.7.7 and 2.7.8, respectively.

2.2.9. Square Brackets

Use square brackets around a parenthesis within a parenthesis, so that the levels of subordination can be easily distinguished. Insert square brackets by hand if they are not available on your word processor or typewriter.

```
The sect known as the Jansenists (after Cornelius Jansen
[1585-1638]) faced opposition from both the king and the
pope.
```

```
The labors of Heracles (Hercules) included the slaying
of the Nemean lion (so called because Hera [Juno] sent
it to destroy the Nemean plain).
```

For square brackets around an ellipsis or an interpolation in a quotation, see 2.7.5 and 2.7.6, respectively. For square brackets around missing, unverified, or interpolated data in documentation, see 4.6.1, 4.6.23, and 4.6.25.

2.2.10. Slashes

The slash, or diagonal, is rarely necessary in formal prose. Other than in quotations of poetry (see 2.7.3), the slash has a place mainly between two terms paired as opposites or alternatives and used together as a noun.

```
The writer discussed how fundamental oppositions like
good/evil, East/West, and aged/young affect the way
cultures view historical events.
```

But use a hyphen when such a compound precedes and modifies a noun.

```
nature-nurture conflict
either-or situation
East-West relations
```

2.2.11. Periods, Question Marks, and Exclamation Points

A sentence can end with a period, a question mark, or an exclamation point. Periods end declarative sentences. (For the use of periods with ellipsis points, see 2.7.5.) Question marks follow interrogative sentences. Except in direct quotation, avoid exclamation points in research writing.

Place a question mark inside a closing quotation mark if the quoted passage is a question. Place a question mark outside if the quotation ends a sentence that is a question. If a question mark occurs where a comma or period would normally be required, omit the comma or period. Note the use of the question mark and other punctuation marks in the following sentences:

```
Whitman asks, "Have you felt so proud to get at the
meaning of poems?"
```

```
Where does Whitman speak of "the meaning of poems"?
```

```
"Have you felt so proud to get at the meaning of poems?"
Whitman asks.
```

2.3. ITALICS (UNDERLINING)

Italic is a style of type in which the characters slant to the right (*Casablanca*). In research papers and manuscripts submitted for publication, words that would be italicized in print are usually underlined.

```
Casablanca
```

Many word-processing programs and computer printers permit the reproduction of italic type. In material that will be graded, edited, or typeset, however, the type style of every letter and punctuation mark must be easily recognizable. Italic type is sometimes not distinctive enough for this purpose, and you can avoid ambiguity by using underlining when you intend italics. If you wish to use italics rather than underlining, check your instructor's preferences.

In electronic environments that do not permit text formatting, it is common to place one underline before and after each word or group of words that would be italicized in print.

```
_Casablanca_
```

```
_Life Is a Dream_
```

The rest of this section discusses using italics for words and letters referred to as words and letters (2.3.1), foreign words in an English text (2.3.2), and emphasis (2.3.3). (See 2.6.2 for italicizing of titles.)

2.3.1. Words and Letters Referred to as Words and Letters

Underline words and letters that are referred to as words and letters.

```
Shaw spelled Shakespeare without the final e.
```

> The word <u>albatross</u> probably derives from the Spanish and
> Portuguese word <u>alcatraz</u>.

2.3.2. Foreign Words in an English Text

In general, underline foreign words used in an English text.

> The Renaissance courtier was expected to display
> <u>sprezzatura</u>, or nonchalance, in the face of adversity.

The numerous exceptions to this rule include quotations entirely in another language ("Julius Caesar said, 'Veni, vidi, vici'"); non-English titles of short works (poems, short stories, essays, articles), which are placed in quotation marks and not underlined ("El sueño," the title of a poem by Quevedo); proper names (Marguerite de Navarre); and foreign words anglicized through frequent use. Since American English rapidly naturalizes words, use a dictionary to decide whether a foreign expression requires italics. Following are some adopted foreign words, abbreviations, and phrases commonly not underlined:

ad hoc	et al.	laissez-faire
cliché	etc.	lieder
concerto	genre	raison d'être
e.g.	hubris	versus

2.3.3. Emphasis

Italics for emphasis ("Booth *does* concede, however [. . .]") is a device that rapidly becomes ineffective. It is rarely appropriate in research writing.

2.4. NAMES OF PERSONS

2.4.1. First and Subsequent Uses of Names

In general, the first time you use a person's name in the text of your research paper, state it fully and accurately, exactly as it appears in your source.

```
Arthur George Rust, Jr.
Victoria M. Sackville-West
```

Do not change Arthur George Rust, Jr., to Arthur George Rust, for example, or drop the hyphen in Victoria M. Sackville-West. In subsequent references to the person, you may give the last name only (Rust, Sackville-West)—unless, of course, you refer to two or more persons with the same last name—or you may give the most common form of the name (e.g., Garcilaso for Garcilaso de la Vega). In casual references to the very famous—say, Mozart, Shakespeare, or Michelangelo—it is not necessary to give the full name initially.

In some languages (e.g., Chinese, Hungarian, Japanese, Korean, and Vietnamese), surnames precede given names; consult the *MLA Style Manual and Guide to Scholarly Publishing* (2nd ed. [New York: MLA, 1998], 3.6.7, 3.6.12) and other relevant reference works for guidance on these names. For rules concerning names of persons in other languages, see 2.8.

2.4.2. Titles of Persons

In general, do not use formal titles (Mr., Mrs., Miss, Ms., Dr., Professor, Reverend) in referring to men or women, living or dead (Churchill, not Mr. Churchill; Einstein, not Professor Einstein; Hess, not Dame Myra; Montagu, not Lady Montagu). A few women in history are traditionally known by their titles as married women (e.g., Mrs. Humphry Ward, Mme de Staël). Treat other women's names the same as men's.

FIRST USE	SUBSEQUENT USES
Emily Dickinson	Dickinson (not Miss Dickinson)
Harriet Beecher Stowe	Stowe (not Mrs. Stowe)
Margaret Mead	Mead (not Ms. Mead)

The appropriate way to refer to persons with titles of nobility can vary. For example, the full name and title of Henry Howard, earl of Surrey, should be given at first mention, and thereafter Surrey alone may be used. In contrast, for Benjamin Disraeli, first earl of Beaconsfield, it is sufficient to give Benjamin Disraeli initially and Disraeli subsequently. Follow the example of your sources in citing titles of nobility.

2.4.3. Names of Authors and Fictional Characters

It is common and acceptable to use simplified names of famous authors (Vergil for Publius Vergilius Maro, Dante for Dante Alighieri). Also acceptable are pseudonyms of authors.

Molière (Jean-Baptiste Poquelin)

Voltaire (François-Marie Arouet)

George Sand (Amandine-Aurore-Lucie Dupin)

George Eliot (Mary Ann Evans)

Mark Twain (Samuel Clemens)

Stendhal (Marie-Henri Beyle)

Novalis (Friedrich von Hardenberg)

Refer to fictional characters in the same way that the work of fiction does. You need not always use their full names, and you may retain titles (Dr. Jekyll, Mme Defarge).

2.5. NUMBERS

2.5.1. Arabic Numerals

Although there are still a few well-established uses for roman numerals (see 2.5.7), virtually all numbers not spelled out are commonly represented today by arabic numerals. If your keyboard does not have the number *1*, use a small letter el (*l*), not capital *I*, for the arabic numeral. If your keyboard has the number *1*, do not substitute the small el.

2.5.2. Use of Words or Numerals

If you are writing about literature or another subject that involves infrequent use of numbers, you may spell out numbers written in one or two words and represent other numbers by numerals (*one, thirty-six, ninety-nine, one hundred, fifteen hundred, two thousand, three million,* but *2½, 101, 137, 1,275*). To form the plural of a spelled-out number, treat the word like an ordinary noun (*sixes, sevens*).

If your project is one that calls for frequent use of numbers—say, a paper on a scientific subject or a study of statistical findings—use numerals for all numbers that precede technical units of measurement (*16 amperes, 5 milliliters*). In such a project, also use numerals for numbers that are presented together and that refer to similar things, such as in comparisons or reports of experimental data. Spell out other numbers if they can be written in one or two words. In the following example of statistical writing, neither "ten years" nor "six-state region" is presented with related figures, so the numbers are spelled out, unlike the other numbers in the sentence.

```
In the ten years covered by the study, the number of
participating institutions in the United States doubled,
reaching 90, and membership in the six-state region rose
from 4 to 15.
```

But do not begin a sentence with a numeral.

```
Nineteen ninety-two began with several good omens.
```

Except at the beginning of a sentence, always use numerals in the following instances:

WITH ABBREVIATIONS OR SYMBOLS

```
6 lbs.              4:20 p.m.              3%
8 KB                $9                     2"
```

IN ADDRESSES

```
4401 13th Avenue
```

IN DATES

```
1 April 2001
April 1, 2001
```

IN DECIMAL FRACTIONS

```
8.3
```

IN PAGE REFERENCES

```
page 7
```

For large numbers, you may use a combination of numerals and words.

```
4.5 million
```

Express related numbers in the same style.

```
only 5 of the 250 delegates
exactly 3 automobiles and 129 trucks
from 1 billion to 1.2 billion
```

2.5.3. Commas in Numbers

Commas are usually placed between the third and fourth digits from the right, the sixth and seventh, and so on.

```
1,000
20,000
7,654,321
```

Following are some of the exceptions to this practice:

PAGE AND LINE NUMBERS

```
on page 1014
```

ADDRESSES

```
at 4132 Broadway
```

FOUR-DIGIT YEAR NUMBERS

```
in 1999
```

But commas are added in year numbers of five or more figures.

```
in 20,000 BC
```

2.5.4. Percentages and Amounts of Money

Treat percentages and amounts of money like other numbers: use numerals with the appropriate symbols.

```
1%          $5.35          68¢
45%         $35
100%        $2,000
```

In discussions involving infrequent use of numbers, you may spell out a percentage or an amount of money if you can do so in three words or fewer (*five dollars, forty-five percent, two thousand dollars, sixty-eight cents*). Do not combine spelled forms of numbers with symbols.

2.5.5. Dates and Times of the Day

Be consistent in writing dates: use either the day-month-year style (*22 July 1999*) or the month-day-year style (*July 22, 1999*) but not both. (If you begin with the month, be sure to add a comma after the day and also after the year, unless another punctuation mark goes there, such as a period or a question mark.) Do not use a comma between month and year (*August 1998*).

Spell out centuries in lowercase letters.

```
the twentieth century
```

Hyphenate centuries when they are used as adjectives before nouns.

```
eighteenth-century thought

nineteenth- and twentieth-century literature
```

Decades are usually written out without capitalization (*the nineties*), but it is acceptable to express them in figures (*the 1990s, the '60s*). Whichever form you use, be consistent.

The abbreviation *BC* follows the year, but *AD* precedes it.

```
19 BC

AD 565
```

Instead of *BC* and *AD*, some writers prefer to use *BCE*, "before the common era," and *CE*, "common era," both of which follow the year.

Numerals are used to indicate most times of the day (*2:00 p.m., the 6:20 flight*). Exceptions include time expressed in quarter and half hours and in hours followed by *o'clock*.

```
a quarter to twelve

half past ten

five o'clock
```

2.5.6. Inclusive Numbers

In a range of numbers, give the second number in full for numbers through ninety-nine.

```
2-3                      21-48
10-12                    89-99
```

For larger numbers, give only the last two digits of the second number, unless more are necessary.

```
96-101                   923-1003
103-04                   1003-05
395-401                  1608-774
```

In a range of years, write both in full unless they are within the same century.

```
1898-1901                1898-99
```

2.5.7. Roman Numerals

Use capital roman numerals for the primary divisions of an outline (see 1.9) and after the names of individuals in a series.

```
Elizabeth II
John D. Rockefeller IV
John Paul II
```

Use lowercase roman numerals for citing pages of a book that are so numbered (e.g., the pages in a preface). Treat inclusive roman numerals like inclusive arabic numerals (see 2.5.6): *xxv–vi*, *xlvi–li*. Your instructor may prefer that you use roman numerals to designate acts and scenes of plays (see 5.4.8, on citing literary works).

2.6. TITLES OF WORKS IN THE RESEARCH PAPER

2.6.1. Capitalization and Punctuation

Whenever you cite the title of a published work in your research paper, take the title from the title page, not from the cover or from a running head at the top of a page. Do not reproduce any unusual typographic characteristics, such as special capitalization or lowercasing of all letters. A title page may present a title designed like one of the following examples:

> MODERNISM & NEGRITUDE

> **BERNARD BERENSON**
> The Making of a Connoisseur

> Turner's early sketchbooks

These titles should appear in a research paper as follows:

<u>Modernism and Negritude</u>

<u>Bernard Berenson: The Making of a Connoisseur</u>

<u>Turner's Early Sketchbooks</u>

The rules for capitalizing titles are strict. In both titles and subtitles, capitalize the first words, the last words, and all principal words, including those that follow hyphens in compound terms. Therefore, capitalize the following parts of speech:

- Nouns (e.g., *flowers* and *Europe* as in *The Flowers of Europe*)
- Pronouns (e.g., *our* as in *Save Our Children*, *that* as in *The Mouse That Roared*)
- Verbs (e.g., *watches* as in *America Watches Television*, *is* as in *What Is Literature?*)
- Adjectives (e.g., *ugly* as in *The Ugly Duckling*, *that* as in *Who Said That Phrase?*)
- Adverbs (e.g., *slightly* as in *Only Slightly Corrupt*, *down* as in *Go Down, Moses*)

- Subordinating conjunctions (e.g., *after, although, as if, as soon as, because, before, if, that, unless, until, when, where, while* as in *One If by Land* and *Anywhere That Chance Leads*)

Do not capitalize the following parts of speech when they fall in the middle of a title:

- Articles (*a, an, the* as in *Under the Bamboo Tree*)
- Prepositions (e.g., *against, between, in, of, to* as in *The Merchant of Venice* and "A Dialogue between the Soul and Body")
- Coordinating conjunctions (*and, but, for, nor, or, so, yet* as in *Romeo and Juliet*)
- The *to* in infinitives (as in *How to Play Chess*)

Use a colon and a space to separate a title from a subtitle, unless the title ends in a question mark, an exclamation point, or a dash. Include other punctuation only if it is part of the title.

The following examples illustrate how to capitalize and punctuate a variety of titles. For a discussion of which titles to underline and which to place in quotation marks, see 2.6.2–3.

<u>Death of a Salesman</u>

<u>The Teaching of Spanish in English-Speaking Countries</u>

<u>Storytelling and Mythmaking: Images from Film and</u>

<u>Literature</u>

<u>Life As I Find It</u>

<u>The Artist as Critic</u>

<u>What Are You Doing in My Universe?</u>

<u>Whose Music? A Sociology of Musical Language</u>

<u>Where Did You Go? Out. What Did You Do? Nothing.</u>

"Ode to a Nightingale"

"Italian Literature before Dante"

"What Americans Stand For"

"Why Fortinbras?"

When the first line of a poem serves as the title of the poem, reproduce the line exactly as it appears in the text.

Dickinson's poem "I heard a Fly buzz--when I died--" contrasts the everyday and the momentous.

For rules concerning capitalization of titles in languages other than English, see 2.8. See 2.6.4 for titles and quotations within titles.

2.6.2. Underlined Titles

In general, underline the titles of works published independently (for works published within larger works, see 2.6.3). Titles to be underlined include the names of books, plays, long poems published as books, pamphlets, periodicals (newspapers, magazines, and journals), films, radio and television programs, compact discs, audiocassettes, record albums, ballets, operas and other long musical compositions (except those identified simply by form, number, and key; see 2.6.5), paintings, works of sculpture, ships, aircraft, and spacecraft. In the following examples, note that the underlining is not broken between words. While there is no need to underline the spaces between words, a continuous line is often the default in word-processing programs, and it guards against the error of failing to underline the punctuation within a title.

<u>The Awakening</u> (book)

<u>The Importance of Being Earnest</u> (play)

<u>The Waste Land</u> (long poem published as a book)

<u>New Jersey Driver Manual</u> (pamphlet)

<u>Wall Street Journal</u> (newspaper)

<u>Time</u> (magazine)

<u>It's a Wonderful Life</u> (film)

<u>Star Trek</u> (television program)

<u>Sgt. Pepper's Lonely Hearts Club Band</u> (compact disc, audiocassette, record album)

<u>The Nutcracker</u> (ballet)

<u>Rigoletto</u> (opera)

Berlioz's <u>Symphonie fantastique</u> (long musical composition identified by name)

Chagall's <u>I and My Village</u> (painting)

French's <u>The Minute Man</u> (sculpture)

HMS <u>Vanguard</u> (ship)

<u>Spirit of St. Louis</u> (aircraft)

<u>Challenger</u> (spacecraft)

2.6.3. Titles in Quotation Marks

Use quotation marks for the titles of works published within larger works. Such titles include the names of articles, essays, short stories, short poems, chapters of books, individual episodes of television and radio programs, and short musical compositions (e.g., songs). Also use quotation marks for unpublished works, such as lectures and speeches.

"Rise in Aid to Education Is Proposed" (newspaper article)

"Sources of Energy in the Next Century" (magazine article)

"Etruscan" (encyclopedia article)

"The Fiction of Langston Hughes" (essay in a book)

"The Lottery" (short story)

"Kubla Khan" (poem)

"The American Economy before the Civil War" (chapter in a book)

"The Trouble with Tribbles" (episode of the television program *Star Trek*)

"Mood Indigo" (song)

"Preparing for a Successful Interview" (lecture)

2.6.4. Titles and Quotations within Titles

Underline a title normally indicated by underlining when it appears within a title enclosed in quotation marks.

"<u>Romeo and Juliet</u> and Renaissance Politics" (an article about a play)

"Language and Childbirth in <u>The Awakening</u>" (an article about a novel)

Enclose in single quotation marks a title normally indicated by quotation marks when it appears within another title requiring quotation marks.

"Lines after Reading 'Sailing to Byzantium'" (a poem about a poem)

"The Uncanny Theology of 'A Good Man Is Hard to Find'"
(an article about a short story)

Also place single quotation marks around a quotation that appears
within a title requiring quotation marks.

"Emerson's Strategies against 'Foolish Consistency'" (an
article with a quotation in its title)

Use quotation marks around a title normally indicated by quotation
marks when it appears within an underlined title.

"The Lottery" and Other Stories (a book of short stories)

New Perspectives on "The Eve of St. Agnes" (a book about a
poem)

If a period is required after an underlined title that ends with a quotation mark, place the period before the quotation mark.

The study appears in New Perspectives on "The Eve of
St. Agnes."

There are two common methods for identifying a normally underlined title when it appears within an underlined title. In one practice,
the title within is neither underlined nor enclosed in quotation marks.
This method is preferred in publications of the Modern Language
Association.

Approaches to Teaching Murasaki Shikibu's The Tale of
Genji (a book about a novel)

From The Lodger to The Lady Vanishes: Hitchcock's
Classic British Thrillers (a book about films)

In the other method, all titles within underlined titles are placed in
quotation marks and underlined.

Approaches to Teaching Murasaki Shikibu's "The Tale of
Genji"

From "The Lodger" to "The Lady Vanishes": Hitchcock's
Classic British Thrillers

Each approach has advantages and disadvantages. In the first
method, the titles of works published independently and the material

containing them are always given opposite treatments. This practice has the advantage of consistency, but it can lead to ambiguity: it is hard to tell where a title like *Approaches to Teaching Murasaki Shikibu's* The Tale of Genji ends and where the adjacent text begins.

The second method prevents confusion between titles and the adjacent text. However, it treats titles of works published independently two ways: they receive quotation marks in underlined titles but nowhere else. In addition, within underlined titles this method abandons the distinction between works that are published independently and those that are not.

Whichever practice you choose or your instructor requires, follow it consistently throughout your paper.

2.6.5. Exceptions

The convention of using underlining and quotation marks to indicate titles does not apply to the names of sacred writings (including all books and versions of the Bible); of laws, acts, and similar political documents; of instrumental musical compositions identified by form, number, and key; of series, societies, buildings, and monuments; and of conferences, seminars, workshops, and courses. These terms all appear without underlining or quotation marks.

SACRED WRITINGS

Bible	Gospels
King James Version	Talmud
Old Testament	Koran
Genesis	Upanishads

But underline titles of individual published editions of sacred writings (*The Interlinear Bible, The Talmud of the Land of Israel: A Preliminary Translation and Explanation, The Upanishads: A Selection for the Modern Reader*) and treat the editions in the works-cited list like any other published book.

LAWS, ACTS, AND SIMILAR POLITICAL DOCUMENTS

Magna Carta

Declaration of Independence

Bill of Rights

Treaty of Trianon

INSTRUMENTAL MUSICAL COMPOSITIONS IDENTIFIED BY FORM,
NUMBER, AND KEY

Beethoven's Symphony no. 7 in A, op. 92

Vivaldi's Concerto for Two Trumpets and Strings in C,
  RV539

SERIES

Bollingen Series

University of North Carolina Studies in Comparative
  Literature

Masterpiece Theatre

SOCIETIES

American Medical Association

Renaissance Society of America

BUILDINGS AND MONUMENTS

Moscone Center

Sears Tower

Arch of Constantine

CONFERENCES, SEMINARS, WORKSHOPS, AND COURSES

Strengthening the Cooperative Effort in Biomedical
  Research: A National Conference for Universities and
  Industry

Geographic Information Analysis Workshop

MLA Annual Convention

Introduction to Calculus

Anthropology 102

Words designating the divisions of a work are also not underlined or put within quotation marks, nor are they capitalized when used in the text ("The author says in her preface [. . .]," "In canto 32 Ariosto writes [. . .]").

preface	appendix	scene 7
introduction	index	stanza 20
list of works cited	chapter 2	canto 32
bibliography	act 4	

2.6.6. Shortened Titles

If you cite a title often in the text of your paper, you may, after stating the title in full at least once, use a shortened form, preferably a familiar or obvious one (e.g., "Nightingale" for "Ode to a Nightingale"), or an abbreviation (for standard abbreviated titles of literary and religious works, see 6.7).

2.7. QUOTATIONS

2.7.1. Use and Accuracy of Quotations

Quotations are effective in research papers when used selectively. Quote only words, phrases, lines, and passages that are particularly interesting, vivid, unusual, or apt, and keep all quotations as brief as possible. Overquotation can bore your readers and might lead them to conclude that you are neither an original thinker nor a skillful writer.

The accuracy of quotations in research writing is extremely important. They must reproduce the original sources exactly. Unless indicated in brackets or parentheses (see 2.7.6), changes must not be made in the spelling, capitalization, or interior punctuation of the source. You must construct a clear, grammatically correct sentence that allows you to introduce or incorporate a quotation with complete accuracy. Alternatively, you may paraphrase the original and quote only fragments, which may be easier to integrate into the text. If you change a quotation in any way, make the alteration clear to the reader, following the rules and recommendations below.

2.7.2. Prose

If a prose quotation runs no more than four lines and requires no special emphasis, put it in quotation marks and incorporate it into the text.

> "It was the best of times, it was the worst of times,"
> wrote Charles Dickens of the eighteenth century.

You need not always reproduce complete sentences. Sometimes you may want to quote just a word or phrase as part of your sentence.

> For Charles Dickens the eighteenth century was both "the
> best of times" and "the worst of times."

You may put a quotation at the beginning, middle, or end of your sentence or, for the sake of variety or better style, divide it by your own words.

> Joseph Conrad writes of the company manager in <u>Heart of</u>
> <u>Darkness</u>, "He was obeyed, yet he inspired neither love
> nor fear, nor even respect."

or

> "He was obeyed," writes Joseph Conrad of the company
> manager in <u>Heart of Darkness</u>, "yet he inspired neither
> love nor fear, nor even respect."

If a quotation ending a sentence requires a parenthetical reference, place the sentence period after the reference. (For more information on punctuating quotations, see 2.7.7.)

> For Charles Dickens the eighteenth century was both "the
> best of times" and "the worst of times" (35).

> "He was obeyed," writes Joseph Conrad of the company
> manager in <u>Heart of Darkness</u>, "yet he inspired neither
> love nor fear, nor even respect" (87).

If a quotation runs to more than four lines in your paper, set it off from your text by beginning a new line, indenting one inch (or ten spaces if you are using a typewriter) from the left margin, and typing it double-spaced, without adding quotation marks. A colon generally

introduces a quotation displayed in this way, though sometimes the
context may require a different mark of punctuation or none at all. If
you quote only a single paragraph or part of one, do not indent the first
line more than the rest. A parenthetical reference to a prose quotation
set off from the text follows the last line of the quotation.

> At the conclusion of <u>Lord of the Flies</u>, Ralph and the
> other boys realize the horror of their actions:
>
>> The tears began to flow and sobs shook him. He
>> gave himself up to them now for the first time
>> on the island; great, shuddering spasms of
>> grief that seemed to wrench his whole body. His
>> voice rose under the black smoke before the
>> burning wreckage of the island; and infected by
>> that emotion, the other little boys began to
>> shake and sob too. (186)

If you need to quote two or more paragraphs, indent the first line of
each paragraph an additional quarter inch (or three spaces on a typewriter). If the first sentence quoted does not begin a paragraph in the
source, however, do not indent it the additional amount. Indent only
the first lines of the successive paragraphs.

> In <u>Moll Flanders</u> Defoe maintains the
> pseudoautobiographical narration typical of the
> picaresque tradition:
>
>> My true name is so well known in the
>> records, or registers, at Newgate and in the
>> Old Bailey, and there are some things of such
>> consequence still depending there relating to
>> my particular conduct, that it is not to be
>> expected I should set my name or the account of
>> my family to this work [. . .].
>>
>> It is enough to tell you, that [. . .] some
>> of my worst comrades, who are out of the way of
>> doing me harm [. . .] know me by the name of
>> Moll Flanders [. . .]. (1)

On omitting words within quotations, see 2.7.5. For translations of quotations, see 2.7.8.

2.7.3. Poetry

If you quote part or all of a single line of verse that does not require special emphasis, put it in quotation marks within your text. You may also incorporate two or three lines in this way, using a slash with a space on each side (/) to separate them.

```
Bradstreet frames the poem with a sense of mortality:
"All things within this fading world hath end" (1).

Reflecting on the "incident" in Baltimore, Cullen
concludes, "Of all the things that happened there /
That's all that I remember" (11-12).
```

Verse quotations of more than three lines should begin on a new line. Unless the quotation involves unusual spacing, indent each line one inch (or ten spaces on a typewriter) from the left margin and double-space between lines, adding no quotation marks that do not appear in the original. A parenthetical reference for a verse quotation set off from the text follows the last line of the quotation (as in quotations of prose); a parenthetical reference that will not fit on the line should appear on a new line, flush with the right margin of the page.

```
Elizabeth Bishop's "In the Waiting Room" is rich in
evocative detail:
                 It was winter. It got dark
                 early. The waiting room
                 was full of grown-up people,
                 arctics and overcoats,
                 lamps and magazines. (6-10)
```

A line that is too long to fit within the right margin should be continued on the next line and the continuation indented an additional quarter inch (or three spaces). You may reduce the indentation of the quotation to less than one inch (or ten spaces) from the left margin if doing so will eliminate the need for such continuations. If the spatial arrangement of the original lines, including indentation and spacing within and between them, is unusual, reproduce it as accurately as possible.

```
E. E. Cummings concludes the poem with this vivid
description of a carefree scene, reinforced by the
carefree form of the lines themselves:
            it's
            spring
            and
                the
                    goat-footed
            balloonMan        whistles
            far
            and
            wee (16-24)
```

When a verse quotation begins in the middle of a line, the partial line should be positioned where it is in the original and not shifted to the left margin.

```
In a poem on Thomas Hardy ("T. H."), Molly Holden recalls
her encounter with a "young dog fox" one morning:
                                    I remember
        he glanced at me in just that way, independent
        and unabashed, the handsome sidelong look
        that went round and about but never directly
        met my eyes, for that would betray his soul.
        He was not being sly, only careful. (43-48)
```

For translations of quotations, see 2.7.8.

2.7.4. Drama

If you quote dialogue between two or more characters in a play, set the quotation off from your text. Begin each part of the dialogue with the appropriate character's name indented one inch (or ten spaces if you are using a typewriter) from the left margin and written in all capital letters: HAMLET. Follow the name with a period, and start the quotation. Indent all subsequent lines in that character's speech an additional quarter inch (or three spaces). When the dialogue shifts to another character, start a new line indented one inch (or ten spaces) from the left margin. Maintain this pattern throughout the entire quotation. For the other aspects of formatting, follow the recommendations above for quoting prose and poetry (2.7.2–3).

```
Marguerite Duras's screenplay for Hiroshima mon amour
suggests at the outset the profound difference between
observation and experience:
               HE. You saw nothing in Hiroshima. Nothing.
               SHE. I saw everything. Everything. [. . .] The
                  hospital, for instance, I saw it. I'm sure
                  I did. There is a hospital in Hiroshima. How
                  could I help seeing it?
               HE. You did not see the hospital in Hiroshima.
                  You saw nothing in Hiroshima. (2505-06)
```

```
A short time later Lear loses the final symbol of his
former power, the soldiers who make up his train:
               GONERIL.                      Hear me, my lord.
                  What need you five-and-twenty, ten or five,
                  To follow in a house where twice so many
                  Have a command to tend you?
               REGAN.                         What need one?
               LEAR. 0, reason not the need! (2.4.254-58)
```

2.7.5. Ellipsis

Whenever you wish to omit a word, a phrase, a sentence, or more from a quoted passage, you should be guided by two principles: fairness to the author quoted and the grammatical integrity of your writing. A quotation should never be presented in a way that could cause a reader to misunderstand the sentence structure of the original source. If you quote only a word or a phrase, it will be obvious that you left out some of the original sentence.

```
In his inaugural address, John F. Kennedy spoke of a
"new frontier."
```

But if omitting material from the original sentence or sentences leaves a quotation that appears to be a sentence or a series of sentences, you must use ellipsis points, or three spaced periods, to indicate that your quotation does not completely reproduce the original. To distinguish between your ellipses and the spaced periods that sometimes appear in works, place square brackets around the ellipsis points that you add. Leave a space before the second and third periods but no space before the first or after the third. Whenever you omit words from a quotation, the resulting passage—your prose and the quotation integrated into it—should be grammatically complete and correct.

For an ellipsis within a sentence, leave a space before the first bracket and a space after the last bracket.

ORIGINAL

Medical thinking, trapped in the theory of astral influences, stressed air as the communicator of disease, ignoring sanitation or visible carriers. (Barbara W. Tuchman, *A Distant Mirror: The Calamitous Fourteenth Century* [1978; New York: Ballantine, 1979] 101–02)

QUOTATION WITH AN ELLIPSIS IN THE MIDDLE

In surveying various responses to plagues in the Middle Ages, Barbara W. Tuchman writes, "Medical thinking [. . .] stressed air as the communicator of disease, ignoring sanitation or visible carriers."

QUOTATION WITH AN ELLIPSIS IN THE MIDDLE AND A
PARENTHETICAL REFERENCE

In surveying various responses to plagues in the Middle Ages, Barbara W. Tuchman writes, "Medical thinking [. . .] stressed air as the communicator of disease, ignoring sanitation or visible carriers" (101-02).

When the ellipsis coincides with the end of your sentence, leave a space before the first bracket, and immediately follow the last bracket with the sentence period and the closing quotation mark.

QUOTATION WITH AN ELLIPSIS AT THE END

In surveying various responses to plagues in the Middle
Ages, Barbara W. Tuchman writes, "Medical thinking,
trapped in the theory of astral influences, stressed air
as the communicator of disease [. . .]."

If a parenthetical reference follows the ellipsis at the end of your
sentence, however, leave a space before the first bracket, and immediately follow the last bracket with the closing quotation mark, a space,
the parenthetical reference, and the sentence period.

QUOTATION WITH AN ELLIPSIS AT THE END FOLLOWED BY A
PARENTHETICAL REFERENCE

In surveying various responses to plagues in the Middle
Ages, Barbara W. Tuchman writes, "Medical thinking,
trapped in the theory of astral influences, stressed air
as the communicator of disease [. . .]" (101-02).

In a quotation of more than one sentence, an ellipsis in the middle
can indicate the omission of any amount of text. With such an omission, the first bracket of the ellipsis is always preceded by a space, but
what comes before this space and after the last bracket varies, depending on the material that the ellipsis replaces.

ORIGINAL

Presidential control reached its zenith under Andrew Jackson, the
extent of whose attention to the press even before he became a
candidate is suggested by the fact that he subscribed to twenty
newspapers. Jackson was never content to have only one organ
grinding out his tune. For a time, the *United States Telegraph* and
the *Washington Globe* were almost equally favored as party
organs, and there were fifty-seven journalists on the government
payroll. (William L. Rivers, *The Mass Media: Reporting, Writing,
Editing*, 2nd ed. [New York: Harper, 1975] 7)

QUOTATION OMITTING A SENTENCE

In discussing the historical relation between politics
and the press, William L. Rivers notes, "Presidential
control reached its zenith under Andrew Jackson, the
extent of whose attention to the press even before he

became a candidate is suggested by the fact that he
subscribed to twenty newspapers. [. . .] For a time, the
United States Telegraph and the Washington Globe were
almost equally favored as party organs, and there were
fifty-seven journalists on the government payroll" (7).

QUOTATION WITH AN OMISSION FROM THE MIDDLE OF ONE
SENTENCE TO THE END OF ANOTHER

In discussing the historical relation between politics
and the press, William L. Rivers notes, "Presidential
control reached its zenith under Andrew Jackson
[. . .]. For a time, the United States Telegraph and
the Washington Globe were almost equally favored as
party organs, and there were fifty-seven journalists on
the government payroll" (7).

QUOTATION WITH AN OMISSION FROM THE MIDDLE OF ONE
SENTENCE TO THE MIDDLE OF ANOTHER

In discussing the historical relation between politics
and the press, William L. Rivers notes that when
presidential control "reached its zenith under Andrew
Jackson, [. . .] there were fifty-seven journalists on
the government payroll" (7).

The omission of words and phrases from quotations of poetry is also
indicated by three periods within brackets (as in quotations of prose).

ORIGINAL

In Worcester, Massachusetts,
I went with Aunt Consuelo
to keep her dentist's appointment
and sat and waited for her
in the dentist's waiting room.
It was winter. It got dark
early. The waiting room
was full of grown-up people,
arctics and overcoats,
lamps and magazines.
(Elizabeth Bishop, "In the Waiting Room," lines 1–10)

QUOTATION WITH AN ELLIPSIS AT THE END

Elizabeth Bishop's "In the Waiting Room" is rich in
evocative detail:

> In Worcester, Massachusetts,
> I went with Aunt Consuelo
> to keep her dentist's appointment
> and sat and waited for her
> in the dentist's waiting room.
> It was winter. It got dark
> early. The waiting room
> was full of grown-up people [. . .]. (1-8)

The omission of a line or more in the middle of a poetry quotation that is set off from the text is indicated by a line of spaced periods, within square brackets, approximately the length of a complete line of the quoted poem.

QUOTATION OMITTING A LINE OR MORE IN THE MIDDLE

Elizabeth Bishop's "In the Waiting Room" is rich in
evocative detail:

> In Worcester, Massachusetts,
> I went with Aunt Consuelo
> to keep her dentist's appointment
> [. . . . .]
> It was winter. It got dark
> early. (1-3, 6-7)

2.7.6. Other Alterations of Sources

Occasionally, you may decide that a quotation will be unclear or confusing to your reader unless you provide supplementary information. For example, you may need to insert material missing from the original, to add *sic* (from the Latin for "thus" or "so") to assure readers that the quotation is accurate even though the spelling or logic might make them think otherwise, or to underline words for emphasis. While such contributions to a quotation are permissible, you should keep them to a minimum and make sure to distinguish them from the original, usually by explaining them in parentheses after the quotation or by putting them in square brackets within the quotation.

A comment or an explanation that immediately follows the closing quotation mark appears in parentheses.

> Shaw admitted, "Nothing can extinguish my interest in Shakespear" (sic).

> Lincoln specifically advocated a government "<u>for</u> the people" (emphasis added).

A comment or an explanation that goes inside the quotation must appear within square brackets, not parentheses.

> He claimed he could provide "hundreds of examples [of court decisions] to illustrate the historical tension between church and state."

> Milton's Satan speaks of his "study [pursuit] of revenge."

Similarly, if a pronoun in a quotation seems unclear, you may add an identification in square brackets.

> Why she would hang on him [Hamlet's father]
> As if increase of appetite had grown
> By what it fed on [. . .].

2.7.7. Punctuation with Quotations

Whether set off from the text or run into it, quoted material is usually preceded by a colon if the quotation is formally introduced and by a comma or no punctuation if the quotation is an integral part of the sentence structure.

> Shelley held a bold view: "Poets are the unacknowledged legislators of the World" (794).

> Shelley thought poets "the unacknowledged legislators of the World" (794).

> "Poets," according to Shelley, "are the unacknowledged legislators of the World" (794).

Do not use opening and closing quotation marks to enclose quotations set off from the text. Use double quotation marks around quotations incorporated into the text, single quotation marks around quotations within those quotations.

In "Memories of West Street and Lepke," Robert Lowell, a
conscientious objector (or "C.O."), recounts meeting a
Jehovah's Witness in prison: "'Are you a C.O.?' I asked
a fellow jailbird. / 'No,' he answered, 'I'm a J.W.'"
(38-39).

Except for changing internal double quotation marks to single ones when you incorporate quotations into your text, you should reproduce internal punctuation exactly as in the original. The closing punctuation, though, depends on where the quoted material appears in your sentence. Suppose, for example, that you want to quote the following sentence: "You've got to be carefully taught." If you begin your sentence with this line, you have to replace the closing period with a punctuation mark appropriate to the new context.

"You've got to be carefully taught," wrote Oscar
Hammerstein II about how racial prejudice is perpetuated.

If the quotation ends with a question mark or an exclamation point, however, the original punctuation is retained, and no comma is required.

"How can I describe my emotions at this catastrophe, or
how delineate the wretch whom with such infinite pains
and care I had endeavoured to form?" wonders the doctor
in Mary Shelley's Frankenstein (42).

"What a wonderful little almanac you are, Celia!"
Dorothea Brooke responds to her sister (7).

By convention, commas and periods that directly follow quotations go inside the closing quotation marks, but a parenthetical reference should intervene between the quotation and the required punctuation. Thus, if a quotation ends with a period, the period appears after the reference.

> N. Scott Momaday's <u>House Made of Dawn</u> begins with an
> image that also concludes the novel: "Abel was
> running" (7).

If a quotation ends with both single and double quotation marks, the comma or period precedes both.

> "Read 'Kubla Khan,'" he told me.

All other punctuation marks—such as semicolons, colons, question marks, and exclamation points—go outside a closing quotation mark, except when they are part of the quoted material.

ORIGINAL

I believe taxation without representation is tyranny!

QUOTATIONS

> He attacked "taxation without representation" (32).
> Did he attack "taxation without representation"?
> What dramatic events followed his attack on "taxation
>   without representation"!

but

> He declared, "I believe taxation without representation
>   is tyranny!"

If a quotation ending with a question mark or an exclamation point concludes your sentence and requires a parenthetical reference, retain the original punctuation within the quotation mark and follow with the reference and the sentence period outside the quotation mark.

> In Mary Shelley's <u>Frankenstein</u>, the doctor wonders, "How
> can I describe my emotions at this catastrophe, or how
> delineate the wretch whom with such infinite pains and
> care I had endeavoured to form?" (42).

> Dorothea Brooke responds to her sister, "What a
> wonderful little almanac you are, Celia!" (7).

2.7.8 Translations of Quotations

If you believe that a significant portion of your audience will not be familiar with the language of a quotation you present, you should add a translation. If the translation is not yours, give its source in addition to the source of the quotation. In general, the translation should immediately follow the quotation whether they are run into or set off from the text, although their order may be reversed if most readers will not likely be able to read the original. If the quotation is run into the text, use double quotation marks around a translation placed in parentheses following the quotation but single quotation marks around a translation that immediately follows without intervening punctuation.

```
Chaucer's setting is April, the time of "shoures soote"
  ("sweet showers"; GP 1).
Chaucer's setting is April, the time of "shoures soote"
  'sweet showers' (GP 1).
```

Do not use quotation marks around quotations and translations set off from the text.

```
Dante's Inferno begins literally in the middle of
things:

          Nel mezzo del cammin di nostra vita
          mi ritrovai per una selva oscura,
          ché la diritta via era smarrita.
          Ahi quanto a dir qual era è cosa dura
          esta selva selvaggia e aspra e forte
          che nel pensier rinova la paura! (1.1-6)
          Midway in our life's journey, I went astray
          from the straight road and woke to find myself
          alone in a dark wood. How shall I say
          what wood that was! I never saw so drear,
          so rank, so arduous a wilderness!
          Its very memory gives a shape to fear.
                                    (Ciardi 28)
```

See also 2.2.8b for guidelines on translating a foreign word or phrase within a sentence.

2.8. CAPITALIZATION AND PERSONAL NAMES IN LANGUAGES OTHER THAN ENGLISH

The following section contains recommendations for writing personal names and for capitalizing in French, German, Italian, Spanish, and Latin. If you need such rules for other languages or if you need information on transliterating from languages that do not use the Latin alphabet, such as Russian or Chinese, consult the *MLA Style Manual and Guide to Scholarly Publishing*.

2.8.1. French

Personal Names

With some exceptions, especially in English-language contexts, French *de* following a first name or a title such as *Mme* or *duc* is not used with the last name alone.

    La Boétie (Etienne de La Boétie)
    La Bruyère (Jean de La Bruyère)
    Maupassant (Guy de Maupassant)
    Nemours (Louis-Charles d'Orléans, duc de Nemours)
    Ronsard (Pierre de Ronsard)
    Scudéry (Madeleine de Scudéry)

but

    De Quincey (Thomas De Quincey)

When the last name has only one syllable, however, *de* is usually retained.

    de Gaulle (Charles de Gaulle)

The preposition also remains, in the form *d'*, when it elides with a last name beginning with a vowel.

    d'Arcy (Pierre d'Arcy)
    d'Arsonval (Arsène d'Arsonval)

The forms *du* and *des*—combinations of *de* with *le* and *les*—are always used with last names and are capitalized.

```
Des Périers (Bonaventure Des Périers)
Du Bos (Charles Du Bos)
```

A hyphen is frequently used between French given names, as well as between their initials (Marie-Joseph Chénier, M.-J. Chénier). Note that *M.* and *P.* before names may be abbreviations for the titles *Monsieur* 'Mr.' and *Père* 'Father' (M. René Char, P. J. Reynard).

Capitalization

In prose and verse, French capitalization is the same as English except that the following terms are not capitalized in French unless they begin sentences or, sometimes, lines of verse: (1) the subject pronoun *je* 'I,' (2) the names of months and days of the week, (3) the names of languages, (4) adjectives derived from proper nouns, (5) titles preceding personal names, and (6) the words meaning "street," "square," "lake," "mountain," and so on, in most place-names.

```
Un Français m'a parlé anglais près de la place de
la Concorde.

Hier j'ai vu le docteur Maurois qui conduisait une
voiture Ford.

Le capitaine Boutillier m'a dit qu'il partait pour Rouen
le premier jeudi d'avril avec quelques amis normands.
```

There are two widely accepted methods of capitalizing French titles and subtitles of works. One method is to capitalize only the first word and all proper nouns in a title or subtitle. This method is normally followed in publications of the Modern Language Association.

```
L'ami du peuple

Du côté de chez Swann

Le grand Meaulnes

La guerre de Troie n'aura pas lieu

Nouvelle revue d'onomastique
```

In the other method, when a title or subtitle begins with an article, the first noun and any preceding adjectives are also capitalized.

```
L'Ami du peuple

Du côté de chez Swann
```

<u>Le Grand Meaulnes</u>

<u>La Guerre de Troie n'aura pas lieu</u>

In this system, all major words in titles of series and periodicals are sometimes capitalized.

<u>Nouvelle Revue d'Onomastique</u>

Whichever practice you choose or your instructor requires, follow it consistently throughout your paper.

2.8.2. German

Personal Names

German *von* is generally not used with the last name alone, but there are some exceptions, especially in English-language contexts, where the *von* is firmly established by convention.

Droste-Hülshoff (Annette von Droste-Hülshoff)

Kleist (Heinrich von Kleist)

but

Von Braun (Wernher Von Braun)

Von Trapp (Maria Von Trapp)

In alphabetizing a German name with an umlaut (the mark over the vowel in *ä, ö, ü*), Germanists treat the umlauted vowel as if it were followed by an *e*; thus *Götz* would be alphabetized as *Goetz* and would precede *Gott* in an alphabetical listing. Nonspecialists, however, and many libraries in English-speaking countries alphabetize such names without regard to the umlaut; in this practice, *Götz* would be alphabetized as *Gotz* and would therefore follow *Gott* in an alphabetical listing.

Capitalization

In prose and verse, German capitalization differs considerably from English. Always capitalized in German are all nouns—including adjectives, infinitives, pronouns, prepositions, and other parts of speech used as nouns—as well as the pronoun *Sie* 'you' and its possessive, *Ihr* 'your,' and their inflected forms. Not capitalized unless they begin sentences or, usually, lines of verse are (1) the subject pronoun *ich* 'I,' (2) the names of languages and of days of the week used as adjectives, adverbs, or complements of prepositions, and (3) adjectives and adverbs formed from proper nouns, except when the proper nouns are names of persons and the adjectives and adverbs refer to the persons' works or deeds.

```
Ich glaube an das Gute in der Welt.

Er schreibt, nur um dem Auf und Ab der Buch-Nachfrage zu
entsprechen.

Fahren Sie mit Ihrer Frau zurück?

Ein französischer Schriftsteller, den ich gut kenne,
arbeitet sonntags immer an seinem neuen Buch über die
platonische Liebe.

Der Staat ist eine der bekanntesten Platonischen
Schriften.
```

In letters and ceremonial writings, the pronouns *du* and *ihr* 'you' and their derivatives are capitalized.

In a title or a subtitle, capitalize the first word and all words normally capitalized.

```
Thomas Mann und die Grenzen des Ich

Ein treuer Diener seines Herrn

Zeitschrift für vergleichende Sprachforschung
```

2.8.3. Italian

Personal Names

The names of many Italians who lived before or during the Renaissance are alphabetized by first name.

```
Bonvesin da la Riva

Cino da Pistoia

Dante Alighieri

Iacopone da Todi

Michelangelo Buonarroti
```

But other names of the period follow the standard practice.

```
Boccaccio, Giovanni

Cellini, Benvenuto

Stampa, Gaspara
```

The names of members of historic families are also usually alphabetized by last name.

```
Este, Beatrice d'

Medici, Lorenzo de'
```

In modern times, Italian *da, de, del, della, di*, and *d'* are used with the last name. They are usually capitalized and are treated as an integral part of the name, even though a space may separate the prepositional from the nominal part of the name.

```
Da Ponte (Lorenzo Da Ponte)

D'Azeglio (Massimo D'Azeglio)

Del Buono (Oreste Del Buono)

Della Casa (Giovanni Della Casa)

De Sica (Vittorio De Sica)

Di Costanzo (Angelo Di Costanzo)
```

Capitalization

In prose and verse, Italian capitalization is the same as English except that in Italian centuries and other large divisions of time are capitalized (*il Seicento*) and the following terms are not capitalized unless they begin sentences or, usually, lines of verse: (1) the subject pronoun *io* 'I,' (2) the names of months and days of the week, (3) the names of languages and nationalities, (4) nouns, adjectives, and adverbs derived from proper nouns, (5) titles preceding personal names, and (6) the words meaning "street," "square," and so on, in most place-names.

```
Un italiano parlava francese con uno svizzero in piazza
di Spagna.

Il dottor Bruno ritornerà dall'Italia giovedì otto
agosto e io partirò il nove.
```

In a title or a subtitle, capitalize only the first word and all words normally capitalized.

L'arte tipografica in Urbino

Bibliografia della critica pirandelliana

Collezione di classici italiani

Dizionario letterario Bompiani

Studi petrarcheschi

2.8.4. Spanish

Personal Names

Spanish *de* is not used before the last name alone.

Las Casas (Bartolomé de Las Casas)

Madariaga (Salvador de Madariaga)

Rueda (Lope de Rueda)

Timoneda (Juan de Timoneda)

Spanish *del*, formed from the fusion of the preposition *de* and the definite article *el*, is capitalized and used with the last name alone.

Del Río (Angel Del Río)

A Spanish surname may include both the paternal name and the maternal name, with or without the conjunction *y*. The surname of a married woman usually includes her paternal surname and her husband's paternal surname, connected by *de*. Alphabetize Spanish names by the full surnames (consult your sources or a biographical dictionary for guidance in distinguishing surnames and given names).

Carreño de Miranda, Juan

Cervantes Saavedra, Miguel de

Díaz del Castillo, Bernal

García Márquez, Gabriel

Larra y Sánchez de Castro, Mariano José

López de Ayala, Pero

Matute, Ana María

Ortega y Gasset, José

Quevedo y Villegas, Francisco Gómez de

Sinues de Marco, María del Pilar

Zayas y Sotomayor, María de

Even persons commonly known by the maternal portions of their surnames, such as Galdós and Lorca, should be indexed under their full surnames.

```
García Lorca, Federico
Pérez Galdós, Benito
```

Capitalization

In prose and verse, Spanish capitalization is the same as English except that the following terms are not capitalized in Spanish unless they begin sentences or, sometimes, lines of verse: (1) the subject pronoun *yo* 'I,' (2) the names of months and days of the week, (3) the names of languages and nationalities, (4) nouns and adjectives derived from proper nouns, (5) titles preceding personal names, and (6) the words meaning "street," "square," and so on, in most place-names.

```
El francés hablaba inglés en la plaza Colón.

Ayer yo vi al doctor García en un coche Ford.

Me dijo don Jorge que iba a salir para Sevilla el primer
martes de abril con unos amigos neoyorkinos.
```

In a title or a subtitle, capitalize only the first word and words normally capitalized.

```
Breve historia del ensayo hispanoamericano
Extremos de América
La gloria de don Ramiro
Historia verdadera de la conquista de la Nueva España
Revista de filología española
Trasmundo de Goya
```

Some instructors follow other rules. In titles of series and periodicals, they capitalize all major words: *Revista de Filología Española*.

2.8.5. Latin

Personal Names

Roman male citizens generally had three names: a praenomen (given name), a nomen (clan name), and a cognomen (family or familiar name). Men in this category are usually referred to by nomen, cognomen, or both; your source or a standard reference book such as *The Oxford Classical Dictionary* will provide guidance.

Brutus (Marcus Iunius Brutus)

Calpurnius Siculus (Titus Calpurnius Siculus)

Cicero (Marcus Tullius Cicero)

Lucretius (Titus Lucretius Carus)

Plautus (Titus Maccius Plautus)

Roman women usually had two names—a nomen (the clan name in the feminine form) and a cognomen (often derived from the father's cognomen): Livia Drusilla (daughter of Marcus Livius Drusus). Sometimes a woman's cognomen indicates her chronological order among the daughters of the family: Antonia Minor (younger daughter of Marcus Antonius). Most Roman women are referred to by nomen: Calpurnia, Clodia, Octavia, Sulpicia. Some, however, are better known by cognomen: Agrippina (Vipsania Agrippina).

When citing Roman names, use the forms most common in English.

Horace (Quintus Horatius Flaccus)

Julius Caesar (Gaius Iulius Caesar)

Juvenal (Decimus Iunius Iuvenalis)

Livy (Titus Livius)

Ovid (Publius Ovidius Naso)

Quintilian (Marcus Fabius Quintilianus)

Terence (Publius Terentius Afer)

Vergil (Publius Vergilius Maro)

Finally, some medieval and Renaissance figures are best known by their adopted or assigned Latin names.

Albertus Magnus (Albert von Bollstädt)

Comenius (Jan Amos Komenský)

Copernicus (Niklas Koppernigk)

Paracelsus (Theophrastus Bombast von Hohenheim)

Capitalization

Although practice varies, Latin most commonly follows the English rules for capitalization, except that *ego* 'I' is not capitalized.

Semper ego auditor tantum? Numquamne reponam / Vexatus
totiens rauci Theseide Cordi?

Quidquid id est, timeo Danaos et dona ferentes.

Nil desperandum.

Quo usque tandem abutere, Catilina, patientia nostra?

In a title or a subtitle, however, capitalize only the first word and all
words normally capitalized.

De senectute

Liber de senectute

Medievalia et humanistica

3 The Format of the Research Paper

If your instructor has specific requirements for the format of a research paper, check them before preparing your final draft. The recommendations presented in this chapter are the most common.

3.1. PRINTING OR TYPING

If you composed your paper on a computer, use a high-quality printer. Always choose a standard, easily readable typeface. Do not justify the lines of your paper at the right margin; turn off your word processor's automatic hyphenation feature. Be sure to keep a backup copy on disk. If you are using a typewriter, make certain the ribbon produces dark, clear type. Print or type on one side of the paper; do not use the other side for any purpose. Instructors who accept handwritten work similarly require neatness, legibility, dark blue or black ink, and the use of only one side of the paper. Be sure to keep a copy of the paper.

3.2. PAPER

Use only white, 8½-by-11-inch paper of good quality. Do not submit work typed on erasable paper, which smudges easily. If you find erasable paper convenient to use for your final draft, submit a high-quality photocopy to your instructor.

3.3. MARGINS

Except for page numbers, leave margins of one inch at the top and bottom and on both sides of the text. (For placement of page numbers, see 3.6.) Indent the first word of a paragraph one-half inch (or five spaces) from the left margin. Indent set-off quotations one inch (or ten spaces) from the left margin. (For examples, see 2.7 and the sample first page of a research paper at the end of this book.)

3.4. SPACING

A research paper must be double-spaced throughout, including quotations, notes, and the list of works cited. In a handwritten paper, skip every other ruled line. (See the sample pages of a research paper at the end of this book.)

3.5. HEADING AND TITLE

A research paper does not need a title page. Instead, beginning one inch from the top of the first page and flush with the left margin, type your name, your instructor's name, the course number, and the date on separate lines, double-spacing between the lines. Double-space again and center the title. Double-space also between the lines of the title, and double-space between the title and the first line of the text (see fig. 4). Do not underline your title or put it in quotation marks or type it in all capital letters. Follow the rules for capitalization in 2.6.1, and underline only the words that you would underline in the text (see 2.3, 2.6.2).

```
Local Television Coverage of International News Events
The Attitude toward Violence in A Clockwork Orange
```

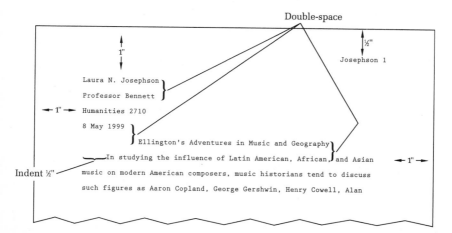

Fig. 4. The top of the first page of a research paper.

The Use of the Words <u>Fair</u> and <u>Foul</u> in Shakespeare's
<u>Macbeth</u>

Romanticism in England and the <u>Scapigliatura</u> in Italy

Do not use a period after your title or after any heading in the paper (e.g., *Works Cited*).

If your teacher requires a title page, format it according to the instructions you are given.

3.6. PAGE NUMBERS

Number all pages consecutively throughout the research paper in the upper right-hand corner, one-half inch from the top and flush with the right margin. Type your last name before the page number, as a precaution in case of misplaced pages. Word processors with automatic page numbering will save you the time and effort of numbering every page. A word processor allows you to create a running head that consists of your last name followed by a space and the page number. Do not use the abbreviation *p.* before a page number or add a period, a hyphen, or any other mark or symbol. Position the first line of text one inch from the top of the page (see fig. 5). The word processor may automatically insert your running head on every page of your paper if you do not specify otherwise. Some teachers, however, prefer that no number appear on the first page. Follow your teacher's preference.

Fig. 5. The running head of a research paper.

3.7. TABLES AND ILLUSTRATIONS

Place tables and illustrations as close as possible to the parts of the text to which they relate. A table is usually labeled *Table*, given an arabic numeral, and captioned. Type both label and caption flush left on separate lines above the table, and capitalize them as you would a title (do not use all capital letters). Give the source of the table and any notes immediately below the table. To avoid confusion between notes to the text and notes to the table, designate notes to the table with lowercase letters rather than with numerals. Double-space throughout, making dividing lines as needed (see fig. 6).

Table 1

Earned Degrees in Modern Foreign Languages Conferred by
  Institutions of Higher Education in the United States[a]

Year	Bachelor's Degrees	Master's Degrees	Doctor's Degrees
1984-85	9,675	1,611	387
1985-86	9,808	1,655	426
1986-87	9,858	1,692	403
1987-88	9,790	1,795	380
1988-89	10,498	1,821	389
1989-90	11,092	1,931	475
1990-91	11,724	1,973	477
1991-92	12,367	2,119	537
1992-93	12,819	2,353	535
1993-94	12,785	2,343	578

Source: United States, Dept. of Educ., Office of Educ.
  Research and Improvement, Natl. Center for Educ.
  Statistics, Digest of Education Statistics, 1996
  (Washington: GPO, 1996) table 282.

  [a] These figures include degrees conferred in a single
modern foreign language or a combination of modern foreign
languages and exclude degrees in linguistics, Latin, classical
Greek, and some not commonly taught modern languages.

Fig. 6. A table in a research paper.

Any other type of illustrative visual material—for example, a photograph, map, line drawing, graph, or chart—should be labeled *Figure* (usually abbreviated *Fig.*), assigned an arabic numeral, and given a title or caption: "Fig. 1. Mary Cassatt, *Mother and Child*, Wichita Art Museum, Wichita." A label and title or caption ordinarily appear directly below the illustration and have the same one-inch margins as the text of the paper (see fig. 7).

If your research papers have many illustrations, you will probably want to become familiar with the various kinds of drafting software, for the creation of tables, graphs, drawings, and so forth, on a computer. These programs automatically number tables and illustrations, set them appropriately into the text, and generate a listing of all tables and illustrations created for the paper.

Musical illustrations are labeled *Example* (usually abbreviated *Ex.*), assigned an arabic numeral, and given a title or caption: "Ex. 1. Pyotr Ilich Tchaikovsky, Symphony no. 6 in B, op. 74 (*Pathétique*), finale." A label and title or caption ordinarily appear directly below the example and have the same one-inch margins as the text of the paper (see fig. 8).

Fig. 1. Manticore, woodcut from Edward Topsell, <u>The History of Four-Footed Beasts and Serpents [. . .]</u> (London, 1658) 344; rpt. in Konrad Gesner, <u>Curious Woodcuts of Fanciful and Real Beasts</u> (New York: Dover, 1971) 8.

Fig. 7. A figure in a research paper.

Ex. 1. Ludwig van Beethoven, Symphony no. 3 in E flat, op. 55 (Eroica), first movement, opening.

Fig. 8. A musical example in a research paper.

3.8. CORRECTIONS AND INSERTIONS

Proofread and correct your research paper carefully before submitting it. If you find a mistake in the final copy and you are using a word processor, recall the file, make the appropriate revisions, and reprint the corrected page or pages. Be sure to save the changed file. Some writers find such software as spelling checkers and usage checkers helpful when used with caution (see 1.10). If you are not using a computer and if your instructor permits brief corrections, write them neatly and legibly in ink directly above the lines involved, using carets (∧) to indicate where they go. Do not use the margins or write a change below the line it affects. If corrections on any page are numerous or substantial, retype the page.

3.9. BINDING

Pages of your research paper may get misplaced or lost if they are left unattached or merely folded down at a corner. Although a plastic folder or some other kind of binder may seem an attractive finishing touch, most instructors find such devices a nuisance in reading and commenting on students' work. Many prefer that a paper be secured with a simple paper clip, which can be easily removed and restored.

3.10. ELECTRONIC SUBMISSION

There are at present no commonly accepted standards for the electronic submission of research papers. If you are asked to submit your paper electronically, obtain from your teacher guidelines for formatting, mode of submission (e.g., on disk, by e-mail), and so forth, and follow them closely.

To facilitate discussion of your work, you should incorporate in the paper reference markers that can be cited the way page numbers in a printed paper are. Numbering paragraphs is becoming common in electronic publications. If you use this system, place the appropriate number, in brackets—"[12]"—and followed by a space, at the beginning of each paragraph.

4 Documentation: Preparing the List of Works Cited

4.1. DOCUMENTING SOURCES

Nearly all research builds on previous research. Researchers commonly begin a project by studying past work in the area and deriving relevant information and ideas from their predecessors. This process is largely responsible for the continual expansion of human knowledge. In presenting their work, researchers generously acknowledge their debts to predecessors by carefully documenting each source, so that earlier contributions receive appropriate credit.

As you prepare your paper, you should similarly seek to build on the work of previous writers and researchers. And whenever you draw on another's work, you must also document your source by indicating what you borrowed—whether facts, opinions, or quotations—and where you borrowed it from. If you have not already done so, read carefully the earlier section on plagiarism (1.8) to learn what you must document in your paper.

4.2. MLA STYLE

In MLA documentation style, you acknowledge your sources by keying brief parenthetical citations in your text to an alphabetical list of works that appears at the end of the paper. The parenthetical citation that concludes the following sentence is typical of MLA style.

```
Ancient writers attributed the invention of the
monochord to Pythagoras, who lived in the sixth century
BC (Marcuse 197).
```

The citation "(Marcuse 197)" tells readers that the information in the sentence was derived from page 197 of a work by an author named Marcuse. If readers want more information about this source, they can turn to the works-cited list, where, under the name Marcuse, they would find the following information.

```
Marcuse, Sibyl. A Survey of Musical Instruments. New
York: Harper, 1975.
```

This entry states that the work's author is Sibyl Marcuse and its title is *A Survey of Musical Instruments*. The remaining information relates, in shortened form, that the work was published in New York City by Harper and Row in 1975.

A citation in MLA style contains only enough information to enable readers to find the source in the works-cited list. If the author's name is mentioned in the text, only the page number appears in the citation: "(197)." If more than one work by the author is in the list of works cited, a shortened version of the title is given: "(Marcuse, *Survey* 197)." (See ch. 5 for a fuller discussion of parenthetical citations in MLA style.)

MLA style is not the only way to document sources. Many disciplines have their own documentation systems. MLA style is widely used in the humanities. Although generally simpler and more economical than other documentation styles, it shares with most others its central feature: parenthetical citations keyed to a works-cited list. If you learn MLA documentation style at an early stage in your school career, you will probably have little difficulty in adapting to other styles.

Documentation styles differ according to discipline because they are shaped by the kind of research and scholarship undertaken. For example, in the sciences, where timeliness of research is crucial, the date of publication is usually given prominence. Thus, in the style recommended by the American Psychological Association (APA), a typical citation includes the date of publication (as well as the abbreviation *p.* before the page number). Compare APA and MLA parenthetical citations for the same source.

APA

(Marcuse, 1975, p. 197)

MLA

(Marcuse 197)

In the humanities, where most important scholarship remains relevant for a substantial period, publication dates receive less attention: though always stated in the works-cited list, they are omitted in parenthetical references. An important reason for this omission is that many humanities scholars like to keep their texts as readable and as free of disruptions as possible.

In an entry in an APA-style works-cited list, the date (in parentheses) immediately follows the name of the author (whose first name is written only as an initial), just the first word of the title is capitalized, and the publisher's full name is provided. In APA style, the first line of the entry is indented; second and subsequent lines are flush with the left margin.

APA

>   Marcuse, S. (1975). <u>A survey of musical instruments</u>. New York: Harper and Row.

By contrast, in an MLA-style entry, the author's name appears as given in the work (normally in full), every important word of the title is capitalized, the publisher's name is shortened, and the publication date is placed at the end. In MLA style, the first line of the entry is flush with the left margin, and second and subsequent lines are indented. This format helps readers locate authors' names in the alphabetical listing.

MLA

Marcuse, Sibyl. <u>A Survey of Musical Instruments</u>. New
>   York: Harper, 1975.

Chapters 4 and 5 offer an authoritative and comprehensive presentation of MLA style. For descriptions of other systems of documentation, including one using endnotes and footnotes, see appendix B.

4.3. THE LIST OF WORKS CITED AND OTHER SOURCE LISTS

Although the list of works cited appears at the end of your paper, you need to draft the section in advance, so that you will know what information to give in parenthetical references as you write. For example, you have to include shortened titles if you cite two or more works by the same author, and you have to add initials or first names if two of the cited authors have the same last name: "(K. Roemer 123–24)," "(M. Roemer 67)." This chapter therefore explains how to prepare a list of works cited, and the next chapter demonstrates how to document sources where you use them in your text.

As the heading *Works Cited* indicates, this list contains all the works that you will cite in your text. The list simplifies documentation by permitting you to make only brief references to these works in the text. For example, when you have the following entry in your list of works cited, a citation such as "(Thompson 32–35)" fully identifies your source to readers (provided that you cite no other work by an author with the same last name).

```
Thompson, Stith. The Folktale. New York: Dryden, 1946.
```

Other names for such a listing are *Bibliography* (literally, "description of books") and *Literature Cited*. Usually, however, the broader title *Works Cited* is most appropriate, since research papers often draw on not only books and articles but also films, recordings, television programs, and other nonprint sources.

Titles used for other kinds of source lists include *Annotated Bibliography*, *Works Consulted*, and *Selected Bibliography*. An annotated bibliography, also called *Annotated List of Works Cited*, contains descriptive or evaluative comments on the sources. (For more information on such listings, see James L. Harner, *On Compiling an Annotated Bibliography*, rev. ed. [New York: MLA, 1991].)

```
Thompson, Stith. The Folktale. New York: Dryden, 1946. A
    comprehensive survey of the most popular folktales,
    including their histories and their uses in
    literary works.
```

The title *Works Consulted* indicates that the list is not confined to works cited in the paper. The heading *Selected Bibliography*, or *Selected List of Works Consulted*, is appropriate for lists suggesting readings in the field.

4.4. PLACEMENT OF THE LIST OF WORKS CITED

The list of works cited appears at the end of the paper. Begin the list on a new page and number each page, continuing the page numbers of the text. For example, if the text of your research paper ends on page 10, the works-cited list begins on page 11. The page number appears in the upper right-hand corner, half an inch from the top and flush with the right margin. Center the title, *Works Cited*, an inch from the top of the page. Double-space between the title and the first entry. Begin each entry flush with the left margin; if an entry runs more than one line, indent the subsequent line or lines one-half inch (or five spaces if you are using a typewriter) from the left margin. Double-space the entire list, both between and within entries (see fig. 9). Continue the list on as many pages as necessary.

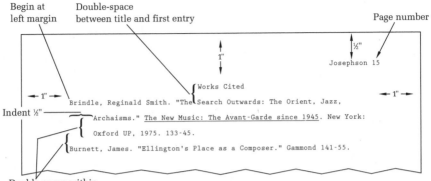

Fig. 9. The top of the first page of a works-cited list.

4.5. ARRANGEMENT OF ENTRIES

In general, alphabetize entries in the list of works cited by the author's last name, using the letter-by-letter system. In this system, the alphabetical order of names is determined by the letters before the commas that separate last names and first names. Spaces and other punctuation marks are ignored. The letters after the commas are considered only when two or more last names are identical. The following examples are alphabetized letter by letter. (For more information on alphabetizing foreign names, see 2.8.)

```
Descartes, René
De Sica, Vittorio

MacDonald, George
McCullers, Carson

Morris, Robert
Morris, William
Morrison, Toni

Saint-Exupéry, Antoine de
St. Denis, Ruth
```

If two or more entries citing coauthors begin with the same name, alphabetize by the last names of the second authors listed.

```
Scholes, Robert, and Robert Kellogg

Scholes, Robert, Carl H. Klaus, and Michael Silverman

Scholes, Robert, and Eric S. Rabkin
```

If the author's name is unknown, alphabetize by the title, ignoring any initial *A*, *An*, or *The*. For example, the title *An Encyclopedia of the Latin-American Novel* would be alphabetized under *e* rather than *a*. An alphabetical listing makes it easy for the reader to find the entry corresponding to a citation in the text.

Other kinds of bibliographies may be arranged differently. An annotated list, a list of works consulted, or a list of selected readings for a historical study, for example, may be organized chronologically by publication date. Some bibliographies are divided into sections and the items alphabetized in each section. A list may be broken down into primary and secondary sources or into different research media (books, articles, recordings). Alternatively, it may be arranged by subject matter (literature and law, law in literature, law as literature), by period (classical utopia, Renaissance utopia), or by area (Egyptian mythology, Greek mythology, Norse mythology).

4.6. CITING BOOKS AND OTHER NONPERIODICAL PUBLICATIONS

4.6.1. The Basic Entry: A Book by a Single Author

One of the most common items in students' works-cited lists is the entry for a book by a single author. Such an entry characteristically has three main divisions:

```
Author's name. Title of the book. Publication
     information.
```

Here is an example:

```
Wilson, Frank R. The Hand: How Its Use Shapes the Brain,
     Language, and Human Culture. New York: Pantheon,
     1998.
```

Author's Name

Reverse the author's name for alphabetizing, adding a comma after the last name (Porter, Katherine Anne). Put a period after the complete name.

```
Wilson, Frank R.
```

Apart from reversing the order, give the author's name as it appears on the title page. Never abbreviate a name given in full. If, for example, the title page lists the author as "Carleton Brown," do not enter the name as "Brown, C." But use initials if the title page does.

```
Eliot, T. S.
McLuhan, H. Marshall.
```

You may spell out a name abbreviated on the title page if you think the additional information would be helpful to readers. Put square brackets around the material you add.

```
Hinton, S[usan] E[loise].
Tolkien, J[ohn] R[onald] R[euel].
```

Similarly, you may give the real name of an author listed under a pseudonym, enclosing the added name in square brackets.

```
Le Carré, John [David Cornwell].
```

In general, omit titles, affiliations, and degrees that precede or follow names.

ON TITLE PAGE	IN WORKS-CITED LIST
Anthony T. Boyle, PhD	Boyle, Anthony T.
Sister Jean Daniel	Daniel, Jean.
Gerard Manley Hopkins, SJ	Hopkins, Gerard Manley.
Lady Mary Wortley Montagu	Montagu, Mary Wortley.
Sir Philip Sidney	Sidney, Philip.
Saint Teresa de Jesús	Teresa de Jesús.

A suffix that is an essential part of the name—like *Jr.* or a roman numeral—appears after the given name, preceded by a comma.

```
Rockefeller, John D., IV.
Rust, Arthur George, Jr.
```

Title of the Book

In general, follow the recommendations for titles given in 2.6. State the full title of the book, including any subtitle. If the book has a subtitle, put a colon directly after the main title, unless the main title ends in a question mark, an exclamation point, or a dash. Place a period after the entire title (including any subtitle), unless it ends in another punctuation mark. Underline the entire title, including any colon, subtitle, and punctuation in the title, but do not underline the period that follows the title.

> Wilson, Frank R. <u>The Hand: How Its Use Shapes the Brain, Language, and Human Culture</u>.

Publication Information

In general, give the city of publication, publisher's name, and year of publication. Take these facts directly from the book, not from a source such as a bibliography or a library catalog. The publisher's name that appears on the title page is generally the name to cite. The name may be accompanied there by the city and date. Any publication information not available on the title page can usually be found on the copyright page (i.e., the reverse of the title page) or, particularly in books published outside the United States, on a page at the back of the book. Use a colon between the place of publication and the publisher, a comma between the publisher and the date, and a period after the date.

> Wilson, Frank R. <u>The Hand: How Its Use Shapes the Brain, Language, and Human Culture</u>. New York: Pantheon, 1998.

If several cities are listed in the book, give only the first. For cities outside the United States, add an abbreviation of the country (or of the province for cities in Canada) if the name of the city may be ambiguous or unfamiliar to your reader (see 6.3 for abbreviations of geographic names).

> Manchester, Eng.
>
> Sherbrooke, PQ

Shorten the publisher's name, following the guidelines in 6.5. If the year of publication is not recorded on the title page, use the latest copyright date.

Here are some additional examples of the basic book entry:

Berlage, Gai Ingham. <u>Women in Baseball: The Forgotten
    History</u>. Westport: Greenwood, 1994.

Freedman, Richard R. <u>What Do Unions Do?</u> New York: Basic,
    1984.

Hinton, S[usan] E[loise]. <u>Tex</u>. New York: Delacorte, 1979.

Le Carré, John [David Cornwell]. <u>The Russia House</u>. New
    York: Knopf, 1989.

Silver, Lee M. <u>Remaking Eden: Cloning and Beyond in a
    Brave New World</u>. New York: Avon, 1997.

Tatar, Maria. <u>Off with Their Heads! Fairy Tales and the
    Culture of Childhood</u>. Princeton: Princeton
    UP, 1992.

Townsend, Robert M. <u>The Medieval Village Economy</u>.
    Princeton: Princeton UP, 1993.

Sometimes additional information is required. This list shows most
of the possible components of a book entry and the order in which
they are normally arranged:

1. Author's name
2. Title of a part of the book (see esp. 4.6.7–9)
3. Title of the book
4. Name of the editor, translator, or compiler (see esp. 4.6.7 and
   4.6.12–13)
5. Edition used (see 4.6.14)
6. Number(s) of the volume(s) used (see 4.6.15)
7. Name of the series (see 4.6.16)
8. Place of publication, name of the publisher, and date of
   publication
9. Page numbers (see esp. 4.6.7)
10. Supplementary bibliographic information and annotation (see
    esp. 4.6.13 and 4.6.15)

The rest of 4.6 explains how to cite these items. To cite an online book,
see 4.9.3.

4.6.2. An Anthology or a Compilation

To cite an anthology or a compilation (e.g., a bibliography) that was edited or compiled by someone whose name appears on the title page, begin your entry with the name of the editor or compiler, followed by a comma and the abbreviation *ed.* or *comp.* If the person named performed more than one function—serving, say, as editor and translator—give both roles in the order in which they appear on the title page.

Feldman, Paula R., ed. British Women Poets of the
        Romantic Era. Baltimore: Johns Hopkins UP, 1997.

Lopate, Phillip, ed. The Art of the Personal Essay: An
        Anthology from the Classical Era to the Present.
        New York: Anchor-Doubleday, 1994.

McRae, Murdo William, ed. The Literature of Science:
        Perspectives on Popular Science Writing. Athens:
        U of Georgia P, 1993.

Sevillano, Mando, comp. The Hopi Way: Tales from a
        Vanishing Culture. Flagstaff: Northland, 1986.

Spafford, Peter, comp. and ed. Interference: The Story
        of Czechoslovakia in the Words of Its Writers.
        Cheltenham: New Clarion, 1992.

See also the sections on works in an anthology (4.6.7); introductions, prefaces, and similar parts of books (4.6.9); editions (4.6.12); and translations (4.6.13).

4.6.3. Two or More Books by the Same Author

To cite two or more books by the same author, give the name in the first entry only. Thereafter, in place of the name, type three hyphens, followed by a period and the title. The three hyphens stand for exactly the same name as in the preceding entry. If the person named edited, translated, or compiled the book, place a comma (not a period) after the three hyphens, and write the appropriate abbreviation (*ed., trans.,* or *comp.*) before giving the title. If the same person served as, say, the editor of two or more works listed consecutively, the abbreviation *ed.*

must be repeated with each entry. This sort of label does not affect the order in which entries appear; works listed under the same name are alphabetized by title.

Borroff, Marie. <u>Language and the Past: Verbal Artistry in Frost, Stevens, and Moore</u>. Chicago: U of Chicago P, 1979.

---, trans. <u>Sir Gawain and the Green Knight</u>. New York: Norton, 1967.

---, ed. <u>Wallace Stevens: A Collection of Critical Essays</u>. Englewood Cliffs: Prentice, 1963.

Frye, Northrop. <u>Anatomy of Criticism: Four Essays</u>. Princeton: Princeton UP, 1957.

---, ed. <u>Design for Learning: Reports Submitted to the Joint Committee of the Toronto Board of Education and the University of Toronto</u>. Toronto: U of Toronto P, 1962.

---. <u>The Double Vision: Language and Meaning in Religion</u>. Toronto: U of Toronto P, 1991.

---, ed. <u>Sound and Poetry</u>. New York: Columbia UP, 1957.

4.6.4. A Book by Two or More Authors

To cite a book by two or three authors, give their names in the same order as on the title page—not necessarily in alphabetical order. Reverse only the name of the first author, add a comma, and give the other name or names in normal form (Wellek, René, and Austin Warren). Place a period after the last name. Even if the authors have the same last name, state each name in full (Durant, Will, and Ariel Durant). If the persons listed on the title page are editors, translators, or compilers, place a comma (not a period) after the final name and add the appropriate abbreviation (*eds., trans.,* or *comps.* for "editors," "translators," or "compilers").

Eggins, Suzanne, and Diane Slade. <u>Analysing Casual Conversation</u>. London: Cassell, 1997.

Marquart, James W., Sheldon Ekland Olson, and Jonathan R. Sorensen. <u>The Rope, the Chair, and the Needle:</u>

> Capital Punishment in Texas, 1923-1990. Austin: U of
>   Texas P, 1994.
> Rabkin, Eric S., Martin H. Greenberg, and Joseph D.
>   Olander, eds. No Place Else: Explorations in Utopian
>   and Dystopian Fiction. Carbondale: Southern Illinois
>   UP, 1983.
> Welsch, Roger L., and Linda K. Welsch. Cather's Kitchens:
>   Foodways in Literature and Life. Lincoln: U of
>   Nebraska P, 1987.

If there are more than three authors, you may name only the first and add *et al.* ("and others"), or you may give all names in full in the order in which they appear on the title page.

> Gilman, Sander, et al. Hysteria beyond Freud. Berkeley:
>   U of California P, 1993.
> Quirk, Randolph, et al. A Comprehensive Grammar of the
>   English Language. London: Longman, 1985.

or

> Gilman, Sander, Helen King, Roy Porter, George Rousseau,
>   and Elaine Showalter. Hysteria beyond Freud.
>   Berkeley: U of California P, 1993.
> Quirk, Randolph, Sidney Greenbaum, Geoffrey Leech, and
>   Jan Svartvik. A Comprehensive Grammar of the
>   English Language. London: Longman, 1985.

If a single author cited in an entry is also the first of multiple authors in the following entry, repeat the name in full; do not substitute three hyphens. Repeat the name in full whenever you cite the same person as part of a different authorship. The three hyphens are never used in combination with persons' names.

> Scholes, Robert. Protocols of Reading. New Haven: Yale
>   UP, 1989.
> ---. Textual Power: Literary Theory and the Teaching of
>   English. New Haven: Yale UP, 1985.
> Scholes, Robert, and Robert Kellogg. The Nature of
>   Narrative. New York: Oxford UP, 1966.

Scholes, Robert, and Eric S. Rabkin. Science Fiction:
      History, Science, Vision. New York: Oxford UP, 1977.

Tannen, Deborah, ed. Gender and Conversational
      Interaction. New York: Oxford UP, 1993.

---. You Just Don't Understand: Women and Men in
      Conversation. New York: Morrow, 1990.

Tannen, Deborah, and James E. Alatis, eds. Languages and
      Linguistics: The Interdependence of Theory, Data,
      and Application. Washington: Georgetown UP, 1986.

Tannen, Deborah, and Muriel Saville-Troike, eds.
      Perspectives on Silence. Norwood: Ablex, 1985.

4.6.5. Two or More Books by the Same Authors

To cite two or more books by the same authors, give the names in the
first entry only. Thereafter, in place of the names, type three hyphens,
followed by a period and the title. The three hyphens stand for exactly
the same names as in the preceding entry.

Durant, Will, and Ariel Durant. The Age of Voltaire. New
      York: Simon, 1965.

---. A Dual Autobiography. New York: Simon, 1977.

Gilbert, Sandra M. Emily's Bread: Poems. New York:
      Norton, 1984.

---. Ghost Volcano: Poems. New York: Norton, 1995.

Gilbert, Sandra M., and Susan Gubar. The Madwoman in the
      Attic: The Woman Writer and the Nineteenth-Century
      Literary Imagination. New Haven: Yale UP, 1979.

---, eds. The Norton Anthology of Literature by Women:
      The Tradition in English. 2nd ed. New York:
      Norton, 1996.

4.6.6. A Book by a Corporate Author

A corporate author may be a commission, an association, a committee,
or any other group whose individual members are not identified on the

title page. Cite the book by the corporate author, even if the corporate author is the publisher. (On citing government publications, see 4.6.21.)

American Medical Association. <u>The American Medical</u>
 <u>Association Encyclopedia of Medicine</u>. New York:
 Random, 1989.

National Research Council. <u>China and Global Change:</u>
 <u>Opportunities for Collaboration</u>. Washington: Natl.
 Acad., 1992.

Public Agenda Foundation. <u>The Health Care Crisis:</u>
 <u>Containing Costs, Expanding Coverage</u>. New York:
 McGraw, 1992.

4.6.7. A Work in an Anthology

If you are citing an essay, a short story, a poem, or another work that appears within an anthology or some other book collection, you need to add the following information to the basic book entry (4.6.1).

Author, title, and (if relevant) translator of the part of the book being cited. Begin the entry with the author and title of the piece, normally enclosing the title in quotation marks.

Allende, Isabel. "Toad's Mouth."

But if the work was originally published independently (as, e.g., autobiographies, plays, and novels generally are), underline its title instead (see the sample entries below for Douglass and Hansberry). Follow the title of the part of the book with a period. If the anthology contains the work of more than one translator, give the translator's name next, preceded by the abbreviation *Trans.* ("Translated by").

Allende, Isabel. "Toad's Mouth." Trans. Margaret Sayers
 Peden.

Then state the title of the anthology (underlined).

Allende, Isabel. "Toad's Mouth." Trans. Margaret Sayers
 Peden. <u>A Hammock beneath the Mangoes: Stories from</u>
 <u>Latin America</u>.

Name of the editor, translator, or compiler of the book being cited.
If all the works in the collection have the same translator or if the book
has an editor or compiler, write *Trans.*, *Ed.*, or *Comp.* ("Translated by,"
"Edited by," or "Compiled by"), as appropriate, after the book title and
give that person's name.

> Allende, Isabel. "Toad's Mouth." Trans. Margaret Sayers
>
>   Peden. <u>A Hammock beneath the Mangoes: Stories from</u>
>
>   <u>Latin America</u>. Ed. Thomas Colchie.

If someone served in more than one role—say, as editor and translator—state the roles in the order in which they appear on the title page
(e.g., "Ed. and trans."; see the entry below for Hanzlík). Similarly, if
more than one person served in different roles, give the names in the
order in which they appear on the title page: "Trans. Jessie Coulson.
Ed. George Gibian."

Page numbers of the cited piece. Give the inclusive page numbers of
the piece you are citing. Be sure to provide the page numbers for the
entire piece, not just for the material you used. Inclusive page numbers, usually without any identifying abbreviation, follow the publication date and a period. (If the book has no page numbers, see 4.6.25.)

> Allende, Isabel. "Toad's Mouth." Trans. Margaret Sayers
>
>   Peden. <u>A Hammock beneath the Mangoes: Stories from</u>
>
>   <u>Latin America</u>. Ed. Thomas Colchie. New York: Plume,
>
>   1992. 83-88.

Here are some additional sample entries for works in anthologies:

> Calvino, Italo. "Cybernetics and Ghosts." <u>The Uses of</u>
>
>   <u>Literature: Essays</u>. Trans. Patrick Creagh. San
>
>   Diego: Harcourt, 1982. 3-27.
>
> Hansberry, Lorraine. <u>A Raisin in the Sun</u>. <u>Black Theater:</u>
>
>   <u>A Twentieth-Century Collection of the Work of Its</u>
>
>   <u>Best Playwrights</u>. Ed. Lindsay Patterson. New York:
>
>   Dodd, 1971. 221-76.
>
> Hanzlík, Josef. "Vengeance." Trans. Ewald Osers.
>
>   <u>Interference: The Story of Czechoslovakia in the</u>
>
>   <u>Words of Its Writers</u>. Comp. and ed. Peter Spafford.
>
>   Cheltenham: New Clarion, 1992. 54.

More, Hannah. "The Black Slave Trade: A Poem." <u>British</u>
    <u>Women Poets of the Romantic Era</u>. Ed. Paula R.
    Feldman. Baltimore: Johns Hopkins UP, 1997. 472-82.
"A Witchcraft Story." <u>The Hopi Way: Tales from a</u>
    <u>Vanishing Culture</u>. Comp. Mando Sevillano.
    Flagstaff: Northland, 1986. 33-42.

Often the works in anthologies have been published before. If you
wish to inform your reader of the date when a previously published
piece other than a scholarly article first appeared, you may follow the
title of the piece with the year of original publication and a period.

Douglass, Frederick. <u>Narrative of the Life of Frederick</u>
    <u>Douglass, an American Slave, Written by Himself</u>.
    1845. <u>Classic American Autobiographies</u>. Ed. William
    L. Andrews. New York: Mentor, 1992. 229-327.
Franklin, Benjamin. "Emigration to America." 1782. <u>The</u>
    <u>Faber Book of America</u>. Ed. Christopher Ricks and
    William L. Vance. Boston: Faber, 1992. 24-26.

To cite a previously published scholarly article in a collection, give
the complete data for the earlier publication and then add *Rpt. in*
("Reprinted in"), the title of the collection, and the new publication
facts. (On citing articles in periodicals, see 4.7.)

Frye, Northrop. "Literary and Linguistic Scholarship in
    a Postliterate Age." <u>PMLA</u> 99 (1984): 990-95. Rpt.
    in <u>Myth and Metaphor: Selected Essays, 1974-88</u>. Ed.
    Robert D. Denham. Charlottesville: UP of Virginia,
    1990. 18-27.
Roberts, Sheila. "A Confined World: A Rereading of
    Pauline Smith." <u>World Literature Written in English</u>
    24 (1984): 232-38. Rpt. in <u>Twentieth-Century</u>
    <u>Literary Criticism</u>. Ed. Dennis Poupard. Vol. 25.
    Detroit: Gale, 1988. 399-402.

If the article was originally published under a different title, first state
the new title and publication facts, followed by *Rpt. of* ("Reprint of"),
the original title, and the original publication facts.

Lewis, C. S. "Viewpoints: C. S. Lewis." <u>Twentieth-Century</u>
     <u>Interpretations of</u> Sir Gawain and the Green Knight.
     Ed. Denton Fox. Englewood Cliffs: Prentice, 1968.
     100-01. Rpt. of "The Anthropological Approach."
     <u>English and Medieval Studies Presented to J. R. R.</u>
     <u>Tolkien on the Occasion of His Seventieth Birthday</u>.
     Ed. Norman Davis and C. L. Wrenn. London: Allen,
     1962. 219-23.

If you refer to more than one piece from the same collection, you
may wish to cross-reference each citation to a single entry for the book
(see 4.6.10). On citing articles in reference books, see 4.6.8. On citing
introductions, prefaces, and the like, see 4.6.9. On citing a piece in a
multivolume anthology, see 4.6.15.

4.6.8. An Article in a Reference Book

Treat an encyclopedia article or a dictionary entry as you would a piece
in a collection (4.6.7), but do not cite the editor of the reference work. If
the article is signed, give the author first (often articles in reference
books are signed with initials identified elsewhere in the work); if it is
unsigned, give the title first. If the encyclopedia or dictionary arranges
articles alphabetically, you may omit volume and page numbers.

When citing familiar reference books, especially those that frequently
appear in new editions, do not give full publication information. For
such works, list only the edition (if stated) and the year of publication.

"Azimuthal Equidistant Projection." <u>Merriam-Webster's</u>
     <u>Collegiate Dictionary</u>. 10th ed. 1993.
"Ginsburg, Ruth Bader." <u>Who's Who in America</u>. 52nd ed.
     1998.
"Mandarin." <u>The Encyclopedia Americana</u>. 1994 ed.
Mohanty, Jitendra M. "Indian Philosophy." <u>The New</u>
     <u>Encyclopaedia Britannica: Macropaedia</u>. 15th
     ed. 1987.
"Noon." <u>The Oxford English Dictionary</u>. 2nd ed. 1989.

If you are citing a specific definition, among several, add the abbreviation *Def.* ("Definition") and the appropriate designation (e.g., number, letter).

> "Noon." Def. 4b. <u>The Oxford English Dictionary</u>. 2nd ed.
>   1989.

When citing less familiar reference books, however, especially those that have appeared in only one edition, give full publication information.

> Allen, Anita L. "Privacy in Health Care." <u>Encyclopedia</u>
>   <u>of Bioethics</u>. Ed. Warren T. Reich. Rev. ed. 5 vols.
>   New York: Macmillan-Simon, 1995.
> Le Patourel, John. "Normans and Normandy." <u>Dictionary of</u>
>   <u>the Middle Ages</u>. Ed. Joseph R. Strayer. 13 vols.
>   New York: Scribner's, 1987.

4.6.9. An Introduction, a Preface, a Foreword, or an Afterword

To cite an introduction, a preface, a foreword, or an afterword, begin with the name of its author and then give the name of the part being cited, capitalized but neither underlined nor enclosed in quotation marks (*Introduction, Preface, Foreword, Afterword*). If the writer of the piece is different from the author of the complete work, cite the author of the work after its title, giving the full name, in normal order, preceded by the word *By.* If the writer of the piece is also the author of the complete work, use only the last name after *By.* Continue with full publication information and, finally, the inclusive page numbers.

> Borges, Jorge Luis. Foreword. <u>Selected Poems, 1923-1967</u>.
>   By Borges. Ed. Norman Thomas Di Giovanni. New York:
>   Delta-Dell, 1973. xv-xvi.
> Doctorow, E. L. Introduction. <u>Sister Carrie</u>. By Theodore
>   Dreiser. New York: Bantam, 1982. v-xi.
> Drabble, Margaret. Introduction. <u>Middlemarch</u>. By George
>   Eliot. New York: Bantam, 1985. vii-xvii.
> Elliott, Emory. Afterword. <u>The Jungle</u>. By Upton
>   Sinclair. New York: Signet, 1990. 342-50.

Hamill, Pete. Introduction. <u>The Brooklyn Reader: Thirty</u>
     <u>Writers Celebrate America's Favorite Borough</u>. Ed.
     Andrea Wyatt Sexton and Alice Leccese Powers. New
     York: Harmony, 1994. xi-xiv.
Marsalis, Wynton. Foreword. <u>Beyond Category: The Life</u>
     <u>and Genius of Duke Ellington</u>. By John Edward Hasse.
     New York: Simon, 1993. 13-14.

If the introduction, preface, foreword, or afterword has a title, give the
title, enclosed in quotation marks, immediately before the name of the
part.

Brodsky, Joseph. "Poetry as a Form of Resistance to
     Reality." Foreword. <u>Winter Dialogue</u>. By Tomas
     Venclova. Trans. Diana Senechal. Evanston: Hydra-
     Northwestern UP, 1997. vii-xviii.
Doody, Margaret Anne. "In Search of the Ancient Novel."
     Introduction. <u>The True Story of the Novel</u>. New
     Brunswick: Rutgers UP, 1996. 1-11.

4.6.10. Cross-References

To avoid unnecessary repetition in citing two or more works from the
same collection, you may create a complete entry for the collection
and cross-reference individual pieces to the entry. In a cross-reference,
state the author and the title of the piece, the last name of the editor of
the collection, and the inclusive page numbers. If the piece is a translation, add the name of the translator after the title, unless one person
translated the entire volume.

Hamill, Pete. Introduction. Sexton and Powers xi-xiv.
Mayakovsky, Vladimir. "Brooklyn Bridge." Trans. Max
     Hayward and George Reavey. Sexton and Powers 136-41.
McCullers, Carson. "Brooklyn Is My Neighborhood." Sexton
     and Powers 143-47.
Sexton, Andrea Wyatt, and Alice Leccese Powers, eds. <u>The</u>
     <u>Brooklyn Reader: Thirty Writers Celebrate America's</u>
     <u>Favorite Borough</u>. New York: Harmony, 1994.

Walcott, Derek. "A Letter from Brooklyn." Sexton and
        Powers 264-65.

Whitman, Walt. "Crossing Brooklyn Ferry." Sexton and
        Powers 267-74.

If you list two or more works under the editor's name, however, add
the title (or a shortened version of it) to the cross-reference.

Angelou, Maya. "Pickin Em Up and Layin Em Down." Baker,
        Norton 276-78.

Baker, Russell, ed. The Norton Book of Light Verse. New
        York: Norton, 1986.

---, ed. Russell Baker's Book of American Humor. New
        York: Norton, 1993.

Hurston, Zora Neale. "Squinch Owl Story." Baker, Russell
        Baker's Book 458-59.

Lebowitz, Fran. "Manners." Baker, Russell Baker's Book
        556-59.

Lennon, John. "The Fat Budgie." Baker, Norton 357-58.

4.6.11. An Anonymous Book

If a book has no author's or editor's name on the title page, begin the
entry with the title. Do not use either *Anonymous* or *Anon.* Alphabetize the entry by the title, ignoring any initial *A*, *An*, or *The*. (Note in
the sample entries that *A Guide to Our Federal Lands* is alphabetized
under *g*.)

Encyclopedia of Virginia. New York: Somerset, 1993.

A Guide to Our Federal Lands. Washington: Natl.
        Geographic Soc., 1984.

New York Public Library American History Desk Reference.
        New York: Macmillan, 1997.

4.6.12. An Edition

Every published book is, in at least one sense, an edition; for example, a book may be a first edition, a second edition, and so forth (see 4.6.14). Researchers also use the term *edition*, however, to denote a work that was prepared for publication by someone other than the author—by an editor. For example, a 1999 printing of Shakespeare's *Hamlet* was obviously not prepared for publication by Shakespeare. An editor selected a version of *Hamlet* from the various versions available, decided on any changes in spelling or punctuation, and perhaps added explanatory notes or wrote an introduction. This 1999 version of *Hamlet* would be called an "edition," and the editor's name would most likely appear on the title page along with Shakespeare's.

To cite an edition, begin with the author (or the title, for an anonymous work) if you refer primarily to the text itself; give the editor's name, preceded by the abbreviation *Ed.* ("Edited by"), after the title. If for clarity you wish to indicate the original date of publication, place the year directly after the title (see the entry for Crane).

Crane, Stephen. <u>The Red Badge of Courage: An Episode of the American Civil War</u>. 1895. Ed. Fredson Bowers. Charlottesville: UP of Virginia, 1975.

Edgeworth, Maria. Castle Rackrent <u>and</u> Ennui. Ed. Marilyn Butler. London: Penguin, 1992.

<u>Octovian</u>. Ed. Frances McSparran. Early English Text Soc. 289. London: Oxford UP, 1986.

Rossetti, Christina. <u>Selected Prose of Christina Rossetti</u>. Ed. David A. Kent and P. G. Stanwood. New York: St. Martin's, 1998.

Shakespeare, William. <u>Hamlet</u>. Ed. Barbara A. Mowat and Paul Werstine. New York: Washington Square-Pocket, 1992.

Twain, Mark. <u>Roughing It</u>. Ed. Harriet E. Smith and Edgar M. Branch. Berkeley: U of California P, 1993.

Wollstonecraft, Mary. <u>A Vindication of the Rights of Woman</u>. Ed. Carol H. Poston. New York: Norton, 1975.

If your citations are generally to the work of the editor (e.g., the introduction, the notes, or editorial decisions regarding the text), begin the entry with the editor's name, followed by a comma and the abbreviation *ed.* ("editor"), and give the author's name, preceded by the word *By*, after the title.

> Bowers, Fredson, ed. <u>The Red Badge of Courage: An</u>
>   <u>Episode of the American Civil War</u>. By Stephen
>   Crane. 1895. Charlottesville: UP of Virginia, 1975.

Consult 4.6.15 if you are citing more than one volume of a multivolume work or if the book is a part of a multivolume edition—say, *The Works of Mark Twain*—and you wish to give supplementary information about the entire project.

4.6.13. A Translation

To cite a translation, state the author's name first if you refer primarily to the work itself; give the translator's name, preceded by *Trans.* ("Translated by"), after the title. If the book has an editor as well as a translator, give the names, with appropriate abbreviations, in the order in which they appear on the title page (see the sample entry for Dostoevsky).

> Dostoevsky, Feodor. <u>Crime and Punishment</u>. Trans. Jessie
>   Coulson. Ed. George Gibian. New York: Norton, 1964.
> Esquivel, Laura. <u>Like Water for Chocolate: A Novel in</u>
>   <u>Monthly Installments, with Recipes, Romances, and</u>
>   <u>Home Remedies</u>. Trans. Carol Christensen and Thomas
>   Christensen. New York: Doubleday, 1992.
> Homer. <u>The Odyssey</u>. Trans. Robert Fagles. New York:
>   Viking, 1996.
> Murasaki Shikibu. <u>The Tale of Genji</u>. Trans. Edward G.
>   Seidensticker. New York: Knopf, 1976.

If your citations are mostly to the translator's comments or choice of wording, begin the bibliographic entry with the translator's name, followed by a comma and the abbreviation *trans.* ("translator"), and give the author's name, preceded by the word *By*, after the title. (On citing anthologies of translated works by different authors, see 4.6.7.)

```
Coulson, Jessie, trans. Crime and Punishment. By Feodor
     Dostoevsky. Ed. George Gibian. New York: Norton,
     1964.
```

Although not required, some or all of the original publication facts may be added as supplementary information at the end of the entry.

```
Grimal, Pierre. Love in Ancient Rome. Trans. Arthur
     Train, Jr. Norman: U of Oklahoma P, 1986. Trans. of
     L'amour à Rome. 1980.
Levi, Primo. Survival in Auschwitz: The Nazi Assault on
     Humanity. Trans. Stuart Woolf. New York: Collier-
     Macmillan, 1987. Trans. of Se questo è un uomo.
     Torino: Einaudi, 1958.
```

On citing a book in a language other than English, see 4.6.23.

4.6.14. A Book Published in a Second or Subsequent Edition

A book with no edition number or name on its title page is probably a first edition. Unless informed otherwise, readers assume that bibliographic entries refer to first editions. When you use a later edition of a work, identify the edition in your entry by number (*2nd ed.*, *3rd ed.*, *4th ed.*), by name (*Rev. ed.*, for "Revised edition"; *Abr. ed.*, for "Abridged edition"), or by year (*1999 ed.*)—whichever the title page indicates. The specification of edition comes after the name of the editor, translator, or compiler, if there is one, or otherwise after the title of the book. (On citing encyclopedias, dictionaries, and similar works revised regularly, see 4.6.8.)

```
Chaucer, Geoffrey. The Works of Geoffrey Chaucer. Ed.
     F. W. Robinson. 2nd ed. Boston: Houghton, 1957.
Cheyfitz, Eric. The Poetics of Imperialism: Translation
     and Colonization from The Tempest to Tarzan.
     Expanded ed. Philadelphia: U of Pennsylvania P,
     1997.
Hyde, Margaret O., and Elizabeth Held Forsyth. Suicide:
     The Hidden Epidemic. Rev. ed. New York: Watts, 1986.
```

Murasaki Shikibu. <u>The Tale of Genji</u>. Trans. Edward G. Seidensticker. Abr. ed. New York: Vintage-Random, 1985.

Newcomb, Horace, ed. <u>Television: The Critical View</u>. 5th ed. New York: Oxford UP, 1994.

4.6.15. A Multivolume Work

If you are using two or more volumes of a multivolume work, cite the total number of volumes in the work ("5 vols."). This information comes after the title—or after any editor's name or identification of edition—and before the publication information. Specific references to volume and page numbers ("3: 212–13") belong in the text. (See ch. 5 for parenthetical documentation.)

Blanco, Richard L., ed. <u>The American Revolution, 1775-1783: An Encyclopedia</u>. 2 vols. Hamden: Garland, 1993.

Doyle, Arthur Conan. <u>The Oxford Sherlock Holmes</u>. Ed. Owen Dudley Edwards. 9 vols. New York: Oxford UP, 1993.

Lauter, Paul, et al., eds. <u>The Heath Anthology of American Literature</u>. 2nd ed. 2 vols. Lexington: Heath, 1994.

Martin, Michael T., ed. <u>New Latin American Cinema</u>. 2 vols. Detroit: Wayne State UP, 1997.

Sadie, Stanley, ed. <u>The New Grove Dictionary of Music and Musicians</u>. 20 vols. London: Macmillan, 1980.

Schlesinger, Arthur M., gen. ed. <u>History of U.S. Political Parties</u>. 4 vols. New York: Chelsea, 1973.

If the volumes of the work were published over a period of years, give the inclusive dates at the end of the citation ("1952–70"). If the work is still in progress, write *to date* after the number of volumes ("3 vols. to date") and leave a space after the hyphen that follows the beginning date ("1982– ").

Boswell, James. <u>The Life of Johnson</u>. Ed. George
  Birkbeck Hill and L. F. Powell. 6 vols. Oxford:
  Clarendon, 1934-50.

Cassidy, Frederic, ed. <u>Dictionary of American Regional</u>
  <u>English</u>. 3 vols. to date. Cambridge: Belknap-
  Harvard UP, 1985- .

Churchill, Winston S. <u>A History of the English-Speaking</u>
  <u>Peoples</u>. 4 vols. New York: Dodd, 1956-58.

Crane, Stephen. <u>The University of Virginia Edition of</u>
  <u>the Works of Stephen Crane</u>. Ed. Fredson Bowers. 10
  vols. Charlottesville: UP of Virginia, 1969-76.

Wellek, René. <u>A History of Modern Criticism, 1750-1950</u>.
  8 vols. New Haven: Yale UP, 1955-92.

If you are using only one volume of a multivolume work, state the number of the volume in the bibliographic entry ("Vol. 2") and give publication information for that volume alone; then you need give only page numbers when you refer to that work in the text.

Doyle, Arthur Conan. <u>The Oxford Sherlock Holmes</u>. Ed. Owen
  Dudley Edwards. Vol. 8. New York: Oxford UP, 1993.

Parker, Hershel. <u>Melville: A Biography</u>. Vol. 1.
  Baltimore: Johns Hopkins UP, 1996.

Stowe, Harriet Beecher. "Sojourner Truth, the Libyan
  Sibyl." 1863. <u>The Heath Anthology of American</u>
  <u>Literature</u>. Ed. Paul Lauter et al. 2nd ed. Vol. 1.
  Lexington: Heath, 1994. 2425-33.

Wellek, René. <u>A History of Modern Criticism, 1750-1950</u>.
  Vol. 5. New Haven: Yale UP, 1986.

Although not required, the complete number of volumes may be added as supplementary information at the end of the listing, along with other relevant publication facts, such as inclusive dates of publication if the volumes were published over a period of years (see the sample entry for Wellek).

Doyle, Arthur Conan. <u>The Oxford Sherlock Holmes</u>. Ed. Owen
  Dudley Edwards. Vol. 8. New York: Oxford UP, 1993.
  9 vols.

Stowe, Harriet Beecher. "Sojourner Truth, the Libyan
     Sibyl." 1863. <u>The Heath Anthology of American</u>
     <u>Literature</u>. Ed. Paul Lauter et al. 2nd ed. Vol. 1.
     Lexington: Heath, 1994. 2425-33. 2 vols.
Wellek, René. <u>A History of Modern Criticism, 1750-1950</u>.
     Vol. 5. New Haven: Yale UP, 1986. 8 vols. 1955-92.

If you are using only one volume of a multivolume work and the
volume has an individual title, you may cite the book without reference to the other volumes in the work.

Churchill, Winston S. <u>The Age of Revolution</u>. New York:
     Dodd, 1957.
Durant, Will, and Ariel Durant. <u>The Age of Voltaire</u>. New
     York: Simon, 1965.

Although not required, supplementary information about the complete multivolume work may follow the basic citation: the volume
number, preceded by *Vol.* and followed by the word *of*; the title of the
complete work; the total number of volumes; and, if the work
appeared over a period of years, the inclusive publication dates.

Churchill, Winston S. <u>The Age of Revolution</u>. New York:
     Dodd, 1957. Vol. 3 of <u>A History of the English-</u>
     <u>Speaking Peoples</u>. 4 vols. 1956-58.
Durant, Will, and Ariel Durant. <u>The Age of Voltaire</u>. New
     York: Simon, 1965. Vol. 9 of <u>The Story of</u>
     <u>Civilization</u>. 11 vols. 1935-75.

If the volume you are citing is part of a multivolume scholarly edition
(see 4.6.12), you may similarly give supplementary information about
the entire edition. Follow the publication information for the volume
with the appropriate volume number, preceded by *Vol.* and followed
by the word *of*; the title of the complete work; the name of the general
editor of the multivolume edition, followed by a comma and *gen. ed.*;
the total number of volumes; and the inclusive publication dates for
the edition (see the entry for Howells). If the entire edition was edited
by one person, state the editor's name after the title of the edition
rather than after the title of the volume (see the entry for Crane).

Crane, Stephen. <u>The Red Badge of Courage: An Episode of</u>
     <u>the American Civil War</u>. 1895. Charlottesville: UP
     of Virginia, 1975. Vol. 2 of <u>The University of</u>
     <u>Virginia Edition of the Works of Stephen Crane</u>. Ed.
     Fredson Bowers. 10 vols. 1969-76.

Howells, W. D. <u>Their Wedding Journey</u>. Ed. John K. Reeves.
     Bloomington: Indiana UP, 1968. Vol. 5 of <u>A Selected</u>
     <u>Edition of W. D. Howells</u>. Edwin H. Cady, gen. ed.
     32 vols. 1968-83.

4.6.16. A Book in a Series

If the title page or the preceding page (the half-title page) indicates that
the book you are citing is part of a series, include the series name, neither underlined nor enclosed in quotation marks, and the series number, followed by a period, before the publication information. Use
common abbreviations for words in the series name (see 6.4), including *Ser.* if *Series* is part of the name.

Charrière, Isabelle de. <u>Letters of Mistress Henley</u>
     <u>Published by Her Friend</u>. Trans. Philip Stewart and
     Jean Vaché. Texts and Trans. 1. New York: MLA,
     1993.

Neruda, Pablo. <u>Canto General</u>. Trans. Jack Schmitt. Latin
     Amer. Lit. and Culture 7. Berkeley: U of California
     P, 1991.

Pihl, Marshall R. <u>The Korean Singer of Tales</u>. Harvard-
     Yenching Inst. Monograph Ser. 37. Cambridge:
     Harvard UP, 1994.

Wilson, Sharon R., Thomas B. Friedman, and Shannon
     Hengen, eds. <u>Approaches to Teaching Atwood's</u> The
     Handmaid's Tale <u>and Other Works</u>. Approaches to
     Teaching World Lit. 56. New York: MLA, 1996.

4.6.17. A Republished Book

To cite a republished book—for example, a paperback version of a book originally published in a clothbound version—give the original publication date, followed by a period, before the publication information for the book you are citing.

> Atwood, Margaret. <u>Surfacing</u>. 1972. New York: Doubleday,
>   1998.
>
> Doctorow, E. L. <u>Welcome to Hard Times</u>. 1960. New York:
>   Vintage-Random, 1988.
>
> Douglas, Mary. <u>Purity and Danger: An Analysis of the</u>
>   <u>Concepts of Pollution and Taboo</u>. 1966. London:
>   Routledge, 1993.

Although not required, supplementary information pertaining to the original publication may precede the original publication date.

> Ishiguro, Kazuo. <u>The Remains of the Day</u>. London: Faber,
>   1989. New York: Knopf, 1990.

New material added to the republication, such as an introduction, should be cited after the original publication facts.

> Dreiser, Theodore. <u>Sister Carrie</u>. 1900. Introd. E. L.
>   Doctorow. New York: Bantam, 1982.

To cite a republished book that was originally issued under a different title, first state the new title and publication facts, followed by *Rpt. of* ("Reprint of"), the original title, and the original date.

> <u>The WPA Guide to 1930s New Jersey</u>. New Brunswick:
>   Rutgers UP, 1986. Rpt. of <u>New Jersey: A Guide to</u>
>   <u>Its Past and Present</u>. 1939.

4.6.18. A Publisher's Imprint

Publishers often group some of their books under imprints, or special names. Among Doubleday's many imprints, for example, have been Anchor Books, Crime Club, and Double D Western. If an imprint appears on a title page along with the publisher's name, state the imprint and follow it by a hyphen and the name of the publisher ("Anchor-Doubleday," "Collier-Macmillan," "Vintage-Random").

Cassidy, Frederic, ed. <u>Dictionary of American Regional English</u>. 3 vols. to date. Cambridge: Belknap-Harvard UP, 1985- .

Findlater, Mary, and Jane Findlater. <u>Crossriggs</u>. 1908. Introd. Paul Binding. New York: Virago-Penguin, 1986.

Lopate, Phillip, ed. <u>The Art of the Personal Essay: An Anthology from the Classical Era to the Present</u>. New York: Anchor-Doubleday, 1994.

4.6.19. A Book with Multiple Publishers

If the title page lists two or more publishers—not just two or more offices of the same publisher—include all of them, in the order given, as part of the publication information, putting a semicolon after the name of each but the last.

Duff, J. Wight. <u>A Literary History of Rome: From the Origins to the Close of the Golden Age</u>. Ed. A. M. Duff. 3rd ed. 1953. London: Benn; New York: Barnes, 1967.

Wells, H. G. <u>The Time Machine</u>. 1895. London: Dent; Rutland: Tuttle, 1992.

4.6.20. A Pamphlet

Treat a pamphlet as you would a book.

<u>London</u>. New York: Trip Builder, 1996.
<u>Renoir Lithographs</u>. New York: Dover, 1994.

4.6.21. A Government Publication

Government publications emanate from many sources and so present special problems in bibliographic citation. In general, if you do not know the writer of the document, cite as author the government agency that issued it—that is, state the name of the government first, followed by the name of the agency, using an abbreviation if the context makes it clear. (But see below for citing a document whose author is known.)

```
California. Dept. of Industrial Relations.
United States. Cong. House.
```

If you are citing two or more works issued by the same government, substitute three hyphens for the name in each entry after the first. If you also cite more than one work by the same government agency, use an additional three hyphens in place of the agency in the second entry and each subsequent one.

```
United States. Cong. House.
---. ---. Senate.
---. Dept. of Health and Human Services.
```

The title of the publication, underlined, should follow immediately.

In citing the *Congressional Record* (abbreviated *Cong. Rec.*), give only the date and page numbers.

```
Cong. Rec. 7 Feb. 1973: 3831-51.
```

In citing other congressional documents, include such information as the number and session of Congress, the house (*S* stands for Senate, *H* and *HR* for House of Representatives), and the type and number of the publication. Types of congressional publications include bills (S 33, HR 77), resolutions (S. Res. 20, H. Res. 50), reports (S. Rept. 9, H. Rept. 142), and documents (S. Doc. 333, H. Doc. 222, Misc. Doc. 67).

The usual publication information comes next (i.e., place, publisher, and date). Most federal publications, regardless of the branch of government issuing them, are published by the Government Printing Office (GPO), in Washington, DC; its British counterpart is Her (or His) Majesty's Stationery Office (HMSO), in London. Documents issued by the United Nations and most local governments, however, do not all emanate from a central office; give the publication information that appears on the title page.

Great Britain. Ministry of Agriculture, Fisheries, and
     Food. National Food Survey. London: HMSO, 1993.
New York State. Commission on the Adirondacks in the
     Twenty-First Century. The Adirondack Park in the
     Twenty-First Century. Albany: State of New York,
     1990.
---. Committee on State Prisons. Investigation of the
     New York State Prisons. 1883. New York: Arno, 1974.
United Nations. Consequences of Rapid Population Growth
     in Developing Countries. New York: Taylor, 1991.
---. Centre on Transnational Corporations. Foreign Direct
     Investment, the Service Sector, and International
     Banking. New York: United Nations, 1987.
---. Economic Commission for Africa. Industrial Growth
     in Africa. New York: United Nations, 1963.
United States. Cong. Joint Committee on the Investigation
     of the Pearl Harbor Attack. Hearings. 79th Cong.,
     1st and 2nd sess. 32 vols. Washington: GPO, 1946.
---. ---. Senate. Subcommittee on Constitutional
     Amendments of the Committee on the Judiciary.
     Hearings on the "Equal Rights" Amendment. 91st
     Cong., 2nd sess. S. Res. 61. Washington: GPO, 1970.
---. Dept. of Labor. Child Care: A Workforce Issue.
     Washington: GPO, 1988.
---. Dept. of State. The Global 2000 Report to the
     President: Entering the Twenty-First Century. 3
     vols. Washington: GPO, 1981.

If known, the name of the document's author may either begin the
entry or, if the agency comes first, follow the title and the word *By* or
an abbreviation (such as *Ed.* or *Comp.*).

Poore, Benjamin Perley, comp. A Descriptive Catalogue of
     the Government Publications of the United States,
     September 5, 1774-March 4, 1881. US 48th Cong., 2nd
     sess. Misc. Doc. 67. Washington: GPO, 1885.

or

United States. Cong. <u>A Descriptive Catalogue of the
Government Publications of the United States,
September 5, 1774-March 4, 1881</u>. Comp. Benjamin
Perley Poore. 48th Cong., 2nd sess. Misc. Doc. 67.
Washington: GPO, 1885.

To cite an online government document, see 4.9.3d. To cite a legal
source, see 4.8.14.

4.6.22. The Published Proceedings of a Conference

Treat the published proceedings of a conference like a book, but add
pertinent information about the conference (unless the book title
includes such information).

Freed, Barbara F., ed. <u>Foreign Language Acquisition
Research and the Classroom</u>. Proc. of Consortium for
Lang. Teaching and Learning Conf., Oct. 1989, U of
Pennsylvania. Lexington: Heath, 1991.

Hall, Kira, Michael Meacham, and Richard Shapiro, eds.
<u>Proceedings of the Fifteenth Annual Meeting of the
Berkeley Linguistics Society, February 18-20, 1989:
General Session and Parasession on Theoretical
Issues in Language Reconstruction</u>. Berkeley:
Berkeley Linguistics Soc., 1989.

Cite a presentation in the proceedings like a work in a collection of
pieces by different authors (see 4.6.7).

Mann, Jill. "Chaucer and the 'Woman Question.'" <u>This
Noble Craft: Proceedings of the Tenth Research
Symposium of the Dutch and Belgian University
Teachers of Old and Middle English and Historical
Linguistics, Utrecht, 19-20 January 1989</u>. Ed. Erik
Kooper. Amsterdam: Rodopi, 1991. 173-88.

4.6.23. A Book in a Language Other Than English

Cite a book published in a language other than English like any other book. Give the author's name, title, and publication information as they appear in the book. You may need to look in the colophon, at the back of the book, for some or all of the publication information found on the title or copyright page of English-language books. If it seems necessary to clarify the title, provide a translation, in brackets: "*Gengangere [Ghosts]*." Similarly, you may use brackets to give the English name of a foreign city—"Wien [Vienna]"—or you may substitute the English name, depending on your reader's knowledge of the language. Shorten the publisher's name appropriately (see 6.5). For capitalization in languages other than English, see 2.8.

> Bessière, Jean, ed. <u>Mythologies de l'écriture: Champs critiques</u>. Paris: PUF, 1990.
>
> Dahlhaus, Carl. <u>Musikästhetik</u>. Köln: Gerig, 1967.
>
> Eco, Umberto. <u>Isola del giorno primo</u>. Milano: Bompiani, 1994.
>
> Esquivel, Laura. <u>Como agua para chocolate: Novelas de entregas mensuales, con recetas, amores y remedios caseros</u>. Madrid: Mondadori, 1990.
>
> Poche, Emanuel. <u>Prazské Palace</u>. Praha [Prague]: Odeon, 1977.

4.6.24. A Book Published before 1900

When citing a book published before 1900, you may omit the name of the publisher and use a comma, instead of a colon, after the place of publication.

> Brome, Richard. <u>The Dramatic Works of Richard Brome</u>. 3 vols. London, 1873.
>
> Dewey, John. <u>The School and Society</u>. Chicago, 1899.
>
> Segni, Bernardo. <u>Rettorica et poetica d'Aristotile</u>. Firenze, 1586.

4.6.25. A Book without Stated Publication Information or Pagination

When a book does not indicate the publisher, the place or date of publication, or pagination, supply as much of the missing information as you can, using brackets to show that it did not come from the source.

```
New York: U of Gotham P, [1999].
```

If the date can only be approximated, put it after a *c.*, for *circa* 'around': "[c. 1999]." If you are uncertain about the accuracy of the information you supply, add a question mark: "[1993?]." Use the following abbreviations for information you cannot supply.

n.p.	No place of publication given
n.p.	No publisher given
n.d.	No date of publication given
n. pag.	No pagination given

Inserted before the colon, the abbreviation *n.p.* indicates *no place*; after the colon, it indicates *no publisher*. *N. pag.* explains the absence of page references in citations of the work.

NO PLACE

```
N.p.: U of Gotham P, 1999.
```

NO PUBLISHER

```
New York: n.p., 1999.
```

NO DATE

```
New York: U of Gotham P, n.d.
```

NO PAGINATION

```
New York: U of Gotham P, 1999. N. pag.
```

The examples above are hypothetical; the following ones are entries for actual books.

```
Bauer, Johann. Kafka und Prag. [Stuttgart]: Belser,
     [1971?].
Malachi, Zvi, ed. Proceedings of the International
     Conference on Literary and Linguistic Computing.
     [Tel Aviv]: [Fac. of Humanities, Tel Aviv U], n.d.
```

```
Michelangelo. The Sistine Chapel. New York: Wings, 1992.
     N. pag.
Photographic View Album of Cambridge. [England]: n.p.,
     n.d. N. pag.
Sendak, Maurice. Where the Wild Things Are. New York:
     Harper, 1963. N. pag.
```

4.6.26. An Unpublished Dissertation

Enclose the title of an unpublished dissertation in quotation marks; do not underline it. Then write the descriptive label *Diss.*, and add the name of the degree-granting university, followed by a comma and the year.

```
Boyle, Anthony T. "The Epistemological Evolution of
     Renaissance Utopian Literature, 1516-1657." Diss.
     New York U, 1983.
Sakala, Carol. "Maternity Care Policy in the United
     States: Toward a More Rational and Effective
     System." Diss. Boston U, 1993.
```

For citing a dissertation abstract published in *Dissertation Abstracts* or *Dissertation Abstracts International*, see 4.7.8. For documenting other unpublished writing, see 4.8.12.

4.6.27. A Published Dissertation

Cite a published dissertation like a book, but add pertinent dissertation information before the publication facts. If the work was published by University Microfilms International (UMI), you may add the order number as supplementary information.

```
Dietze, Rudolf F. Ralph Ellison: The Genesis of an
     Artist. Diss. U Erlangen-Nürnberg, 1982. Erlanger
     Beiträge zur Sprach- und Kunstwissenschaft 70.
     Nürnberg: Carl, 1982.
Valentine, Mary-Blair Truesdell. An Investigation of
     Gender-Based Leadership Styles of Male and Female
```

```
Officers in the United States Army. Diss. George
Mason U, 1993. Ann Arbor: UMI, 1993. 9316566.
```

4.7. CITING ARTICLES AND OTHER PUBLICATIONS IN PERIODICALS

4.7.1. The Basic Entry: An Article in a Scholarly Journal with Continuous Pagination

A periodical is a publication that appears regularly at fixed intervals, such as a newspaper, a magazine, or a scholarly journal. Unlike newspapers and magazines, scholarly journals usually appear only about four times a year, and the issues present learned articles containing original research and original interpretations of data and texts. Such journals are intended not for general readers but for professionals and students. Since the research you do for your papers will inevitably lead you to consult scholarly journals, the entry for an article in a scholarly journal will be among the most common in the works-cited lists you compile.

The entry for an article in a periodical, like that for a book, has three main divisions:

```
Author's name. "Title of the article." Publication
    information.
```

Here is an example:

```
Most, Andrea. "'We Know We Belong to the Land': The
    Theatricality of Assimilation in Rodgers and
    Hammerstein's Oklahoma!" PMLA 113 (1998): 77-89.
```

Author's Name

In general, follow the recommendations for citing names of authors of books (4.6.1). Take the author's name from the beginning or the end of the article. Reverse the name for alphabetizing, and put a period after it.

```
Most, Andrea.
```

Title of the Article

In general, follow the recommendations for titles given in 2.6. State the full title of the article, enclosed in quotation marks (not underlined). Unless the title has its own concluding punctuation (e.g., a question mark), put a period before the closing quotation mark.

```
Most, Andrea. "'We Know We Belong to the Land': The
     Theatricality of Assimilation in Rodgers and
     Hammerstein's Oklahoma!"
```

Publication Information

In general, after the title of the article, give the journal title (underlined), the volume number, the year of publication (in parentheses), a colon, the inclusive page numbers, and a period.

```
Most, Andrea. "'We Know We Belong to the Land': The
     Theatricality of Assimilation in Rodgers and
     Hammerstein's Oklahoma!" PMLA 113 (1998): 77-89.
```

Take these facts directly from the journal, not from a source such as a bibliography. Publication information usually appears on the cover or title page of a journal. Omit any introductory article in the title of an English-language journal (*William and Mary Quarterly*, not *The William and Mary Quarterly*). For newspaper titles, see 4.7.5. Do not precede the volume number with the word *volume* or the abbreviation *vol.*

In addition to the volume number, the journal's cover or title page may include an issue number ("Number 3") or a month or season before the year ("January 1999," "Fall 1998"). In general, the issues of a journal published in a single year compose one volume. Volumes are usually numbered in continuous sequence—each new volume is numbered one higher than its predecessor—while the numbering of issues starts over with 1 in each new volume. You may ignore the issue number and the month or season if the journal's pages are numbered continuously throughout each annual volume. In a journal with such pagination, if the first issue for a year ends on page 130, for instance, the second issue begins on page 131.

Most scholarly journals are paginated continuously throughout each annual volume. Then, at the end of the year, the issues in the volume are bound together and shelved in the library by year number. If you are looking for the article by Andrea Most cited above, for example, which was published in 1998 in an issue of the scholarly journal *PMLA*, you will likely find it in your library in what appears to be a book with "*PMLA* 1998" printed on the spine. In that volume, you will find all the issues of *PMLA* published during 1998, and the page numbering of the volume will be continuous, from page 1 of the first issue through to the final page of the last issue published in the year. Suppose, then, that you wish to cite the article in your research paper. The title page of the issue containing the article includes this publication information: "Volume 113, Number 1, January 1998." But since *PMLA* is paged continuously by volume, you should omit the issue number and the month from your entry, for the reader will be able to find the source by knowing simply the volume number and the page numbers of the article.

Some scholarly journals do not use continuous pagination throughout the annual volume, however, and some use issue numbers alone without volume numbers; on citing articles in such journals, see 4.7.2–3. In addition, entries for newspapers and magazines do not require volume numbers (see 4.7.5–6). Your instructor or a librarian will help you if you are uncertain whether a periodical is a magazine or a scholarly journal. If any doubt remains, include the volume number.

The inclusive page numbers cited should encompass the complete article, not just the portion you used. (Specific page references appear parenthetically at appropriate places in your text; see ch. 5.) Follow the rules for writing inclusive numbers in 2.5.6. Write the page reference for the first page exactly as shown in the source ("198–232," "A32–34," "28/WETA–29," "TV-15–18," "lxii–lxv"). If an article is not printed on consecutive pages—if, for example, after beginning on page 6 it skips to page 10 and then to page 22—write only the first page number and a plus sign, leaving no intervening space: "6+." (See examples in 4.7.5.)

Here are some additional examples of the basic entry for an article in a scholarly journal with continuous pagination:

Craner, Paul M. "New Tool for an Ancient Art: The
        Computer and Music." <u>Computers and the Humanities</u>
        25 (1991): 303-13.

Fitzgerald, John. "The Misconceived Revolution: State and
        Society in China's Nationalist Revolution, 1923-26."
        Journal of Asian Studies 49 (1990): 323-43.

McKenna, Bernard. "How Engineers Write: An Empirical
        Study of Engineering Report Writing." Applied
        Linguistics 18 (1997): 189-211.

White, Sabina, and Andrew Winzelberg. "Laughter and
        Stress." Humor 5 (1992): 343-55.

Sometimes additional information is required in an entry. This list
shows most of the possible components of an entry for an article in a
periodical and the order in which they are normally arranged:

1. Author's name
2. Title of the article
3. Name of the periodical
4. Series number or name (if relevant; see 4.7.4)
5. Volume number (for a scholarly journal)
6. Issue number (if needed; see 4.7.2–3)
7. Date of publication
8. Page numbers
9. Supplementary information (see esp. 4.7.12)

The rest of 4.7 explains how to cite these items. To document an
article in an online periodical, see 4.9.4.

4.7.2. An Article in a Scholarly Journal That Pages Each Issue Separately

Some scholarly journals do not number pages continuously throughout an annual volume but begin each issue on page 1. For such journals, you must include the issue number to identify the source. Add a
period and the issue number directly after the volume number, without any intervening space: "14.2" signifies volume 14, issue 2;
"10.3–4," volume 10, issues 3 and 4 combined.

Barthelme, Frederick. "Architecture." Kansas Quarterly
        13.3-4 (1981): 77-80.

Hallin, Daniel C. "Sound Bite News: Television Coverage
        of Elections, 1968-1988." Journal of Communication
        42.2 (1992): 5-24.

Vickery, Laurie. "The Politics of Abuse: The Traumatized
   Child in Toni Morrison and Marguerite Duras."
   <u>Mosaic</u> 29.2 (1996): 91-109.

4.7.3. An Article in a Scholarly Journal That Uses Only Issue Numbers

Some scholarly journals do not use volume numbers at all, numbering issues only. Treat the issue numbers of such journals as you would volume numbers.

Bowering, George. "Baseball and the Canadian
   Imagination." <u>Canadian Literature</u> 108 (1986):
   115-24.

Lajolo, Marisa. "The Female Reader on Trial." <u>Brasil</u> 14
   (1995): 61-81.

4.7.4. An Article in a Scholarly Journal with More Than One Series

Some scholarly journals have been published in more than one series. In citing a journal with numbered series, write the number (an arabic digit with the appropriate ordinal suffix: *2nd, 3rd, 4th*, etc.) and the abbreviation *ser.* between the journal title and the volume number (see the sample entry for Daniels). For a journal divided into a new series and an original series, indicate the series with *ns* or *os* before the volume number (see the entry for Spivack).

Daniels, John. "Indian Population of North America in
   1492." <u>William and Mary Quarterly</u> 3rd ser. 49
   (1992): 298-320.

Spivack, Kathleen. "Between Two Cultures." <u>Kenyon Review</u>
   ns 17.3-4 (1995): 118-26.

4.7.5. An Article in a Newspaper

To cite an English-language newspaper, give the name as it appears on the masthead but omit any introductory article (*New York Times*, not *The New York Times*). If the city of publication is not included in the name of a locally published newspaper, add the city in square brackets, not underlined, after the name: "*Star-Ledger* [Newark]." For nationally published newspapers (e.g., *USA Today, Wall Street Journal, Chronicle of Higher Education*), you need not add the city of publication. Next give the complete date—day, month, and year. Abbreviate the names of all months except May, June, and July (see 6.2). Do not give the volume and issue numbers even if they are listed. If an edition is named on the masthead, add a comma after the date and specify the edition (e.g., *natl. ed., late ed.*). It is important to state the edition because different editions of the same issue of a newspaper contain different material. Follow the edition—or the date if there is no edition—with a colon and the page number or numbers. Here are examples illustrating how an article appeared in different sections of two editions of the *New York Times* on the same day:

```
Lohr, Steve. "Now Playing: Babes in Cyberspace." New
     York Times 3 Apr. 1998, late ed.: C1+.

Lohr, Steve. "Now Playing: Babes in Cyberspace." New
     York Times 3 Apr. 1998, New England final ed.: D1+.
```

If each section is paginated separately, indicate the appropriate section number or letter. Determining how to indicate a section can sometimes be complicated. The *New York Times*, for example, is currently divided in two distinct ways, depending on the day of the week, and each system calls for a different method of indicating section and page. On Monday through Saturday, there are normally several sections, labeled *A, B, C, D*, and so forth, and paginated separately, and the section letter is part of each page number: "A1," "B1," "C5," "D3." Whenever the pagination of a newspaper includes a section designation, give the first page number exactly as it appears.

DAILY *NEW YORK TIMES*

```
Hall, Trish. "IQ Scores Are Up, and Psychologists Wonder
     Why." New York Times 24 Feb. 1998, late ed.: F1+.
```

The Sunday edition contains numerous individually paged sections (covering the arts and entertainment, business, sports, travel, and so on) designated not by letters but by numbers ("Section 4," "Section 7"), which do not appear as parts of the page numbers. Whenever the section designation of a newspaper is not part of the pagination, put a comma after the date (or after the edition, if any) and add the abbreviation *sec.*, the appropriate letter or number, a colon, and the page number or numbers.

SUNDAY *NEW YORK TIMES*

> Goldberg, Vicki. "Photographing a Mexico Where Silence
>   Reigned." <u>New York Times</u> 23 Mar. 1997, late ed.,
>   sec. 2: 39+.

Newspaper articles are often not printed on consecutive pages—for example, an article might begin on page 1, then skip to page 16. For such articles, write only the first page number and a plus sign, leaving no intervening space: "6+," "C3+." The parenthetical reference in the text tells readers the exact page from which material was used.

Here are some additional examples from different newspapers:

> Alaton, Salem. "So, Did They Live Happily Ever After?"
>   <u>Globe and Mail</u> [Toronto] 27 Dec. 1997: D1+.
> Kiernan, Vincent. "Study Finds Errors in Medical
>   Information Available on the Web." <u>Chronicle of
>   Higher Education</u> 12 June 1998: A25.
> Manning, Anita. "Curriculum Battles from Left and
>   Right." <u>USA Today</u> 2 Mar. 1994: 5D.
> Trachtenberg, Jeffrey A. "What's in a Movie Soundtrack?
>   Catchy Tunes and Big Business." <u>Wall Street Journal</u>
>   1 Apr. 1994, eastern ed.: B1.

4.7.6. An Article in a Magazine

To cite a magazine published every week or every two weeks, give the complete date (beginning with the day and abbreviating the month, except for May, June, and July), followed by a colon and the inclusive page numbers of the article. If the article is not printed on consecutive pages, write only the first page number and a plus sign, leaving no

intervening space. Do not give the volume and issue numbers even if
they are listed.

Armstrong, Larry, Dori Jones Yang, and Alice Cuneo.
    "The Learning Revolution: Technology Is Reshaping
    Education--at Home and at School." <u>Business Week</u>
    28 Feb. 1994: 80-88.
Mehta, Pratap Bhanu. "Exploding Myths." <u>New Republic</u> 6
    June 1998: 17-19.

To cite a magazine published every month or every two months,
give the month or months and year. If the article is not printed on consecutive pages, write only the first page number and a plus sign, leaving no intervening space. Do not give the volume and issue numbers
even if they are listed.

Amelar, Sarah. "Restoration on 42nd Street."
    <u>Architecture</u> Mar. 1998: 146-50.
Bender, William H. "How Much Food Will We Need in the
    Twenty-First Century?" <u>Environment</u> Mar. 1997: 6-11.
Csikszentmihalyi, Mihaly. "The Creative Personality."
    <u>Psychology Today</u> July-Aug. 1996: 36-40.
Murphy, Cullen. "Women and the Bible." <u>Atlantic Monthly</u>
    Aug. 1993: 39-64.
Perlstein, Rick. "Abridged Too Far?" <u>Lingua Franca</u> Apr.-
    May 1997: 23-24.

4.7.7. A Review

To cite a review, give the reviewer's name and the title of the review
(if there is one); then write *Rev. of* (neither underlined nor enclosed
in quotation marks), the title of the work reviewed, a comma, the
word *by*, and the name of the author. If the work of someone other
than an author—say, an editor, a translator, or a director—is under
review, use the appropriate abbreviation, such as *ed.*, *trans.*, or *dir.*,
instead of *by*. For a review of a performance, add pertinent information about the production (see the sample entry for Tommasini).
If more than one work is under review, list titles and authors in
the order given at the beginning of the review (see the entry for

Bordewich). Conclude the entry with the name of the periodical and the rest of the publication information.

If the review is titled but unsigned, begin the entry with the title of the review and alphabetize by that title (see the entry for "The Cooling of an Admiration"). If the review is neither titled nor signed, begin the entry with *Rev. of* and alphabetize under the title of the work reviewed (see the entry for *Anthology of Danish Literature*).

Rev. of <u>Anthology of Danish Literature</u>, ed. F. J.
    Billeskov Jansen and P. M. Mitchell. <u>Times Literary</u>
    <u>Supplement</u> 7 July 1972: 785.

Bordewich, Fergus M. Rev. of <u>Once They Moved like the</u>
    <u>Wind: Cochise, Geronimo, and the Apache Wars</u>, by
    David Roberts, and <u>Brave Are My People: Indian</u>
    <u>Heroes Not Forgotten</u>, by Frank Waters. <u>Smithsonian</u>
    Mar. 1994: 125-31.

"The Cooling of an Admiration." Rev. of <u>Pound/Joyce: The</u>
    <u>Letters of Ezra Pound to James Joyce, with Pound's</u>
    <u>Essays on Joyce</u>, ed. Forrest Read. <u>Times Literary</u>
    <u>Supplement</u> 6 Mar. 1969: 239-40.

Kauffmann, Stanley. "A New Spielberg." Rev. of
    <u>Schindler's List</u>, dir. Steven Spielberg. <u>New</u>
    <u>Republic</u> 13 Dec. 1993: 30.

Socha, Thomas J. Rev. of <u>Learning the Rules: The Anatomy</u>
    <u>of Children's Relationships</u>, by B. J. Bigelow, G.
    Tesson, and J. H. Lewko. <u>Communication Education</u> 47
    (1998): 91-92.

Tommasini, Anthony. "A Feminist Look at Sophocles." Rev.
    of <u>Jocasta</u>, by Ruth Schonthal and Hélène Cixous.
    Voice and Vision Theater Co. Cornelia Connelly
    Center for Educ., New York. <u>New York Times</u> 11 June
    1998, late ed.: E5.

Updike, John. "Fine Points." Rev. of <u>The New Fowler's</u>
    <u>Modern English Usage</u>, ed. R. W. Burchfield. <u>New</u>
    <u>Yorker</u> 23-30 Dec. 1996: 142-49.

4.7.8. An Abstract in an Abstracts Journal

An abstracts journal publishes summaries of journal articles and of other literature. If you are citing an abstract, begin the entry with the publication information for the original work. Then add the relevant information for the journal from which you derived the abstract—title (underlined), volume number, year (in parentheses), and either item number or page number, depending on how the journal presents its abstracts. Of the journals cited below, *Current Index to Journals in Education*, *Psychological Abstracts*, and *Sociological Abstracts* use item numbers; *Dissertation Abstracts* and *Dissertation Abstracts International* use page numbers. Precede an item number with the word *item*. If the title of the journal does not make clear that you are citing an abstract, add the word *Abstract*, neither underlined nor in quotation marks, immediately after the original publication information (see the sample entry for McCabe).

Dissertation Abstracts International (*DAI*) has a long and complex history that might affect the way you cite an abstract in it. Before volume 30 (1969), *Dissertation Abstracts International* was titled *Dissertation Abstracts* (*DA*). From volume 27 to volume 36, *DA* and *DAI* were paginated in two series: *A*, for humanities and social sciences, and *B*, for sciences and engineering. With volume 37, *DAI* added a third separately paginated section: *C*, for abstracts of European dissertations; in 1989, this section expanded its coverage to include institutions throughout the world. (For recommendations on citing dissertations themselves, see 4.6.26–27.)

> Ferguson, Tamara J., and Susan L. Crowley. "Gender
> Differences in the Organization of Guilt and
> Shame." <u>Sex Roles</u> 37 (1997): 19-44. <u>Psychological
> Abstracts</u> 85 (1998): item 4265.
>
> Gans, Eric L. "The Discovery of Illusion: Flaubert's
> Early Works, 1835-1837." Diss. Johns Hopkins U,
> 1967. <u>DA</u> 27 (1967): 3046A.
>
> McCabe, Donald L. "Faculty Responses to Academic
> Dishonesty: The Influence of Student Honor Codes."
> <u>Research in Higher Education</u> 34 (1993): 647-58.
> Abstract. <u>Current Index to Journals in Education</u> 26
> (1994): item EJ471017.

```
Neumann, Mark, and Timothy A. Simpson. "Smuggled Sound:
    Bootleg Recording and the Pursuit of Popular
    Memory." Symbolic Interaction 20 (1997): 319-41.
    Sociological Abstracts 46 (1998): item 9804189.
Sakala, Carol. "Maternity Care Policy in the United
    States: Toward a More Rational and Effective
    System." Diss. Boston U, 1993. DAI 54 (1993): 1360B.
```

4.7.9. An Anonymous Article

If no author's name is given for the article you are citing, begin the entry with the title. Ignore any initial *A, An,* or *The* when you alphabetize the entry.

```
"The Decade of the Spy." Newsweek 7 Mar. 1994: 26-27.
"Dubious Venture." Time 3 Jan. 1994: 64-65.
```

4.7.10. An Editorial

If you are citing a signed editorial, begin with the author's name, give the title, and then add the descriptive label *Editorial*, neither underlined nor enclosed in quotation marks. Conclude with the appropriate publication information. If the editorial is unsigned, begin with the title and continue in the same way.

```
"Death of a Writer." Editorial. New York Times 20 Apr.
    1994, late ed.: A18.
Zuckerman, Mortimer B. "Welcome to Communicopia."
    Editorial. US News and World Report 1 Nov. 1993:
    116.
```

4.7.11. A Letter to the Editor

To identify a letter to the editor, add the descriptive label *Letter* after the name of the author, but do not underline the word or place it in quotation marks.

```
Ozick, Cynthia. Letter. Partisan Review 57 (1990):
    493-94.
Safer, Morley. Letter. New York Times 31 Oct. 1993, late
    ed., sec. 2: 4.
```

Identify a published response to a letter as "Reply to letter of [. . .]," adding the name of the writer of the initial letter. Do not underline this phrase or place it in quotation marks.

```
Gilbert, Sandra M. Reply to letter of Jerry W. Ward, Jr.
    PMLA 113 (1998): 131.
```

4.7.12. A Serialized Article

To cite a serialized article or a series of related articles published in more than one issue of a periodical, include all bibliographic information in one entry if each installment has the same author and title.

```
Garbaccia, Donna R., et al. "Food, Recipes, Cookbooks,
    and Italian-American Life." Italian Americana 16
    (1998): 5-23, 125-46.
Meserole, Harrison T., and James M. Rambeau. "Articles
    on American Literature Appearing in Current
    Periodicals." American Literature 52 (1981):
    688-705; 53 (1981): 164-80, 348-59.
```

If the installments bear different titles, list each one separately. You may include a brief supplementary description at the end of the entry to indicate that the article is part of a series.

```
Dugger, Celia W. "Wedding Vows Bind Old World and New."
    New York Times 20 July 1998, late ed.: A1+. Pt. 2
    of a series, Here and There: Immigration Now, begun
    19 July 1998.
Sontag, Deborah. "A Mexican Town That Transcends All
    Borders." New York Times 21 July 1998, late ed.:
    A1+. Pt. 3 of a series, Here and There: Immigration
    Now, begun 19 July 1998.
```

Sontag, Deborah, and Celia W. Dugger. "New Immigrant
      Tide: Shuttle between Worlds." <u>New York Times</u> 19
      July 1998, late ed.: A1+. Pt. 1 of a series, Here
      and There: Immigration Now.

4.7.13. A Special Issue

To cite an entire special issue of a journal, begin the entry with the
name of the person who edited the issue (if given on the title page),
followed by a comma and the abbreviation *ed*. Next give the title of
the special issue (underlined), followed by "Spec. issue of" and the
name of the journal (underlined). Conclude the entry with the journal's volume number as well as the issue number (separated by a
period: "9.1"), the year of publication (in parentheses), a colon, a
space, and the complete pagination of the issue. If the issue has been
republished in book form, add the relevant information about the book
(city of publication, publisher, and date of publication).

Appiah, Kwame Anthony, and Henry Louis Gates, Jr., eds.
      <u>Identities</u>. Spec. issue of <u>Critical Inquiry</u> 18.4
      (1992): 625-884. Chicago: U of Chicago P, 1995.
Perret, Delphine, and Marie-Denise Shelton, eds. <u>Maryse</u>
      <u>Condé</u>. Spec. issue of <u>Callaloo</u> 18.3 (1995):
      535-711.
<u>Science and Culture</u>. Spec. issue of <u>Daedalus</u> 127.1
      (1998): 1-236.

If you are citing one article from a special issue and wish to indicate
complete publication information about the issue, use the following
form:

Ackerman, James. "Leonardo da Vinci: Art in Science."
      <u>Science and Culture</u>. Spec. issue of <u>Daedalus</u> 127.1
      (1998): 207-24.
Makward, Christiane. "Reading Maryse Condé's Theater."
      <u>Maryse Condé</u>. Ed. Delphine Perret and Marie-Denise
      Shelton. Spec. issue of <u>Callaloo</u> 18.3 (1995):
      681-89.

4.7.14. An Article in a Microform Collection of Articles

If you are citing an article that was provided by a reference source such as NewsBank, which selects periodical articles and makes them available on microfiche, begin the entry with the original publication information. Then add the relevant information concerning the micro-form from which you derived the article—title of source (underlined), volume number, year (in parentheses), and appropriate identifying numbers ("fiche 42, grids 5–6").

> Chapman, Dan. "Panel Could Help Protect Children."
>
> Winston-Salem Journal 14 Jan. 1990: 14. NewsBank:
>
> Welfare and Social Problems 12 (1990): fiche 1,
>
> grids A8-11.

4.7.15. An Article Reprinted in a Loose-Leaf Collection of Articles

If you are citing a reprinted article that was provided by an informa-tion service such as the Social Issues Resources Series (SIRS), which selects articles from periodicals and publishes them in loose-leaf vol-umes, each dedicated to a specific topic, begin the entry with the origi-nal publication information. Then add the relevant information for the loose-leaf volume in which the article is reprinted, treating the volume like a book (see 4.6)—title (underlined), name of editor (if any), vol-ume number (if any), city of publication, publisher, year of publica-tion, and article number (preceded by the abbreviation *Art.*).

> Edmondson, Brad. "AIDS and Aging." American Demographics
>
> Mar. 1990: 28+. The AIDS Crisis. Ed. Eleanor
>
> Goldstein. Vol. 2. Boca Raton: SIRS, 1991. Art. 24.

4.8. CITING MISCELLANEOUS PRINT AND NONPRINT SOURCES

4.8.1. A Television or Radio Program

The information in an entry for a television or radio program usually appears in the following order:

1. Title of the episode or segment, if appropriate (in quotation marks)
2. Title of the program (underlined)
3. Title of the series, if any (neither underlined nor in quotation marks)
4. Name of the network
5. Call letters and city of the local station (if any)
6. Broadcast date

For instance, among the examples below, "Frederick Douglass" is an episode of the program *Civil War Journal*; *The Buccaneers* is a program in the series Masterpiece Theatre. Use a comma between the call letters and the city ("KETC, St. Louis"). A period follows each of the other items. For the inclusion of other information that may be pertinent (e.g., performers, director, narrator, number of episodes), see the sample entries.

<u>The Buccaneers</u>. By Edith Wharton. Adapt. Maggie Wadey. Perf. Mira Sorvino, Alison Elliott, and Carla Gugino. 3 episodes. Masterpiece Theatre. Introd. Russell Baker. PBS. WGBH, Boston. 27 Apr.-11 May 1997.

"Death and Society." Narr. Joanne Silberner. <u>Weekend Edition Sunday</u>. Natl. Public Radio. WUWM, Milwaukee. 25 Jan. 1998.

<u>Don Giovanni</u>. By Wolfgang Amadeus Mozart. Perf. James Morris, Bryn Terfel, and Carol Vaness. Cond. Yakov Kreizberg. Lyric Opera of Chicago. Nuveen-Lyric Opera of Chicago Radio Network. WFMT, Chicago. 8 June 1996.

"<u>Frankenstein</u>: The Making of the Monster." <u>Great Books</u>. Narr. Donald Sutherland. Writ. Eugenie Vink. Dir. Jonathan Ward. Learning Channel. 8 Sept. 1993.

"Frederick Douglass." <u>Civil War Journal</u>. Narr. Danny Glover. Dir. Craig Haffner. Arts and Entertainment Network. 6 Apr. 1993.

<u>Passion</u>. By Stephen Sondheim. Dir. James Lapine. Perf. Donna Murphy, Jere Shea, and Marin Mazzie. Amer. Playhouse. PBS. WNET, New York. 7 Mar. 1996.

"Yes . . . but Is It Art?" Narr. Morley Safer. <u>Sixty</u>
   <u>Minutes</u>. CBS. WCBS, New York. 19 Sept. 1993.

If your reference is primarily to the work of a particular individual,
cite that person's name before the title.

Wadey, Maggie, adapt. <u>The Buccaneers</u>. By Edith Wharton.
   Perf. Mira Sorvino, Alison Elliott, and Carla
   Gugino. 3 episodes. Masterpiece Theatre. Introd.
   Russell Baker. PBS. WGBH, Boston. 27 Apr.-11 May
   1997.

Welles, Orson, dir. <u>The War of the Worlds</u>. By H. G.
   Wells. Adapt. Howard Koch. Mercury Theatre on the
   Air. CBS Radio. WCBS, New York. 30 Oct. 1938.

If you are citing a transcript of a program, add the description *Transcript* at the end of the entry.

"Death and Society." Narr. Joanne Silberner. <u>Weekend</u>
   <u>Edition Sunday</u>. Natl. Public Radio. WUWM,
   Milwaukee. 25 Jan. 1998. Transcript.

To cite a music video for a song, begin with the information about
the song that is given before or after the video: performer, title of song,
title of album, name of manufacturer, and date of album. (See 4.8.2 on
citing a song on a sound recording.) Follow this information with the
descriptive label *Music video*, the name of the director of the video (if
given), the channel, and the date you viewed the video.

Sting. "Fields of Gold." <u>Ten Summoner's Tales</u>. A and M,
   1993. Music video. Dir. Kevin Godley. VH1. 5 July
   1998.

See 4.8.7 for interviews on television and radio programs; see also
4.8.2–3 for sound, film, and video recordings, 4.8.4 for performances,
and 4.9.9a for television and radio programs online or on CD-ROM.

4.8.2. A Sound Recording

In an entry for a commercially available recording, which person is
cited first (e.g., the composer, conductor, or performer) depends on

the desired emphasis. List the title of the recording (or the titles of the works included), the artist or artists, the manufacturer ("Capitol"), and the year of issue (if the year is unknown, write *n.d.*). Place a comma between the manufacturer and the date; periods follow the other items. If you are not using a compact disc, indicate the medium, neither underlined nor enclosed in quotation marks, before the manufacturer's name: *Audiocassette* (see the sample entry for Marsalis), *Audiotape* (reel-to-reel tape), or *LP* (long-playing record; see the entry for Ellington).

In general, underline titles of recordings (*Romances for Saxophone*), but do not underline or enclose in quotation marks the titles of musical compositions identified only by form, number, and key (see the entry for Norrington). You may wish to indicate, in addition to the year of issue, the date of recording (see the entry for Ellington).

Bartoli, Cecilia. <u>Chant d'amour</u>. London, 1996.

Ellington, Duke, cond. Duke Ellington Orch. <u>First Carnegie Hall Concert</u>. Rec. 23 Jan. 1943. LP. Prestige, 1977.

Gabriel, Peter. <u>Passion: Music for</u> The Last Temptation of Christ<u>, a Film by Martin Scorsese</u>. Geffen, 1989.

Holiday, Billie. <u>The Essence of Billie Holiday</u>. Columbia, 1991.

Joplin, Scott. <u>Treemonisha</u>. Perf. Carmen Balthrop, Betty Allen, and Curtis Rayam. Houston Grand Opera Orch. and Chorus. Cond. Gunther Schuller. Deutsche Grammophon, 1976.

Marsalis, Branford. <u>Romances for Saxophone</u>. English Chamber Orch. Cond. Andrew Litton. Audiocassette. CBS, 1986.

Norrington, Roger, cond. Symphony no. 1 in C, op. 21, and Symphony no. 6 in F, op. 68. By Ludwig van Beethoven. London Classical Players. EMI, 1988.

Simon, Paul. <u>The Rhythm of the Saints</u>. Warner Bros., 1990.

Sondheim, Stephen. <u>Passion</u>. Orch. Jonathan Tunick. Perf. Donna Murphy, Jere Shea, and Marin Mazzie. Cond. Paul Gemignani. Angel, 1994.

> Sting, narr. <u>Peter and the Wolf</u>, op. 67. By Sergei
>   Prokofiev. Chamber Orch. of Europe. Cond. Claudio
>   Abbado. Deutsche Grammophon, 1990.

If you are citing a specific song, place its title in quotation marks.

> Bartoli, Cecilia. "Les filles de Cadix." By Pauline
>   Viardot. <u>Chant d'amour</u>. London, 1996.
> Bono, Brian Eno, the Edge, and Luciano Pavarotti. "Miss
>   Sarajevo." <u>Pavarotti and Friends for the Children</u>
>   <u>of Bosnia</u>. London, 1996.
> Gabriel, Peter. "A Different Drum." Perf. Gabriel,
>   Shankar, and Youssou N'Dour. <u>Passion: Music for</u> The
>   Last Temptation of Christ<u>, a Film by Martin</u>
>   <u>Scorsese</u>. Geffen, 1989.
> Holiday, Billie. "God Bless the Child." Rec. 9 May 1941.
>   <u>The Essence of Billie Holiday</u>. Columbia, 1991.
> Simon, Paul, and Milton Nascimento. "Spirit Voices." <u>The</u>
>   <u>Rhythm of the Saints</u>. Warner Bros., 1990.

Treat a spoken-word recording as you would a musical recording.
Begin with the speaker, the writer, or the production director, depending on the desired emphasis. You may add the original publication
date of the work immediately after the title.

> Burnett, Frances Hodgson. <u>The Secret Garden</u>. 1911. Read
>   by Helena Bonham Carter. Audiocassette. Penguin-
>   High Bridge, 1993.
> Scott, George C., narr. <u>World War II</u>. Audiocassette.
>   Carmichael, 1990.
> Shakespeare, William. <u>Othello</u>. Perf. Laurence Olivier,
>   Maggie Smith, Frank Finley, and Derek Jacobi. Dir.
>   John Dexter. LP. RCA Victor, 1964.
> Welles, Orson, dir. <u>The War of the Worlds</u>. By H. G.
>   Wells. Adapt. Howard Koch. Mercury Theatre on the
>   Air. Rec. 30 Oct. 1938. LP. Evolution, 1969.
> Whitman, Walt. "America." <u>In Their Own Voices: A Century</u>
>   <u>of Recorded Poetry</u>. Rhino, 1996.

Do not underline or enclose in quotation marks the title of a private or archival recording or tape. Include the date recorded (if known) and the location and identifying number of the recording.

Wilgus, D. K. Southern Folk Tales. Rec. 23-25 Mar. 1965.

   Audiotape. U of California, Los Angeles, Archives

   of Folklore. B.76.82.

In citing the libretto, the booklet, the liner notes, or other material accompanying a recording, give the author's name, the title of the material (if any), and a description of the material (*Libretto*). Then provide the usual bibliographic information for a recording.

Colette. Libretto. L'enfant et les sortilèges. Music by

   Maurice Ravel. Orch. National Bordeaux-Aquitaine.

   Cond. Alain Lombard. Valois, 1993.

Lawrence, Vera Brodsky. "Scott Joplin and Treemonisha."

   Booklet. Treemonisha. By Scott Joplin. Deutsche

   Grammophon, 1976.

Lewiston, David. Liner notes. The Balinese Gamelan:

   Music from the Morning of the World. LP. Nonesuch,

   n.d.

See 4.9.9b for sound recordings online.

4.8.3. A Film or Video Recording

A film entry usually begins with the title, underlined, and includes the director, the distributor, and the year of release. You may include other data that seem pertinent—such as the names of the writer, performers, and producer—between the title and the distributor.

It's a Wonderful Life. Dir. Frank Capra. Perf. James

   Stewart, Donna Reed, Lionel Barrymore, and Thomas

   Mitchell. RKO, 1946.

Like Water for Chocolate [Como agua para chocolate].

   Screenplay by Laura Esquivel. Dir. Alfonso Arau.

   Perf. Lumi Cavazos, Marco Lombardi, and Regina

   Torne. Miramax, 1993.

If you are citing the contribution of a particular individual, begin with that person's name.

```
Chaplin, Charles, dir. Modern Times. Perf. Chaplin and
     Paulette Goddard. United Artists, 1936.
Jhabvala, Ruth Prawer, adapt. A Room with a View. By
     E. M. Forster. Dir. James Ivory. Prod. Ismail
     Merchant. Perf. Maggie Smith, Denholm Eliot, Helena
     Bonham Carter, and Daniel Day-Lewis. Cinecom Intl.
     Films, 1985.
Mifune, Toshiro, perf. Rashomon. Dir. Akira Kurosawa.
     Daiei, 1950.
Rota, Nino, composer. Juliet of the Spirits [Giulietta
     degli spiriti]. Dir. Federico Fellini. Perf.
     Giulietta Masina. Rizzoli, 1965.
```

Cite a videocassette, DVD (digital videodisc), laser disc, slide program, or filmstrip like a film, but include the original release date (if relevant) and the medium, neither underlined nor enclosed in quotation marks, before the name of the distributor.

```
Alcohol Use and Its Medical Consequences: A Comprehensive
     Teaching Program for Biomedical Education. Prod.
     Project Cork, Dartmouth Medical School. Slide
     program. Milner-Fenwick, 1982.
Don Carlo. By Giuseppe Verdi. Dir. Franco Zeffirelli.
     Perf. Luciano Pavarotti and Samuel Ramey. La Scala
     Orch. and Chorus. Cond. Riccardo Muti.
     Videocassette. EMI, 1994.
Hitchcock, Alfred, dir. Suspicion. Perf. Cary Grant and
     Joan Fontaine. 1941. Laser disc. Turner, 1995.
It's a Wonderful Life. Dir. Frank Capra. Perf. James
     Stewart, Donna Reed, Lionel Barrymore, and Thomas
     Mitchell. 1946. DVD. Republic, 1998.
Looking at Our Earth: A Visual Dictionary. Sound
     filmstrip. Natl. Geographic Educ. Services, 1992.
Mifune, Toshiro, perf. Rashomon. Dir. Akira Kurosawa.
     1950. Videocassette. Embassy, 1986.
```

Nureyev, Rudolph, chor. <u>Swan Lake</u>. By Pyotr Ilich
    Tchaikovsky. Perf. Margot Fonteyn and Nureyev.
    Vienna State Opera Ballet. Vienna Symphony Orch.
    Cond. John Lanchbery. 1966. DVD. Philips, 1997.

See 4.9.9c for films or film clips online or on CD-ROM.

4.8.4. A Performance

An entry for a performance (play, opera, ballet, concert) usually begins
with the title, contains facts similar to those given for a film (see 4.8.3),
and concludes with the site of the performance (usually the theater
and city, separated by a comma and followed by a period) and the date
of the performance.

<u>Hamlet</u>. By William Shakespeare. Dir. John Gielgud. Perf.
    Richard Burton. Shubert Theatre, Boston. 4 Mar.
    1964.

<u>Medea</u>. By Euripides. Trans. Alistair Elliot. Dir.
    Jonathan Kent. Perf. Diana Rigg. Longacre Theatre,
    New York. 7 Apr. 1994.

<u>The River</u>. Chor. Alvin Ailey. Dance Theater of Harlem.
    New York State Theater, New York. 15 Mar. 1994.

<u>The Siege of Paris</u>. Marionettes of the Cooperativa
    Teatroarte Cuticchio. Sylvia and Danny Kaye
    Playhouse, New York. 22 Mar. 1997.

<u>Les vêpres siciliennes</u>. By Giuseppe Verdi. Libretto by
    Eugène Scribe and Charles Duveyrier. Dir. Federico
    Tiezzi. Cond. John Nelson. Perf. Daniela Dessì,
    David Kuebler, and Ferruccio Furlanetto. Teatro
    dell'Opera, Rome. 17 Jan. 1997.

If you are citing the contribution of a particular individual or group,
begin with the appropriate name.

Ars Musica Antiqua. <u>In Praise of Women: Music by Women
    Composers from the Twelfth through the Eighteenth
    Centuries</u>. Concert. Scotch Plains Public Lib., NJ.
    5 Apr. 1994.

Freni, Mirella, soprano. <u>Fedora</u>. By Umberto Giordano.
   With Plácido Domingo and Dwayne Croft. Cond.
   Roberto Abbado. Metropolitan Opera. Metropolitan
   Opera House, New York. 26 Apr. 1997.
Joplin, Scott. <u>Treemonisha</u>. Dir. Frank Corsaro. Cond.
   Gunther Schuller. Perf. Carmen Balthrop, Betty
   Allen, and Curtis Rayam. Houston Grand Opera.
   Miller Theatre, Houston. 18 May 1975.
Rigg, Diana, perf. <u>Medea</u>. By Euripides. Trans. Alistair
   Elliot. Dir. Jonathan Kent. Longacre Theatre, New
   York. 7 Apr. 1994.

For television and radio broadcasts of performances, see 4.8.1; for
sound recordings of performances, see 4.8.2; for video recordings of
performances, see 4.8.3.

4.8.5. A Musical Composition

To cite a musical composition, begin with the composer's name.
Underline the title of an opera, a ballet, or a piece of instrumental
music identified by name (*Symphonie fantastique*), but do not underline or enclose in quotation marks the form, number, and key when
used to identify an instrumental composition.

Beethoven, Ludwig van. Symphony no. 8 in F, op. 93.
Berlioz, Hector. <u>Symphonie fantastique</u>, op. 14.
Wagner, Richard. <u>Götterdämmerung</u>.

Treat a published score, however, like a book. Give the title, underlined, as it appears on the title page, and capitalize the abbreviations
no. and *op.*

Beethoven, Ludwig van. <u>Symphony No. 8 in F, Op. 93</u>. New
   York: Dover, 1989.

If you wish to indicate when a musical composition was written, add
the date immediately after the title.

Beethoven, Ludwig van. <u>Symphony No. 8 in F, Op. 93</u>.
   1812. New York: Dover, 1989.

See 4.8.2 for sound recordings of musical compositions, 4.8.1 for television and radio programs of music, and 4.8.4 for performances of music.

4.8.6. A Painting, Sculpture, or Photograph

To cite a painting or sculpture, state the artist's name first. In general, underline the title. Name the institution that houses the work (e.g., a museum) or, for a work in a private collection, the individual who owns it, and follow the name by a comma and the city.

```
Bearden, Romare. The Train. Carole and Alex Rosenberg
     Collection, New York.
Bernini, Gianlorenzo. Ecstasy of St. Teresa. Santa Maria
     della Vittoria, Rome.
Rembrandt van Rijn. Aristotle Contemplating the Bust of
     Homer. Metropolitan Museum of Art, New York.
```

If you use a photograph of a painting or sculpture, indicate not only the institution or private owner and the city but also the complete publication information for the source in which the photograph appears, including the page, slide, figure, or plate number, whichever is relevant.

```
Cassatt, Mary. Mother and Child. Wichita Art Museum.
     American Painting: 1560-1913. By John Pearce. New
     York: McGraw, 1964. Slide 22.
El Greco. Burial of Count Orgaz. San Tomé, Toledo.
     Renaissance Perspectives in Literature and the
     Visual Arts. By Murray Roston. Princeton: Princeton
     UP, 1987. 274.
```

If you wish to indicate when a work of art was created, add the date immediately after the title.

```
Bearden, Romare. The Train. 1974. Carole and Alex
     Rosenberg Collection, New York.
```

```
Cassatt, Mary. Mother and Child. 1890. Wichita Art
     Museum. American Painting: 1560-1913. By John
     Pearce. New York: McGraw, 1964. Slide 22.
```

Cite a photograph in a museum or collection as you would a painting or sculpture.

```
Evans, Walker. Penny Picture Display. 1936. Museum of
     Mod. Art, New York.
```

To cite a personal photograph, begin with a description of its subject, neither underlined nor placed in quotation marks. Indicate the person who took the photograph and the date it was taken.

```
Saint Paul's Cathedral, London. Personal photograph by
     author. 7 Mar. 1999.
```

See 4.9.9d for paintings, sculptures, and photographs online or on CD-ROM.

4.8.7. An Interview

For purposes of documentation, there are three kinds of interviews:

- Published or recorded interviews
- Interviews broadcast on television or radio
- Interviews conducted by the researcher

Begin with the name of the person interviewed. If the interview is part of a publication, recording, or program, enclose the title of the interview, if any, in quotation marks; if the interview was published independently, underline the title. If the interview is untitled, use the descriptive label *Interview*, neither underlined nor enclosed in quotation marks. The interviewer's name may be added if known and pertinent to your paper (see the sample entries for Blackmun and Nader). Conclude with the appropriate bibliographic information.

```
Blackmun, Harry. Interview with Ted Koppel and Nina
     Totenberg. Nightline. ABC. WABC, New York. 5 Apr.
     1994.
```

Fellini, Federico. "The Long Interview." <u>Juliet of the
    Spirits</u>. Ed. Tullio Kezich. Trans. Howard
    Greenfield. New York: Ballantine, 1966. 17-64.
Gordimer, Nadine. Interview. <u>New York Times</u> 10 Oct. 1991,
    late ed.: C25.
Lansbury, Angela. Interview. <u>Off-Camera: Conversations
    with the Makers of Prime-Time Television</u>. By Richard
    Levinson and William Link. New York: Plume-NAL,
    1986. 72-86.
Nader, Ralph. Interview with Ray Suarez. <u>Talk of the
    Nation</u>. Natl. Public Radio. WBUR, Boston. 16 Apr.
    1998.
Wolfe, Tom. Interview. <u>The Wrong Stuff: American
    Architecture</u>. Dir. Tom Bettag. Videocassette.
    Carousel, 1983.

To cite an interview that you conducted, give the name of the person interviewed, the kind of interview (*Personal interview*, *Telephone interview*), and the date.

Pei, I. M. Personal interview. 22 July 1993.
Poussaint, Alvin F. Telephone interview. 10 Dec. 1990.

See 4.9.9e for interviews online.

4.8.8. A Map or Chart

In general, treat a map or chart like an anonymous book (4.6.11), but add the appropriate descriptive label (*Map*, *Chart*).

<u>Japanese Fundamentals</u>. Chart. Hauppauge: Barron, 1992.
<u>Washington</u>. Map. Chicago: Rand, 1995.

See 4.9.9f for maps and charts online. For guidance on how to cite such sources as dioramas, flash cards, games, globes, kits, and models, see Eugene B. Fleischer, *A Style Manual for Citing Microform and Nonprint Media* (Chicago: ALA, 1978).

4.8.9. A Cartoon

To cite a cartoon, state the cartoonist's name; the title of the cartoon (if any), in quotation marks; and the descriptive label *Cartoon*, neither underlined nor enclosed in quotation marks. Conclude with the usual publication information.

```
Chast, Roz. Cartoon. New Yorker 7 Apr. 1997: 72.
Trudeau, Garry. "Doonesbury." Cartoon. Star-Ledger
     [Newark] 17 June 1998: 23.
```

See 4.9.9g for cartoons online.

4.8.10. An Advertisement

To cite an advertisement, state the name of the product, company, or institution that is the subject of the advertisement, followed by the descriptive label *Advertisement*, neither underlined nor enclosed in quotation marks. Conclude with the usual publication information.

```
Air Canada. Advertisement. CNN. 15 May 1998.
The Fitness Fragrance by Ralph Lauren. Advertisement. GQ
     Apr. 1997: 111-12.
```

See 4.9.9h for advertisements online.

4.8.11. A Lecture, a Speech, an Address, or a Reading

In a citation of an oral presentation, give the speaker's name; the title of the presentation (if known), in quotation marks; the meeting and the sponsoring organization (if applicable); the location; and the date. If there is no title, use an appropriate descriptive label (*Address, Lecture, Keynote speech, Reading*), neither underlined nor enclosed in quotation marks.

```
Atwood, Margaret. "Silencing the Scream." Boundaries of
     the Imagination Forum. MLA Convention. Royal York
     Hotel, Toronto. 29 Dec. 1993.
```

Hyman, Earle. Reading of Shakespeare's <u>Othello</u>. Symphony
    Space, New York. 28 Mar. 1994.

Terkel, Studs. Address. Conf. on Coll. Composition and
    Communication Convention. Palmer House, Chicago.
    22 Mar. 1990.

4.8.12. A Manuscript or Typescript

To cite a manuscript or a typescript, state the author, the title or a
description of the material (e.g., *Notebook*), the form of the material
(*ms.* for a manuscript, *ts.* for a typescript), and any identifying number
assigned to it. Give the name and location of any library or other
research institution housing the material.

Chaucer, Geoffrey. <u>The Canterbury Tales</u>. Harley ms. 7334.
    British Lib., London.

<u>Octovian</u>. Ms. 91. Dean and Chapter Lib., Lincoln, Eng.

Salviati, Lionardo. <u>Poetica d'Aristotile parafrasata e</u>
    <u>comentata</u>. Ms. 2.2.11. Biblioteca Nazionale
    Centrale, Firenze.

Smith, Sonia. "Shakespeare's Dark Lady Revisited."
    Unpublished essay, 1993.

Twain, Mark. Notebook 32, ts. Mark Twain Papers. U of
    California, Berkeley.

See 4.9.9i for manuscripts and working papers online.

4.8.13. A Letter or Memo

As bibliographic entries, letters fall into three general categories:
- Published letters
- Unpublished letters in archives
- Letters received by the researcher

Treat a published letter like a work in a collection (see 4.6.7), adding
the date of the letter and the number (if the editor assigned one).

> Woolf, Virginia. "To T. S. Eliot." 28 July 1920. Letter
>   1138 of The Letters of Virginia Woolf. Ed. Nigel
>   Nicolson and Joanne Trautmann. Vol. 2. New York:
>   Harcourt, 1976. 437-38.

If you use more than one letter from a published collection, however, provide a single entry for the entire work and cite the letters individually in the text, following the form recommended for cross-references in works-cited lists (see 4.6.10).

In citing an unpublished letter, follow the guidelines for manuscripts and typescripts (see 4.8.12).

> Benton, Thomas Hart. Letter to Charles Fremont. 22 June
>   1847. John Charles Fremont Papers. Southwest Museum
>   Lib., Los Angeles.

Cite a letter that you received as follows:

> Morrison, Toni. Letter to the author. 17 May 1999.

Treat memos similarly: give the name of the writer of the memo, a description of the memo that includes the recipient, and the date of the document. Any title of the memo should be enclosed in quotation marks and placed immediately after the writer's name.

> Cahill, Daniel J. Memo to English dept. fac., Brooklyn
>   Technical High School, New York. 1 June 1998.

See 4.9.9j for e-mail communications.

4.8.14. A Legal Source

The citation of legal documents and law cases may be complicated. If your paper requires many such references, consult the most recent edition of *The Blue Book: A Uniform System of Citation* (Cambridge: Harvard Law Rev. Assn.), an indispensable guide in this field.

In general, do not underline or enclose in quotation marks the titles of laws, acts, and similar documents in either the text or the list of works cited (Declaration of Independence, Constitution of the United States, Taft-Hartley Act). Such titles are usually abbreviated, and the works are cited by sections. The years are added if relevant. Although lawyers and legal scholars adopt many abbreviations in their citations, use only familiar abbreviations when writing for a more general audience (see ch. 6).

```
21 US Code. Sec. 1401a. 1988.

US Const. Art. 1, sec. 1.
```

Note that references to the United States Code, which is often abbreviated *USC*, begin with the title number; in the above USC entry, for example, title 21 refers to laws concerned with food and drugs. Alphabetize USC entries under *United States Code* even if you use the abbreviation. When including more than one reference to the code, list the individual entries in numerical order.

If you are citing an act, state the name of the act, its Public Law number, the date it was enacted, and its Statutes at Large cataloging number. Use the abbreviations *Pub. L.* for Public Law and *Stat.* for Statutes at Large.

```
Pesticide Monitoring Improvements Act of 1988. Pub. L.
    100-418. 23 Aug. 1988. Stat. 102.1412.
```

Names of law cases are similarly abbreviated ("Brown v. Board of Ed.," for the case of Oliver Brown versus the Board of Education of Topeka, Kansas), but the first important word of each party's name is always spelled out. Names of cases, unlike those of laws, are underlined in the text but not in bibliographic entries. In citing a case, include, in addition to the names of the first plaintiff and the first defendant, the volume, name (not underlined), and page (in that order) of the law report cited; the name of the court that decided the case; and the year of the decision. Once again, considerable abbreviation is the norm. The following citation, for example, refers to page 755 of volume 148 of the *United States Patent Quarterly*, dealing with the case of Stevens against the National Broadcasting Company, which was decided by the California Superior Court in 1966.

```
Stevens v. National Broadcasting Co. 148 USPQ 755. CA
    Super. Ct. 1966.
```

To cite a government publication, see 4.6.21.

4.9. CITING ELECTRONIC PUBLICATIONS

4.9.1. Introduction

Citations of electronic sources and those of print sources should accomplish the same ends and have analogous formats. Both types of citations identify a source and give sufficient information to allow a reader to locate it. Yet each type requires a different kind and amount of information to fulfill these objectives. Print culture has developed standard reference tools (library catalogs, bibliographies, and so on) for locating published works. Electronic media, in contrast, so far lack agreed-on means of organizing works. Moreover, electronic texts are not as fixed and stable as their print counterparts. References to electronic works therefore must provide more information than print citations generally offer.

Publication Dates

Most bibliographic references to printed works contain only one date of publication; rare exceptions are an article reprinted in a collection of essays (see 4.6.7) and a republished book (see 4.6.17). A citation of an electronic work, however, may require two and sometimes more publication dates to be identified fully. Since electronic texts can be readily altered, any accessed version of an online source is potentially different from any past or future version and therefore must be considered unique. Typically, then, a citation for an online text contains the date assigned to the document in the source as well as the date on which the researcher accessed the document. If the work originally had a print existence, it may be necessary to give the date of the original print publication, if provided, along with the date of electronic publication and the date of access, for the document may have been different at each stage. On citing dates for publications on CD-ROM, diskette, and magnetic tape, see 4.9.5.

Uniform Resource Locator (URL)

The most efficient way to find an online publication at present is through its network address, or uniform resource locator (URL). This edition of the *MLA Handbook* recommends including URLs in citations of online works. Since addresses can change, however, and their length and complexity can result in transcription errors, it is crucial to be as accurate as possible in supplying not only URLs but also other identifying information (e.g., author's name, title), so that the reader who cannot locate the material through the stated address might be able to find it with a network searching tool. Moreover, since Internet sites and resources sometimes disappear altogether, you should consider downloading or printing the material you use, so that you can verify it if it is inaccessible later. Enclose URLs in angle brackets. If a URL must be divided between two lines, break it only after a slash; do not introduce a hyphen at the break or allow your word-processing program to do so. Give the complete address, including the access-mode identifier (*http, ftp, gopher, telnet, news*) and, after the first single slash, any relevant path and file names:

`<http://www.princeton.edu/~lancelot/>`

The recommendations in this section largely tend to treat sources for which a considerable amount of relevant publication information is available. In truth, though, many sources do not supply all desired information, for few standards currently govern the presentation of electronic publications—for instance, many texts do not include reference markers, such as paragraph numbers, so it is difficult if not impossible to direct a reader to the exact location of the material you are citing. Thus, while aiming for comprehensiveness, writers must often settle for citing whatever information is available to them.

These recommendations are aimed not at specialists in academic computing but primarily at students who use ideas and facts from electronic sources to complement those derived from traditional print sources. Moreover, since this section cannot possibly cover all materials available in electronic form, its emphasis, like that of the rest of this handbook, is on refereed, authoritative sources (see 1.6) as well as on historical texts. Needless to say, this edition's recommendations on citing electronic works are necessarily not definitive and will doubtless change as technology, scholarly uses of electronic materials, and electronic publication practices evolve.

This section discusses citing the following kinds of electronic publications: online scholarly projects, information databases, and professional and personal sites (4.9.2); online books (4.9.3); articles in online periodicals (4.9.4); publications on CD-ROM, diskette, and magnetic tape (4.9.5); works published in more than one medium (4.9.6); works from online services (4.9.7); publications in an indeterminate medium (4.9.8); and other electronic sources (e.g., audiovisual materials, manuscripts and working papers, e-mail communications, online postings; 4.9.9).

4.9.2. An Online Scholarly Project, Information Database, or Professional or Personal Site

a. A Complete Scholarly Project or Information Database

The typical entry for a complete online scholarly project or information database consists of the following items:

1. Title of the project or database (underlined)
2. Name of the editor of the project or database (if given)
3. Electronic publication information, including version number (if relevant and if not part of the title), date of electronic publication or of the latest update, and name of any sponsoring institution or organization
4. Date of access and network address

If you cannot find some of this information, cite what is available.

```
Britannica Online. Vers. 98.2. Apr. 1998. Encyclopaedia
        Britannica. 8 May 1998 <http://www.eb.com/>.
The Cinderella Project. Ed. Michael N. Salda. Vers. 1.1.
        Dec. 1997. De Grummond Children's Lit. Research
        Collection, U of Southern Mississippi. 15 Apr. 1998
        <http://www-dept.usm.edu/~engdept/cinderella/
        cinderella.html>.
CNN Interactive. 19 June 1998. Cable News Network. 19
        June 1998 <http://www.cnn.com/>.
The Electronic Text Center. Ed. David Seaman. 1998.
        Alderman Lib., U of Virginia. 14 Feb. 1998
        <http://etext.lib.virginia.edu/>.
The History Channel Online. 1998. History Channel. 19
        June 1998 <http://historychannel.com/>.
Hoover's Online. 1998. Hoover's Company Information. 19
        June 1998 <http://www.hoover.com/>.
Nineteenth-Century German Stories. Ed. Robert Godwin-
        Jones. 1994. Foreign Lang. Dept., Virginia
        Commonwealth U. 10 Jan. 1998 <http://
        www.fln.vcu.edu/hasweb/for/menu.html>.
```

Project Bartleby. Ed. Steven van Leeuwen. May 1998.
    Columbia U. 5 May 1998 <http://www.columbia.edu/
    acis/bartleby/>.

Romantic Chronology. Ed. Laura Mandell and Alan Liu.
    Nov. 1997. U of California, Santa Barbara. 22 June
    1998 <http://humanitas.ucsb.edu/projects/pack/
    rom-chrono/chrono.htm>.

Sí, España. Ed. José Félix Barrio. Vers. 2.0. Oct.
    1996. Embassy of Spain, Ottawa. 3 Feb. 1998
    <http://www.docuweb.ca/SiSpain/>.

Thomas: Legislative Information on the Internet. 26 May
    1998. Lib. of Congress, Washington. 19 June 1998
    <http://thomas.loc.gov/>.

UCMP Glossary. Ed. Allen Collins et al. Oct. 1995. U of
    California Museum of Paleontology, Berkeley. 19
    June 1998 <http://www.ucmp.berkeley.edu/glossary/
    glossary.html>.

Victorian Women Writers Project. Ed. Perry Willett.
    June 1998. Indiana U. 26 June 1998 <http://
    www.indiana.edu/~letrs/vwwp/>.

b. A Document within a Scholarly Project or Information Database

To cite an article, a poem, a short story, or a similar short work or document within a project or database, begin the citation with the author's name and, in quotation marks, the title of the work. If no author is given, begin the citation with the title of the material, in quotation marks. Continue with the relevant information for the project or database, the date of access, and the URL; be sure to give the URL of the specific work or document rather than that of the project or database if they are different. (On citing the texts of printed books in online scholarly projects, see 4.9.3.)

"Catalán." Sí, España. Ed. José Félix Barrio. Vers. 2.0.
    Oct. 1996. Embassy of Spain, Ottawa. 3 Feb.
    1998 <http://www.docuweb.ca/SiSpain/spanish/
    language/language/catalan.html>.

"City Profile: San Francisco." <u>CNN Interactive</u>. 19 June
    1998. Cable News Network. 19 June 1998
    <http://www.cnn.com/TRAVEL/CITY.GUIDES/WTR/
    north.america.profiles/nap.sanfrancisco.html>.

Dove, Rita. "Lady Freedom among Us." <u>The Electronic Text</u>
    <u>Center</u>. Ed. David Seaman. 1998. Alderman Lib., U of
    Virginia. 19 June 1998 <http://
    etext.lib.virginia.edu/subjects/afam.html>.

"Fresco." <u>Britannica Online</u>. Vers. 98.2. April 1998.
    Encyclopaedia Britannica. 8 May 1998 <http://
    www.eb.com:180>.

Hoffmann, Heinrich. "Struwwelpeter." Trans. Mark Twain.
    <u>Nineteenth-Century German Stories</u>. Ed. Robert
    Godwin-Jones. 1994. Foreign Lang. Dept., Virginia
    Commonwealth U. 10 Jan. 1998 <http://
    www.fln.vcu.edu/hasweb/for/struwwel/twpete.html>.

"Reebok International Ltd." <u>Hoover's Online</u>. 1998.
    Hoover's Company Information. 19 June 1998
    <http://www.hoover.com/capsules/11266.html>.

"Selected Seventeenth-Century Events." <u>Romantic</u>
    <u>Chronology</u>. Ed. Laura Mandell and Alan Liu. Oct.
    1996. U of California, Santa Barbara. 22 June 1998
    <http://humanitas.ucsb.edu/projects/pack/
    rom-chrono/chronola.htm>.

"Symbiosis." <u>UCMP Glossary</u>. Ed. Allen Collins et al.
    Oct. 1995. U of California Museum of Paleontology,
    Berkeley. 19 June 1998 <http://
    www.ucmp.berkeley.edu/glossary/gloss5ecol.html>.

"This Day in History: August 20." <u>The History Channel</u>
    <u>Online</u>. 1998. History Channel. 19 June 1998
    <http://historychannel.com/thisday/today/
    980820.html>.

c. A Professional or Personal Site

To document an online professional or personal site, begin the entry
with the name of the person who created it (if given and relevant),

reversed for alphabetizing and followed by a period. Continue with the title of the site (underlined) or, if there is no title, with a description such as *Home page* (neither underlined nor in quotation marks); the date of the last update, if given; the name of any organization associated with the site; the date of access; and the network address.

Dawe, James. <u>Jane Austen Page</u>. 15 Sept. 1998 ⟨http://
    nyquist.ee.ualberta.ca/~dawe/austen.html⟩.
Lancashire, Ian. Home page. 1 May 1998 ⟨http://
    www.chass.utoronto.ca:8080/~ian/⟩.
<u>Romance Languages and Literatures Home Page</u>. 1 Jan.
    1997. Dept. of Romance Langs. and Lits., U of
    Chicago. 8 July 1998 ⟨http://
    humanities.uchicago.edu/romance/⟩.

4.9.3. An Online Book

The texts of some printed books are available online, independently or as part of scholarly projects. In general, follow the recommendations in 4.6 for citing books, modifying them as appropriate to the electronic source.

a. An Online Book Available Independently

The typical entry for a complete online book available independently consists of the following items:

1. Author's name (if given). If only an editor, a compiler, or a translator is identified, cite that person's name, followed by the appropriate abbreviation (*ed., comp., trans.*).
2. Title of the work (underlined)
3. Name of the editor, compiler, or translator (if relevant); see, for example, the entries for Hawthorne and Pascal.
4. Publication information. If the version of the text online has not been published before, give the date of electronic publication and the name of any sponsoring institution or organization. State the publication facts about the original print version if they are given in the source (e.g., city of publication, name of publisher, year of publication). You may add in brackets relevant information not stated in the source; see the entry for Pascal.
5. Date of access and network address

If you cannot find some of this information, cite what is available.

Austen, Jane. <u>Pride and Prejudice</u>. Ed. Henry Churchyard.
      1996. 10 Sept. 1998 <http://www.pemberley.com/
      janeinfo/pridprej.html>.

Barsky, Robert F. <u>Noam Chomsky: A Life of Dissent</u>.
      Cambridge: MIT P, 1997. 8 May 1998 <http://
      mitpress.mit.edu/e-books/chomsky/>.

Douglass, Frederick. <u>Narrative of the Life of Frederick
      Douglass</u>. Boston, 1845. 30 Jan. 1997 <gopher://
      gopher.vt.edu:10010/02/73/1>.

Emerson, Ralph Waldo. <u>Essays: First Series</u>. 1841. 12
      Feb. 1997 <ftp://ftp.books.com/ebooks/NonFiction/
      Philosophy/Emerson/history.txt>.

Hawthorne, Nathaniel. <u>Twice-Told Tales</u>. Ed. George
      Parsons Lathrop. Boston: Houghton, 1883. 1 Mar.
      1998 <http://eldred.ne.mediaone.net/nh/
      ttt.html>.

Pascal, Blaise. <u>Pensées</u>. Trans. W. F. Trotter. [1910.]
      29 Apr. 1997 <gopher://gopher.vt.edu:10010/02/
      130/1>.

b. An Online Book within a Scholarly Project

To cite a book that is a part of a scholarly project, give the five items
listed above, as relevant, but follow the information about the printed
book with the publication information for the project (see 4.9.2). Be
sure to end with the URL of the book, not that of the project, if they
differ.

<u>Cinderella</u>. New York: Wrigley, [c. 1800-25]. <u>The
      Cinderella Project</u>. Ed. Michael N. Salda. Vers.
      1.1. Dec. 1997. De Grummond Children's Lit.
      Research Collection, U of Southern Mississippi. 15
      Apr. 1998 <http://www-dept.usm.edu/~engdept/
      cinderella/cind2.html>.

Keats, John. <u>Poetical Works</u>. 1884. <u>Project Bartleby</u>. Ed.
      Steven van Leeuwen. May 1998. Columbia U. 5 May

1998 <http://www.columbia.edu/acis/bartleby/
keats/>.

Nesbit, E[dith]. <u>Ballads and Lyrics of Socialism</u>.
London, 1908. <u>Victorian Women Writers Project</u>. Ed.
Perry Willett. June 1998. Indiana U. 26 June 1998
<http://www.indiana.edu/~letrs/vwwp/nesbit/
ballsoc.html>.

Robinson, Mary. <u>Sappho and Phaon</u>. London, 1796. <u>The
Electronic Text Center</u>. Ed. David Seaman. 1998.
Alderman Lib., U of Virginia. 14 Feb. 1998
<http://etext.lib.virginia.edu/britpo/sappho/
sappho.html>.

c. A Part of an Online Book

If you are citing a part of an online book, place the title or name of the part between the author's name and the title of the book. If the part is a work like a poem or an essay, place its title in quotation marks. If the part is a standard division of the book, such as an introduction or a preface, do not place the title in quotation marks or underline it; see the entry for Barsky. Be sure to give the URL of the specific part instead of that of the book if they differ.

Barsky, Robert F. Introduction. <u>Noam Chomsky: A Life of
Dissent</u>. By Barsky. Cambridge: MIT P, 1997. 8 May
1998 <http://mitpress.mit.edu/e-books/chomsky/
intro.html>.

Emerson, Ralph Waldo. "Self-Reliance." <u>Essays: First
Series</u>. 1841. 12 Feb. 1997 <ftp://ftp.books.com/
ebooks/NonFiction/Philosophy/Emerson/history.txt>.

Hawthorne, Nathaniel. "Dr. Heidegger's Experiment."
<u>Twice-Told Tales</u>. Ed. George Parsons Lathrop.
Boston: Houghton, 1883. 1 Mar. 1998 <http://
eldred.ne.mediaone.net/nh/dhe.html>.

Keats, John. "Ode on a Grecian Urn." <u>Poetical Works</u>.
1884. <u>Project Bartleby</u>. Ed. Steven van Leeuwen. May
1998. Columbia U. 8 May 1998 <http://
www.columbia.edu/acis/bartleby/keats/keats54.html>.

Nesbit, E[dith]. "Marching Song." <u>Ballads and Lyrics of</u>
<u>Socialism</u>. London, 1908. <u>Victorian Women Writers</u>
<u>Project</u>. Ed. Perry Willett. June 1998. Indiana U.
26 Jul. 1998 <http://www.indiana.edu/~letrs/vwwp/
nesbit/ballsoc.html#p9>.

d. An Online Government Publication

To cite an online government publication, begin with the same facts
given for printed government works (see 4.6.21), and conclude with
information appropriate to the electronic source.

United States. Dept. of Justice. Natl. Inst. of Justice.
<u>Prosecuting Gangs: A National Assessment</u>. By Claire
Johnson, Barbara Webster, and Edward Connors. Feb.
1995. 29 June 1998 <http://www.ncjrs.org/txtfiles/
pgang.txt>.

4.9.4. An Article in an Online Periodical

Periodical publications online include scholarly journals, newspapers, and magazines; works and other materials within such publications include articles, reviews, editorials, and letters to the editor. In
general, follow the recommendations in 4.7 for citing parts of print
periodicals, modifying them as appropriate to the electronic source.
The typical entry for a work in an online periodical consists of the following items:

1. Author's name (if given)
2. Title of the work or material (if any; a review or letter to the editor may be untitled), in quotation marks
3. Name of the periodical (underlined)
4. Volume number, issue number, or other identifying number
5. Date of publication
6. The number range or total number of pages, paragraphs, or other
   sections, if they are numbered
7. Date of access and network address

If you cannot find some of this information, cite what is available.

a. An Article in a Scholarly Journal (cf. 4.7.1–4)

Calabrese, Michael. "Between Despair and Ecstasy: Marco Polo's Life of the Buddha." <u>Exemplaria</u> 9.1 (1997). 22 June 1998 <http://web.english.ufl.edu/english/exemplaria/calax.htm>.

Denning, Peter J. "Business Designs for the New University." <u>Educom Review</u> 31.6 (1996). 23 June 1998 <http://educom.edu/web/pubs/review/reviewArticles/31620.html>.

Elam, Diane. "Disciplining Woman: Feminism or Women's Studies." <u>Surfaces</u> 5.101 (1995): 11 pp. 24 June 1998 <http://tornade.ere.umontreal.ca:80/~guedon/Surfaces/vol5/elam.html>.

Miles, Adrian. "<u>Singin' in the Rain</u>: A Hypertextual Reading." <u>Postmodern Culture</u> 8.2 (1998). 25 June 1998 <http://jefferson.village.virginia.edu/pmc/issue.198/8.2miles.html>.

Sohmer, Steve. "12 June 1599: Opening Day at Shakespeare's Globe." <u>Early Modern Literary Studies</u> 3.1 (1997): 46 pars. 26 June 1998 <http://www.humanities.ualberta.ca/emls/03-1/sohmjuli.html>.

Tully, R. Brent, et al. "Global Extinction in Spiral Galaxies." <u>Astronomical Journal</u> 115.6 (1998). 27 June 1998 <http://www.journals.uchicago.edu/AJ/journal/issues/v115n6/980002/980002.html>.

b. An Article in a Newspaper or on a Newswire (cf. 4.7.5)

"Endangered Species Act Upheld." <u>AP Online</u> 22 June 1998. 22 June 1998 <http://www.nytimes.com/aponline/w/AP-Court-Endangered-Species.html>.

Markoff, John. "The Voice on the Phone Is Not Human, but It's Helpful." <u>New York Times on the Web</u> 21 June 1998. 25 June 1998 <http://www.nytimes.com/library/tech/98/06/biztech/articles/21voice.html>.

Reid, T. R. "Druids Return to Stonehenge." <u>Washington Post</u> 22 June 1998. 22 June 1998 <http://www.washingtonpost.com/wp-srv/WPlate/1998-06/22/045I-062298-idx.html>.

c. An Article in a Magazine (cf. 4.7.6)

Guckenberger, Katherine. "A Convent with a View." <u>Atlantic Unbound</u> 22 Jan. 1998. 26 June 1998 <http://www.theAtlantic.com/atlantic/unbound/abroad/kg980122.htm>.

Kinsley, Michael. "Now Is the Summer of Too Much Content." <u>Slate</u> 20 June 1998. 25 June 1998 <http://www.slate.com/98-06-20/Readme.asp>.

d. A Review (cf. 4.7.7)

Angelo, Gretchen V. Rev. of <u>The Book of the Body Politic</u>, by Christine de Pizan. <u>Bryn Mawr Medieval Review</u> 96.1.7 (1996). 26 Jan. 1997 <gopher://gopher.lib.virginia.edu:70/00/alpha/bmmr/v96/96-1-7>.

Ebert, Roger. Rev. of <u>The Truman Show</u>, dir. Peter Weir. <u>Chicago Sun-Times Online</u> 5 June 1998. 16 June 1998 <http://www.suntimes.com/output/ebert1/05show.htm>.

Jenkins, James J. "Comprehending Comprehension." Rev. of <u>Language Comprehension as Structure</u>, by M. A. Gernsbacher. <u>Psycoloquy</u> 95.6.26 (1995): 5 pars. 3 Feb. 1997 <gopher://gopher.lib.virginia.edu:70/00/alpha/psyc/1995/psyc.95.6.26.language-comprehension.6.jenkins>.

Kisselgoff, Anna. "Mourning Schubert with Oblique Simplicity." Rev. of <u>Medium</u>, chor. Mark Morris. Mark Morris Dance Group. Brooklyn Acad. of Music, New York. <u>New York Times on the Web</u> 26 June 1998. 26 June 1998 <http://www.nytimes.com/yr/mo/day/news/arts/morris-dance-review.html>.

Mamigonian, Marc A. Rev. of <u>America on Film: Hollywood and American History</u>, by Kenneth Cameron. <u>Boston Book Review</u> 1 Dec. 1997. 25 June 1998 <http://www.bookwire.com/BBR/Arts-and-Diversions/read.Review$5601>.

e. An Abstract (cf. 4.7.8)

Bullough, Vern L. "Medieval Concepts of Adultery." <u>Arthuriana</u> 7.4 (1997): 5-15. Abstract. 26 June 1998 <http://dc.smu.edu/Arthuriana/Abstract/Ab_list1.htm>.

f. An Anonymous Article (cf. 4.7.9)

"Fleeting Consciousness." <u>US News Online</u> 29 June 1998. 1 July 1998 <http://www.usnews.com/usnews/issue/980629/29brai.htm>.

g. An Editorial (cf. 4.7.10)

"Controlling Deadly Trade." Editorial. <u>Christian Science Monitor: Electronic Edition</u> 26 June 1998. 26 June 1998 <http://www.csmonitor.com/durable/1998/06/26/f-p16s1.htm>.

h. A Letter to the Editor (cf. 4.7.11)

Kung, Cleo. Letter. <u>New York Times on the Web</u> 28 June 1998. 28 June 1998 <http://www.nytimes.com/yr/mo/day/letters/1kung.html>.

i. A Serialized Article (cf. 4.7.12)

Dugger, Celia W. "Wedding Vows Bind Old World and New." <u>New York Times on the Web</u> 20 July 1998. Pt. 2 of a series, Here and There: Immigration Now, begun 19 July 1998. 5 Aug. 1998 <http://www.nytimes.com/library/national/regional/072098.immigration.html>.
Sontag, Deborah. "A Mexican Town That Transcends All Borders." <u>New York Times on the Web</u> 21 July 1998.

Pt. 3 of a series, Here and There: Immigration Now, begun 19 July 1998. 5 Aug. 1998 〈http:// www.nytimes.com/library/national/regional/ 072198.immigration.html〉.

Sontag, Deborah, and Celia W. Dugger. "New Immigrant Tide: Shuttle between Worlds." <u>New York Times on the Web</u> 19 July 1998. Pt. 1 of a series, Here and There: Immigration Now. 5 Aug. 1998 〈http:// www.nytimes.com/library/national/regional/ 071998.immigration.html〉.

4.9.5. A Publication on CD-ROM, Diskette, or Magnetic Tape

Citations for publications on CD-ROM, diskette, and magnetic tape are similar to those for print sources, with the following important differences.

Publication medium. Many works are published in more than one format (e.g., print, online, CD-ROM), and the works may not be the same in each. When you cite a publication on CD-ROM, diskette, or magnetic tape, it is important to state the publication medium in order to differentiate the source from its possible print or online counterpart.

Vendor's name. The persons or groups responsible for supplying the information in publications on CD-ROM, diskette, and magnetic tape are sometimes also the publishers of the works. But many information providers choose instead to lease the data to vendors (e.g., Information Access, SilverPlatter, UMI-ProQuest) for distribution. It is important to state the vendor's name in your works-cited list, if it is given in your source, because the information provider may have leased electronic versions of the data to more than one vendor, and the versions may not be identical (see 4.9.5b).

Publication dates. Many databases published on CD-ROM, diskette, or magnetic tape are updated regularly (e.g., annually, quarterly). Updates add information and may also correct or otherwise alter information that previously appeared in the database. Therefore, a works-cited-list entry for material derived from such a database commonly contains the date of the document used, as indicated in the source, as well as the publication date (or date of the most recent updating) of the database (see 4.9.5b).

The sections below contain recommendations for citing nonperiodical publications on CD-ROM, diskette, or magnetic tape (4.9.5a), materials from periodically published databases on CD-ROM (4.9.5b), and multidisc publications (4.9.5c).

a. A Nonperiodical Publication on CD-ROM, Diskette, or Magnetic Tape

Many publications on CD-ROM, diskette, or magnetic tape are issued as books are—that is, without a plan to update or otherwise revise the work regularly. Cite a nonperiodical publication on CD-ROM, diskette, or magnetic tape as you would a book, but add a description of the medium of publication. Since the information provider and the publisher are usually the same for such publications, no vendor's name appears, and only one publication date is given. The typical works-cited-list entry for the source consists of the following items:

1. Author's name (if given). If only an editor, a compiler, or a translator is identified, cite that person's name, followed by the appropriate abbreviation (*ed.*, *comp.*, *trans.*).
2. Title of the publication (underlined)
3. Name of the editor, compiler, or translator (if relevant)
4. Publication medium (*CD-ROM*, *Diskette*, or *Magnetic tape*)
5. Edition, release, or version (if relevant)
6. Place of publication
7. Name of the publisher
8. Date of publication

If you cannot find some of this information, cite what is available.

Braunmuller, A. R., ed. <u>Macbeth</u>. By William Shakespeare.
    CD-ROM. New York: Voyager, 1994.
<u>English Poetry Full-Text Database</u>. Magnetic tape. Rel.
    2. Cambridge, Eng.: Chadwyck-Healey, 1993.
<u>Magill's Survey of Science</u>. CD-ROM. 1998 ed. Pasadena:
    Salem, 1998.
Thiesmeyer, Elaine C., and John E. Thiesmeyer. <u>Editor: A
    System for Checking Usage, Mechanics, Vocabulary,</u>

and Structure. Diskette. Vers. 5.2. New York: MLA,
        1996.

If publication information for a printed source or printed analogue is
indicated, begin the citation with that information.

Aristotle. The Complete Works of Aristotle: The Revised
        Oxford Translation. Ed. Jonathan Barnes. 2 vols.
        Princeton: Princeton UP, 1984. CD-ROM. Clayton:
        InteLex, 1994.
The Oxford English Dictionary. 2nd ed. CD-ROM. New York:
        Oxford UP, 1992.

If you are citing only a part of the work, state which part. If the part
is a book-length work, underline the title; if the part is a shorter work
like an article, an essay, a poem, or a short story, enclose the title in
quotation marks. If the source supplies page numbers, paragraph numbers, screen numbers, or some other kind of section numbers, state
their total if the numbering starts over with each part (see the entry for
Rodes), but state the range of the numbers in the part if a single numbering encompasses all the parts.

"Albatross." The Oxford English Dictionary. 2nd ed.
        CD-ROM. Oxford: Oxford UP, 1992.
"The Chemistry of Air Pollution." Magill's Survey of
        Science. CD-ROM. 1998 ed. Pasadena: Salem, 1998.
"Children's Television Workshop." Encyclopedia of
        Associations. Magnetic tape. Detroit: Gale, 1994.
Coleridge, Samuel Taylor. "Dejection: An Ode." The
        Complete Poetical Works of Samuel Taylor Coleridge.
        Ed. Ernest Hartley Coleridge. Vol. 1. Oxford:
        Clarendon, 1912. 362-68. English Poetry Full-Text
        Database. CD-ROM. Rel. 2. Cambridge, Eng.:
        Chadwyck-Healey, 1993.
"Ellison, Ralph." DiscLit: American Authors. Diskette.
        Boston: Hall, 1991.
Rodes, David S. "The Language of Ambiguity and
        Equivocation." Macbeth. By William Shakespeare. Ed.

A. R. Braunmuller. CD-ROM. New York: Voyager, 1994.

5 pp.

b. Material from a Periodically Published Database on CD-ROM

Many periodicals (journals, magazines, newspapers) and periodically published reference works, such as annual bibliographies and collections of abstracts, are published both in print and on CD-ROM as databases or as parts of databases. To cite such a work, begin with the publication data for the printed source or printed analogue, as identified in the CD-ROM publication. If the print version is a book or a pamphlet (see the entry for *Guidelines for Family Television Viewing*), follow the guidelines in 4.6; if the print version is an article in a periodical, follow 4.7. The typical works-cited-list entry consists of the following items:

1. Author's name (if given)
2. Publication information for the printed source or printed analogue (including title and date of print publication)
3. Title of the database (underlined)
4. Publication medium (*CD-ROM*)
5. Name of the vendor (if relevant)
6. Electronic publication date

If you cannot find some of this information, cite what is available.

Coates, Steve. "Et Tu, Cybernetica Machina User?" New
    York Times 28 Oct. 1996, late ed.: D4. New York
    Times Ondisc. CD-ROM. UMI-ProQuest. Dec. 1996.

Danzey, Leigh Ann. "The Price of Success: An Analysis of
    Funding Top Ten Men's and Women's Programs in
    Comparative Sports." DAI 58 (1997): 795A. Florida
    State U, 1997. Dissertation Abstracts Ondisc.
    CD-ROM. UMI-ProQuest. Mar. 1998.

Guidelines for Family Television Viewing. Urbana: ERIC
    Clearinghouse on Elementary and Early Childhood
    Educ., 1990. ERIC. CD-ROM. SilverPlatter. June
    1993.

Krach, Peg. "Myth and Facts about Alcohol Abuse in the
    Elderly." Nursing Feb. 1998: 25+. Abstract.

<u>Periodical Abstracts Ondisc</u>. CD-ROM. UMI-ProQuest. Feb. 1998.

Leonard, Mary. "'Boutique Medicine' Is Not for Everybody." <u>Boston Globe</u> 6 July 1997: C1. Abstract. <u>Newspaper Abstracts Ondisc</u>. CD-ROM. UMI-ProQuest. Mar. 1998.

Reese, Elaine, Catherine A. Haden, and Robyn Fivush. "Mothers, Fathers, Daughters, Sons: Gender Differences in Autobiographical Reminiscing." <u>Research on Language and Social Interaction</u> 29 (1996): 27-56. Abstract. <u>Sociofile</u>. CD-ROM. SilverPlatter. Dec. 1996.

Russo, Michelle Cash. "Recovering from Bibliographic Instruction Blahs." <u>RQ: Reference Quarterly</u> 32 (1992): 178-83. <u>InfoTrac: Magazine Index Plus</u>. CD-ROM. Information Access. Dec. 1993.

United States. Cong. House. Committee on the Judiciary. <u>Report on the Fair Use of Copyrighted Works</u>. 11 Aug. 1992. 102nd Cong. 1st sess. <u>Congressional Masterfile</u> 2. CD-ROM. Congressional Information Service. Dec. 1996.

Verma, Anil. "Day-O: A Jamaican Journey." <u>India Currents</u> 30 Nov. 1997: 48+. <u>Ethnic NewsWatch</u>. CD-ROM. Dataware Technologies. Feb. 1998.

c. A Multidisc Publication

If you are citing a CD-ROM publication of more than one disc, follow the publication medium (*CD-ROM*) either with the total number of discs or with a specific disc number if you use material from only one.

<u>Perseus 2.0: Interactive Sources and Studies on Ancient Greece</u>. CD-ROM. 4 discs. New Haven: Yale UP, 1996.

United States. Dept. of State. <u>Patterns of Global Terrorism</u>. 1994. <u>National Trade Data Bank</u>. CD-ROM. Disc 2. US Dept. of Commerce. Dec. 1996.

4.9.6. A Work in More Than One Publication Medium

If the work you are citing is published in various media (e.g., a CD-ROM and a diskette), specify all the media that constitute the publication or cite only the media you used.

> Lancashire, Ian, et al. Using TACT with Electronic
>
> Texts: A Guide to Text-Analysis Computing Tools.
>
> Book, CD-ROM. Vers. 2.1. New York: MLA, 1996.
>
> Perseus 1.0: Interactive Sources and Studies on Ancient
>
> Greece. CD-ROM, laser disc. New Haven: Yale UP,
>
> 1992.

or

> Mann, Thomas. Tonio Kröger. Ed. Barry Joe. Using TACT
>
> with Electronic Texts: A Guide to Text-Analysis
>
> Computing Tools. By Ian Lancashire et al. CD-ROM.
>
> Vers. 2.1. New York: MLA, 1996.

4.9.7. A Work from an Online Service

Two common types of online services are those to which users tend to subscribe personally (e.g., America Online) and those to which libraries more typically subscribe (e.g., ProQuest Direct, Lexis-Nexis, EBSCOhost). If the service you are using provides a URL for accessed material, follow the recommendations in 4.9.2–4. Sometimes, however, these services supply material without giving a URL. If the user retrieves such material by entering a keyword or similar designation, complete the citation by writing *Keyword* and the word itself following the name of the service and the date of access.

> "Table Tennis." Compton's Encyclopedia Online. Vers.
>
> 2.0. 1997. America Online. 4 July 1998. Keyword:
>
> Compton's.

If instead of entering a keyword the user follows a series of topic labels, write the word *Path* and specify the sequence of topics you followed to obtain the material; use semicolons to separate topics.

"Cloning." BioTech's Life and Science Dictionary. 30

June 1998. Indiana U. America Online. 4 July 1998.

Path: Research and Learning; Science; Biology;

Biotechnology Dictionary.

To cite online material without a URL that you derive from a service to which a library subscribes, complete the citation by stating the name of the database used (underlined), if known; the name of the service; the library; and the date of access. If you know the URL of the service's home page, give it, in angle brackets, immediately after the date of access.

Fox, Justin. "What in the World Happened to Economics?"

Fortune 15 Mar. 1999: 90-102. ABI/INFORM Global.

ProQuest Direct. Regional Community Coll. Lib.,

Little Rock. 2 Mar. 1999 <http://www.umi.com/

proquest/>.

4.9.8. A Work in an Indeterminate Medium

If you cannot determine the medium of a source—for example, if you access material through a local network and cannot tell whether the work is stored on the central computer's hard drive (where the contents would be subject to revision) or on a CD-ROM—use the designation *Electronic* for the medium. Give whatever relevant publication information you can, as well as the name of the network or of its sponsoring organization and the date of access.

Bartlett, John. Familiar Quotations. 9th ed. Boston:

Little, 1901. New York: Columbia U, Academic

Information Systems, 1995. Electronic. ColumbiaNet,

Columbia U. 2 July 1998.

"Brontë, Emily." DISCovering Authors. Vers. 1.0. 1992.

Electronic. Nutley Public Lib., NJ. 15 May 1997.

4.9.9. Other Electronic Sources

In general, to document other electronic sources, follow the recommendations in 4.8 on citing miscellaneous print and nonprint sources, modifying the guidelines as appropriate (cf. 4.9.2–8). Some kinds of works need identifying labels (*Interview, Map, Online posting*), neither underlined nor enclosed in quotation marks. In documenting a source such as an online posting or a synchronous communication, try to cite an archival version, if one exists, so that the reader can more easily consult the work.

a. A Television or Radio Program (cf. 4.8.1)

> Fishkin, Fred. "Privacy and the Net." Boot Camp. CBS Radio. WCBS, New York. 5 Mar. 1998. Transcript. 29 June 1998 <http://newsradio88.com/boot/archive/ march_1998/march_5.html>.
>
> "The Threat of Commercial Fishing." Earth Matters. CNN. 18 Jan. 1998. Transcript. Broadcast News. CD-ROM. Primary Source Media. Jan. 1998. 22 screens.

See also the entries for Fishkin and Nader in 4.9.9b.

b. A Sound Recording or Sound Clip (cf. 4.8.2)

> Fishkin, Fred. "Privacy and the Net." Boot Camp. CBS Radio. WCBS, New York. 5 Mar. 1998. 29 June 1998 <http://newsradio88.com/bootcamp-cgi/ ServeRAM.cgi?storyId=889074000>.
>
> Lecuona, Ernesto. "Malagueña." Lecuona Plays Lecuona. BMG, 1997. 2 Feb. 1997 <http://classicalmus.com/ bmgclassics/recording-clip/ 09026-68671-2_011k08bit.aiff>.
>
> Nader, Ralph. Interview with Ray Suarez. Talk of the Nation. Natl. Public Radio. 16 Apr. 1998. 3 July 1998 <http://www.npr.org/ramfiles/ 980416.totn.01.ram>.
>
> Roosevelt, Franklin D. "Americanism." 1920. American Leaders Speak: Recordings from World War I and the 1920 Election. 1996. American Memory. Lib. of Congress, Washington. 19 Mar. 1997 <http:// lcweb2.loc.gov/mbrs/nforum/9000024.ram>.

c. A Film or Film Clip (cf. 4.8.3)

```
Kurosawa, Akira, dir. Throne of Blood. 1957. Macbeth. By
     William Shakespeare. Ed. A. R. Braunmuller. CD-ROM.
     New York: Voyager, 1994.
Murnau, F. W., dir. Nosferatu. 1922. The Sync. 16 June
     1998 <http://www.thesync.com/ram/nosferatu.ram>.
```

d. A Painting, Sculpture, or Photograph (cf. 4.8.6)

```
Delacroix, Eugène. Death of Ophelia. 1853. Louvre,
     Paris. Shakespeare Illustrated. Ed. Harry Rusche.
     Aug. 1996. Emory U. 7 Apr. 1997 <http://
     www.cc.emory.edu/ENGLISH/classes/
     Shakespeare_Illustrated/Delacroix.Ophelia.html>.
Evans, Walker. Penny Picture Display. 1936. Museum of
     Mod. Art, New York. 30 June 1998 <http://
     www.moma.org/collection/photography/pages/
     evans.penny.html>.
Holbein, Hans. The Ambassadors. Microsoft Art Gallery:
     The Collection of the National Gallery, London.
     CD-ROM. Redmond: Microsoft, 1994.
Syrian Woman. 3rd century (?). Tom and Nan Riley
     Collection. Cedar Rapids Museum of Art, IA. Roman
     Portrait Sculptures. 2 July 1998 <http://
     acs.rhodes.edu/~riley/syrian_woman.html>.
```

e. An Interview (cf. 4.8.7)

```
Price, Richard. Interview with Larry Weissman. Bold
     Type. June 1998. 25 June 1998 <http://
     199.29.97.173/0698/price/interview.html>.
```

See also the entry for Nader in 4.9.9b.

f. A Map (cf. 4.8.8)

```
"Phoenix, Arizona." Map. U.S. Gazetteer. US Census
     Bureau. 30 June 1998 <http://www.census.gov/
     cgi-bin/gazetteer>.
```

g. A Cartoon (cf. 4.8.9)

Toles, Tom. "One Way to Solve the Beeper Problem."
     Cartoon. <u>US News Online</u> 1 June 1998. 29 June 1998
     <http://www.usnews.com/usnews/issue/980601/
     1tole.htm>.

h. An Advertisement (cf. 4.8.10)

Lee Mood Ring. Advertisement. 29 June 1998 <http://
     www.leejeans.com/features/moodring.html>.

i. A Manuscript or Working Paper (cf. 4.8.12)

Cacicedo, Al. "Private Parts: Preliminary Notes for an
     Essay on Gender Identity in Shakespeare." Working
     paper, 12 Mar. 1997. 4 July 1998 <http://
     www.arts.ubc.ca/english/iemls/shak/
     PRIVATE_PARTS.txt>.

Gregory, Saint. Frontispiece. <u>Moralia in Job</u>. Ms. 2.
     Bibliothèque Municipale, Dijon. <u>The Electronic
     Beowulf Project</u>. 1995. 4 Aug. 1998 <http://
     www.uky.edu/~kiernan/BL/beowig.html>.

Whitman, Walt. Notebooks. Thomas Bigg Harned Walt
     Whitman Collection. Ms. Div., Lib. of Congress.
     <u>American Memory</u>. Lib. of Congress, Washington. 29
     June 1998 <http://lcweb2.loc.gov/ammem/
     wwcoll.html>.

j. An E-Mail Communication (cf. 4.8.13)

To cite electronic mail, give the name of the writer; the title of the message (if any), taken from the subject line and enclosed in quotation marks; a description of the message that includes the recipient (e.g., "E-mail to the author"); and the date of the message.

Boyle, Anthony T. "Re: Utopia." E-mail to Daniel J.
     Cahill. 21 June 1997.
Harner, James L. E-mail to the author. 20 Aug. 1998.

k. An Online Posting

To cite a posting to an e-mail discussion list, begin with the author's name and the title of the document (in quotation marks), as given in the subject line, followed by the description *Online posting*, the date when the material was posted, the name of the forum (if known; e.g., Humanist Discussion Group), the date of access, and, in angle brackets, the online address of the list's Internet site or, if no Internet site is known, the e-mail address of the list's moderator or supervisor.

    Holland, Norman. "Overcoming Depression." Online
        posting. 19 Mar. 1997. Psyart. 21 Mar. 1997
        <http://web.clas.ufl.edu/ipsa/psyart.htm>.
    Merrian, Joanne. "Spinoff: Monsterpiece Theatre." Online
        posting. 30 Apr. 1994. Shaksper: The Global
        Electronic Shakespeare Conf. 30 Oct. 1996 <http://
        www.arts.ubc.ca/english/iemls/shak/shak-L.html>.
    Piez, Wendell. "Sustained Reading vs. Synchronic
        Access." Online posting. 23 Jan. 1997. Humanist
        Discussion Group. 24 Jan. 1997 <http://
        www.princeton.edu/~mccarty/humanist/>.

Whenever feasible, cite an archival version of the posting, so that your readers can more easily consult your source.

    Merrian, Joanne. "Spinoff: Monsterpiece Theatre." Online
        posting. 30 Apr. 1994. Shaksper: The Global
        Electronic Shakespeare Conf. 27 Aug. 1998 <http://
        www.arts.ubc.ca/english/iemls/shak/
        MONSTERP_SPINOFF.txt>.
    Piez, Wendell. "Sustained Reading vs. Synchronic
        Access." Online posting. 23 Jan. 1997. Humanist
        Discussion Group. 29 June 1998 <http://
        lists.village.virginia.edu/lists_archive/Humanist/
        v10/0238.html>.

To cite a posting to a World Wide Web forum, begin with the author's name and the title of the posting (if there is one), in quotation marks, followed by the description *Online posting*, the date when the material was posted, the name of the forum, the date of access, and, in angle brackets, the network address.

> Gunkel, Patrick. Online posting. 28 Feb. 1998. Measuring
>   Intelligence. 30 June 1998 <http://www.nytimes.com/
>   webin/WebX?13A^41356@.ee992e/0>.

To cite a posting to a Usenet news group, begin with the author's name and the title of the document (in quotation marks), as given in the subject line, followed by the description *Online posting*, the date when the material was posted, the date of access, and, in angle brackets, the name of the news group, with the prefix *news:*.

> Morton, Paul. "Re: Teaching Portuguese." Online posting.
>   25 Feb. 1997. 4 Aug. 1998
>   <news:comp.edu.languages.natural>.

To cite a document forwarded within a posting, begin with the name of the writer, the title, and the date of the document. Then give the name of the person who forwarded it, preceded by *Fwd. by*. Conclude the entry with the description *Online posting*, the date of the posting in which the material was forwarded, and the appropriate remaining information for a posting to a discussion list, an online forum, or a news group.

> Chessid, Estelle. "Women Authors: A New List Now
>   Available." 29 June 1997. Fwd. by Kevin Berland.
>   Online posting. 2 July 1997. C18-L: Resources for
>   Eighteenth-Century Studies across the Disciplines.
>   5 July 1997 <http://cac.psu.edu/~bcj/c18-1.htm>.

l. A Synchronous Communication

To cite a synchronous communication posted in a forum such as a MUD (multiuser domain) or MOO (multiuser domain, object-oriented), give the name of the speaker (if you are citing just one), a description of the event, the date of the event, the forum for the communication (e.g., LinguaMOO), the date of access, and the network address, with the prefix *telnet://*.

> Grigar, Dene. Online defense of dissertation
>   "Penelopeia: The Making of Penelope in Homer's

> Story and Beyond." 25 July 1995. LinguaMOO. 25 July
> 1995 <telnet://lingua.utdallas.edu:8888>.

Whenever feasible, cite an archival version of the communication, so that your readers can more readily consult your source.

> Grigar, Dene. Online defense of dissertation
>   "Penelopeia: The Making of Penelope in Homer's
>   Story and Beyond." 25 July 1995. LinguaMOO. 1 July
>   1998 <http://wwwpub.utdallas.edu/~cynthiah/
>   lingua_archive/phd-defense.txt>.

m. Downloaded Computer Software

> <u>MacCase</u>. Vers. 1.0. 1 Aug. 1998 <ftp://ftp.adfa.oz.au/
>   pub/mac/MacCASE/>.
> <u>TACT: Text-Analysis Computing Tools</u>. Vers. 2.1 gamma. 30
>   Apr. 1997 <gopher://gopher.epas.utoronto.ca:70/
>   11/cch/hum_comp/software/TACT>.

5 Documentation: Citing Sources in the Text

5.1. PARENTHETICAL DOCUMENTATION
AND THE LIST OF WORKS CITED

The list of works cited at the end of your research paper plays an important role in your acknowledgment of sources (see ch. 4), but the list does not in itself provide sufficiently detailed and precise documentation. You must indicate to your readers not only what works you used in writing the paper but also exactly what you derived from each source and exactly where in the work you found the material. The most practical way to supply this information is to insert a brief parenthetical acknowledgment in your paper wherever you incorporate another's words, facts, or ideas. Usually the author's last name and a page reference are enough to identify the source and the specific location from which you borrowed material.

> Medieval Europe was a place both of "raids, pillages,
> slavery, and extortion" and of "traveling merchants,
> monetary exchange, towns if not cities, and active
> markets in grain" (Townsend 10).

The parenthetical reference "(Townsend 10)" indicates that the quotations come from page 10 of a work by Townsend. Given the author's last name, your readers can find complete publication information for the source in the alphabetically arranged list of works cited that follows the text of your paper.

> Townsend, Robert M. <u>The Medieval Village Economy</u>.
>   Princeton: Princeton UP, 1993.

The sample references in 5.4 offer recommendations for documenting many other kinds of sources.

5.2. INFORMATION REQUIRED IN
PARENTHETICAL DOCUMENTATION

In determining the information needed to document sources accurately, keep the following guidelines in mind.

References in the text must clearly point to specific sources in the list of works cited. The information in your parenthetical references in the text must match the corresponding information in the entries in your list of works cited. For a typical works-cited-list entry, which begins with the name of the author (or editor, translator, or narrator), the parenthetical reference begins with the same name. When the list contains only one work by the author cited, you need give only the author's last name to identify the work: "(Patterson 183–85)." If your list contains more than one author with the same last name, you must add the first initial—"(A. Patterson 183–85)" and "(L. Patterson 230)"—or, if the initial is shared too, the full first name. If two or three names begin the entry, give the last name of each person listed: "(Rabkin, Greenberg, and Olander vii)." If the work has more than three authors, follow the form in the bibliographic entry: either give the first author's last name followed by *et al.*, without any intervening punctuation—"(Lauter et al. 2425–33)"—or give all the last names. If there is a corporate author, use its name, shortened or in full (see 5.4.5). If the work is listed by title, use the title, shortened or in full (see 5.4.4). If the list contains more than one work by the author, add the cited title, shortened or in full, after the author's last name (see 5.4.6).

Identify the location of the borrowed information as specifically as possible. For a printed source, give the relevant page number or numbers in the parenthetical reference (see esp. 5.4.2) or, if you cite from more than one volume of a multivolume work, the volume and page numbers (see 5.4.3). In a reference to a literary work or to the Bible, it is helpful to give information other than, or in addition to, the page number—for example, the chapter, book, or stanza number or the numbers of the act, scene, and line (see 5.4.8). You may omit page numbers when citing complete works (see 5.4.1), as well as articles in works arranged alphabetically (like encyclopedias). A page reference is similarly unnecessary if, for example, you use a passage from a one-page work. Of course, nonprint sources such as films, television programs, recordings, and performances and electronic sources with no pagination or other type of reference markers cannot be cited by page number. Such works are usually cited in their entirety (see 5.4.1) and often by title (see 5.4.4). (See 5.4.2 for electronic publications with paragraph numbers or other kinds of reference numbers.)

5.3. READABILITY

Keep parenthetical references as brief—and as few—as clarity and accuracy permit. Give only the information needed to identify a source, and do not add a parenthetical reference unnecessarily. Identify sources by author and, if necessary, title; do not use abbreviations such as *ed.*, *trans.*, and *comp.* after the name. If you are citing an entire work, for example, rather than a specific part of it, the author's name in the text may be the only documentation required. The statement "Booth has devoted an entire book to the subject" needs no parenthetical documentation if the list of works cited includes only one work by Booth. If, for the reader's convenience, you wished to name the book in your text, you could recast the sentence: "Booth has devoted an entire book, *The Rhetoric of Fiction*, to the subject."

Remember that there is a direct relation between what you integrate into your text and what you place in parentheses. If, for example, you include an author's name in a sentence, you need not repeat the name in the parenthetical page citation that follows, provided that the reference is clearly to the work of the author you mention. The paired sentences below illustrate alternative ways of identifying authors. Note that sometimes one version is more concise than the other.

AUTHOR'S NAME IN TEXT

```
Tannen has argued this point (178-85).
```

AUTHOR'S NAME IN REFERENCE

```
This point has already been argued (Tannen 178-85).
```

AUTHORS' NAMES IN TEXT

```
Others, like Jakobson and Waugh (210-15), hold the
opposite point of view.
```

AUTHORS' NAMES IN REFERENCE

```
Others hold the opposite point of view (e.g., Jakobson
and Waugh 210-15).
```

AUTHOR'S NAME IN TEXT

```
Only Daiches has seen this relation (2: 776-77).
```

AUTHOR'S NAME IN REFERENCE

Only one scholar has seen this relation (Daiches 2: 776-77).

AUTHOR'S NAME IN TEXT

It may be true, as Robertson maintains, that "in the appreciation of medieval art the attitude of the observer is of primary importance [. . .]" (136).

AUTHOR'S NAME IN REFERENCE

It may be true that "in the appreciation of medieval art the attitude of the observer is of primary importance [. . .]" (Robertson 136).

To avoid interrupting the flow of your writing, place the parenthetical reference where a pause would naturally occur (preferably at the end of a sentence), as near as possible to the material documented. The parenthetical reference precedes the punctuation mark that concludes the sentence, clause, or phrase containing the borrowed material.

In his Autobiography, Benjamin Franklin states that he prepared a list of thirteen virtues (135-37).

A reference directly after a quotation follows the closing quotation mark.

In the late Renaissance, Machiavelli contended that human beings were by nature "ungrateful" and "mutable" (1240), and Montaigne thought them "miserable and puny" (1343).

If the quotation, whether of poetry or prose, is set off from the text (see 2.7.2–4), type a space after the concluding punctuation mark of the quotation and insert the parenthetical reference.

John K. Mahon adds a further insight to our understanding of the War of 1812:

> Financing the war was very difficult at the time. Baring Brothers, a banking firm of the enemy country, handled routine accounts for the United States overseas, but the firm would take

> on no loans. The loans were in the end absorbed
> by wealthy Americans at great hazard--also, as
> it turned out, at great profit to them. (385)

Elizabeth Bishop's "In the Waiting Room" is rich in
evocative detail:

> It was winter. It got dark
> early. The waiting room
> was full of grown-up people,
> arctics and overcoats,
> lamps and magazines. (6-10)

For guidelines on citing literary works, see 5.4.8.

If you need to document several sources for a statement, you may cite them in a note to avoid unduly disrupting the text (see 5.5). If you quote more than once from the same page within a single paragraph—and no quotation from another source intervenes—you may give a single parenthetical reference after the last quotation.

5.4. SAMPLE REFERENCES

Each of the following sections concludes with a list of the works cited in the examples. Note that the lists for the first five sections (5.4.1–5) do not include more than one work by the same author. On citing two or more works by an author, see 5.4.6.

5.4.1. Citing an Entire Print or Nonprint Work

If you wish to cite an entire work—whether a print source; a nonprint source such as a film, television program, or performance; or an electronic publication that has no pagination or other type of reference markers—it is usually preferable to include in the text, rather than in a parenthetical reference, the name of the person (e.g., author, editor, director, performer) that begins the corresponding entry in the works-cited list. (See 5.4.4 for citing a work by title.)

BOOKS (cf. 4.6)

McRae's <u>The Literature of Science</u> includes many examples of this trend.

Paul Lauter and his coeditors have provided a useful anthology of American literature.

Gilbert and Gubar broke new ground on the subject.

ARTICLES IN PERIODICALS (cf. 4.7)

But Andrea Most has offered another view.

Diction, according to Anthony Tommasini, is more important than vocal prowess in a singer of Gilbert and Sullivan.

MISCELLANEOUS NONPRINT SOURCES (cf. 4.8)

Kurosawa's <u>Rashomon</u> was one of the first Japanese films to attract a Western audience.

I vividly recall Diana Rigg's interpretation of Medea.

Margaret Atwood's remarks drew an enthusiastic response.

ELECTRONIC SOURCES (cf. 4.9)

William J. Mitchell's <u>City of Bits</u> discusses architecture and urban life in the context of the digital telecommunications revolution.

Stempel has tried to develop a "historical sociology" of sport in nineteenth-century America.

Michael Joyce was among the first to write fiction in hypertext.

Joanne Merrian reported on a parody of Shakespeare performed by the Muppets.

Works Cited

Atwood, Margaret. "Silencing the Scream." Boundaries of
    the Imagination Forum. MLA Convention. Royal York
    Hotel, Toronto. 29 Dec. 1993.

Gilbert, Sandra M., and Susan Gubar. The Madwoman in the
    Attic: The Woman Writer and the Nineteenth-Century
    Literary Imagination. New Haven: Yale UP, 1979.

Joyce, Michael. Afternoon: A Story. Diskette. Watertown:
    Eastgate, 1987.

Kurosawa, Akira, dir. Rashomon. Perf. Toshiro Mifune.
    Daiei, 1950.

Lauter, Paul, et al., eds. The Heath Anthology of
    American Literature. 2nd ed. 2 vols. Lexington:
    Heath, 1994.

McRae, Murdo William, ed. The Literature of Science:
    Perspectives on Popular Science Writing. Athens:
    U of Georgia P, 1993.

Merrian, Joanne. "Spinoff: Monsterpiece Theatre." Online
    posting. 30 Apr. 1994. Shaksper: The Global
    Electronic Shakespeare Conf. 27 Aug. 1998
    <http://www.arts.ubc.ca/english/iemls/shak/
    MONSTERP_SPINOFF.txt>.

Mitchell, William J. City of Bits: Space, Place, and the
    Informationbahn. Cambridge: MIT P, 1995. MIT P
    Electronic Books. 9 July 1998 <http://
    mitpress.mit.edu/e-books/City_of_Bits>.

Most, Andrea. "'We Know We Belong to the Land': The
    Theatricality of Assimilation in Rodgers and
    Hammerstein's Oklahoma!" PMLA 113 (1998): 77-89.

Rigg, Diana, perf. Medea. By Euripides. Trans. Alistair
    Elliot. Dir. Jonathan Kent. Longacre Theatre, New
    York. 7 Apr. 1994.

Stempel, Carl William. "Towards a Historical Sociology
    of Sport in the United States, 1825-1875." DAI 53
    (1993): 3374A. U of Oregon, 1992. Dissertation
    Abstracts Ondisc. CD-ROM. UMI-ProQuest. Sept. 1993.

Tommasini, Anthony. "In G. and S., Better to Have More
Words, Less Voice." Rev. of The Mikado, by William
S. Gilbert and Arthur Sullivan. New York City
Opera. New York State Theater, New York. New York
Times 10 Mar. 1997, late ed.: C22.

5.4.2. Citing Part of a Work

If you quote, paraphrase, or otherwise use a specific passage in a book
or article, give the relevant page or section (e.g., paragraph) number or
numbers. When the author's name is in your text, give only the number reference in parentheses, but if the context does not clearly identify the author, add the author's last name before the reference. Leave a
space between them, but do not insert punctuation or, for a page reference, the word *page* or *pages* or the abbreviation *p.* or *pp.* If you used
only one volume of a multivolume work and included the volume
number in the bibliographic entry, you need give only page numbers
in the reference (see the Lauter et al. example), but if you used more
than one volume of the work, you must cite both volume and page
numbers (see 5.4.3).

If your source uses paragraph numbers rather than page numbers—
as, for example, some electronic journals do—give the relevant number or numbers preceded by the abbreviation *par.* or *pars.* (see the
Sohmer example); if the author's name begins such a citation, place a
comma after the name. If another kind of section is numbered in the
source (e.g., screens), either write out the word for the section
or use a standard abbreviation (see ch. 6); if the author's name
begins such a citation, place a comma after the name (see the Gardiner
example). When a source has no page numbers or any other kind of
reference numbers, no number can be given in the parenthetical reference. The work must be cited in its entirety (see 5.4.1).

BOOKS (cf. 4.6)

Brian Taves suggests some interesting conclusions
regarding the philosophy and politics of the adventure
film (153-54, 171).

The anthology by Lauter and his coeditors contains
Stowe's "Sojourner Truth, the Libyan Sibyl" (2425-33).

Among intentional spoonerisms, the "punlike metathesis of distinctive features may serve to weld together words etymologically unrelated but close in their sound and meaning" (Jakobson and Waugh 304).

Although writings describing utopia have always seemed to take place far from the everyday world, in fact "all utopian fiction whirls contemporary actors through a costume dance no place else but here" (Rabkin, Greenberg, and Olander vii).

Another engaging passage is the opening of Isabel Allende's story "Toad's Mouth" (83).

In Hansberry's play <u>A Raisin in the Sun</u>, the rejection of Lindner's tempting offer permits Walter's family to pursue the new life they had long dreamed about (274-75).

ARTICLES IN PERIODICALS (cf. 4.7)

Between 1968 and 1988, television coverage of presidential elections changed dramatically (Hallin 5).

Repetitive strain injury, or RSI, is reported to be "the fastest-growing occupational hazard of the computer age" (Taylor A1).

ELECTRONIC SOURCES (cf. 4.9)

"The study of comparative literature," Bill Readings wrote, "takes off from the idea of humanity" (6).

Beethoven has been called the "first politically motivated composer," for he was "caught up in the whole ferment of ideas that came out of the French Revolution" (Gardiner, screens 2-3).

"The debut of <u>Julius Caesar</u>," according to Sohmer, "proclaimed Shakespeare's Globe a theater of courage and ideas, a place where an audience must observe with the inner eye, listen with the inner ear" (par. 44).

Works Cited

Allende, Isabel. "Toad's Mouth." Trans. Margaret Sayers
    Peden. A Hammock beneath the Mangoes: Stories from
    Latin America. Ed. Thomas Colchie. New York: Plume,
    1992. 83-88.

Gardiner, John Eliot. "The Importance of Beethoven."
    Interview. Charlie Rose. PBS. 25 July 1996.
    Transcript. Broadcast News. CD-ROM. Primary Source
    Media. July 1996. 23 screens.

Hallin, Daniel C. "Sound Bite News: Television Coverage
    of Elections, 1968-1988." Journal of Communication
    42.2 (1992): 5-24.

Hansberry, Lorraine. A Raisin in the Sun. Black Theater:
    A Twentieth-Century Collection of the Work of Its
    Best Playwrights. Ed. Lindsay Patterson. New York:
    Dodd, 1971. 221-76.

Jakobson, Roman, and Linda R. Waugh. The Sound Shape of
    Language. Bloomington: Indiana UP, 1979.

Lauter, Paul, et al., eds. The Heath Anthology of
    American Literature. 2nd ed. Vol. 1. Lexington:
    Heath, 1994.

Rabkin, Eric S., Martin H. Greenberg, and Joseph D.
    Olander. Preface. No Place Else: Explorations in
    Utopian and Dystopian Fiction. Ed. Rabkin,
    Greenberg, and Olander. Carbondale: Southern
    Illinois UP, 1983. vii-ix.

Readings, Bill. "Translatio and Comparative Literature:
    The Terror of European Humanism." Surfaces 1.11
    (1991): 19 pp. 8 July 1998 <http://
    tornade.ere.umontreal.ca/~guedon/Surfaces/vol1/
    readin-a.html>.

Sohmer, Steve. "12 June 1599: Opening Day at
    Shakespeare's Globe." Early Modern Literary Studies
    3.1 (1997): 46 pars. 22 June 1998 <http://
    www.humanities.ualberta.ca/emls/03-1/
    sohmjuli.html>.

Taves, Brian. <u>The Romance of Adventure: The Genre of</u>
    <u>Historical Adventure Movies</u>. Jackson: UP of
    Mississippi, 1993.

Taylor, Paul. "Keyboard Grief: Coping with Computer-
    Caused Injuries." <u>Globe and Mail</u> [Toronto] 27 Dec.
    1993: A1+.

5.4.3. Citing Volume and Page Numbers of a Multivolume Work

When citing a volume number as well as a page reference for a multi-volume work, separate the two by a colon and a space: "(Wellek 2: 1–10)." Use neither the words *volume* and *page* nor their abbreviations. The functions of the numbers in such a citation are understood. If, however, you wish to refer parenthetically to an entire volume of a multivolume work, there is no need to cite pages. Place a comma after the author's name and include the abbreviation *vol.*: "(Wellek, vol. 2)." If you integrate such a reference into a sentence, spell out *volume*: "In volume 2, Wellek deals with [. . .]."

The anthology by Lauter and his coeditors contains both
Stowe's "Sojourner Truth, the Libyan Sibyl" (1: 2425-33)
and Gilman's "The Yellow Wall-Paper" (2: 800-12).

Between the years 1945 and 1972, the political-party
system in the United States underwent profound changes
(Schlesinger, vol. 4).

Wellek admits in the middle of his multivolume history
of modern literary criticism, "An evolutionary history
of criticism must fail. I have come to this resigned
conclusion" (5: xxii).

Works Cited

Lauter, Paul, et al., eds. <u>The Heath Anthology of</u>
    <u>American Literature</u>. 2nd ed. 2 vols. Lexington:
    Heath, 1994.

Schlesinger, Arthur M., Jr., gen. ed. <u>History of U.S.</u>
    <u>Political Parties</u>. 4 vols. New York: Chelsea, 1973.

Wellek, René. <u>A History of Modern Criticism, 1750-1950</u>. 8 vols. New Haven: Yale UP, 1955-92.

5.4.4. Citing a Work Listed by Title

In a parenthetical reference to a work alphabetized by title in the list of works cited, the full title (if brief) or a shortened version precedes the page or section number or numbers (if any; see 5.2), unless the title appears in your text. When abbreviating the title, begin with the word by which it is alphabetized. Do not, for example, shorten *Glossary of Terms Used in Heraldry* to *Heraldry*, since this abbreviation would lead your reader to look for the bibliographic entry under *h* rather than *g*. If you wish to cite a specific definition in a dictionary entry, give the relevant designation (e.g., number, letter) after the abbreviation *def.* (see the "Noon" example under "Electronic Sources").

BOOKS (cf. 4.6)

A presidential commission reported in 1970 that recent campus protests had focused on "racial injustice, war, and the university itself" (<u>Report</u> 3).

The nine grades of mandarins were "distinguished by the color of the button on the hats of office" ("Mandarin").

ARTICLES IN PERIODICALS (cf. 4.7)

International espionage was as prevalent as ever in the 1990s ("Decade").

A <u>New York Times</u> editorial called Ralph Ellison "a writer of universal reach" ("Death").

MISCELLANEOUS NONPRINT SOURCES (cf. 4.8)

Even <u>Sixty Minutes</u> launched an attack on modern art, in a segment entitled "Yes . . . but Is It Art?"

The classical Greek tragedy <u>Medea</u>, one of the most successful Broadway plays of the 1990s, made a lasting impression on me.

ELECTRONIC SOURCES (cf. 4.9)

The database <u>Duecento</u> is an invaluable source for texts of medieval Italian poetry.

<u>Perseus 1.0</u> revolutionized the way scholars conduct research on ancient civilizations.

In fresco painting, "the pigments are completely fused with a damp plaster ground to become an integral part of the wall surface" ("Fresco").

Milton's description of the moon at "her highest noon" signifies the "place of the moon at midnight" ("Noon," def. 4b).

<u>Romance Languages and Literatures Home Page</u> has links to helpful resources.

Works Cited

"Death of a Writer." Editorial. <u>New York Times</u> 20 Apr. 1994, late ed.: A18.

"Decade of the Spy." <u>Newsweek</u> 7 Mar. 1994: 26-27.

<u>Duecento: Repertorio elettronico della poesia italiana dalle origini a Dante</u>. Ed. Francesco Bonomi. 1996. Si.Lab, Firenze. 19 Apr. 1997 <http://www.silab.it/frox/200/pwhomita.htm>.

"Fresco." <u>Britannica Online</u>. Vers. 97.1.1. Mar. 1997. Encyclopaedia Britannica. 29 Mar. 1997 <http://www.eb.com:180>.

"Mandarin." <u>The Encyclopedia Americana</u>. 1993 ed.

<u>Medea</u>. By Euripides. Trans. Alistair Elliot. Dir. Jonathan Kent. Perf. Diana Rigg. Longacre Theatre, New York. 7 Apr. 1994.

"Noon." <u>The Oxford English Dictionary</u>. 2nd ed. CD-ROM. Oxford: Oxford UP, 1992.

<u>Perseus 1.0: Interactive Sources and Studies on Ancient Greece</u>. CD-ROM, laser disc. New Haven: Yale UP, 1992.

<u>Report of the President's Commission on Campus Unrest</u>.
New York: Arno, 1970.

<u>Romance Languages and Literatures Home Page</u>. 1 Jan.
1997. Dept. of Romance Langs. and Lits., U of
Chicago. 8 July 1998 <http://
humanities.uchicago.edu/romance/>.

"Yes . . . but Is It Art?" Narr. Morley Safer. <u>Sixty
Minutes</u>. CBS. WCBS, New York. 19 Sept. 1993.

5.4.5. Citing a Work by a Corporate Author

To cite a work by a corporate author, you may use the author's name followed by a page reference: "(United Nations, Economic Commission for Africa 79–86)." It is better, however, to include a long name in the text, so that the reading is not interrupted with an extended parenthetical reference. When giving the name of a corporate author in parentheses, shorten terms that are commonly abbreviated (see 6.4): "(Natl. Research Council 15)."

According to a study sponsored by the National Research
Council, the population of China around 1990 was
increasing by more than fifteen million annually (15).

By 1992 it was apparent that the American health care
system, though impressive in many ways, needed "to be
fixed and perhaps radically modified" (Public Agenda
Foundation 4).

A study prepared by the United States Department of
State defined terrorism as "premeditated, politically
motivated violence against noncombatant targets by
subnational groups or clandestine agents, usually
intended to influence an audience" (lines 14-16).

In 1963 the United Nations Economic Commission for
Africa predicted that Africa would evolve into an
advanced industrial economy within fifty years (1-2,
4-6).

Works Cited

National Research Council. <u>China and Global Change:</u>
    <u>Opportunities for Collaboration</u>. Washington: Natl.
    Acad., 1992.

Public Agenda Foundation. <u>The Health Care Crisis:</u>
    <u>Containing Costs, Expanding Coverage</u>. New York:
    McGraw, 1992.

United Nations. Economic Commission for Africa.
    <u>Industrial Growth in Africa</u>. New York: United
    Nations, 1963.

United States. Dept. of State. <u>Patterns of Global</u>
    <u>Terrorism</u>. 1994. <u>National Trade Data Bank</u>. CD-ROM.
    Disc 2. US Dept. of Commerce. Dec. 1996.

5.4.6. Citing Two or More Works by the Same Author or Authors

In a parenthetical reference to one of two or more works by the same author, put a comma after the author's last name and add the title of the work (if brief) or a shortened version and the relevant page reference: "(Frye, *Double Vision* 85)," "(Durant and Durant, *Age* 214–48)." If you state the author's name in the text, give only the title and page reference in parentheses: "(*Double Vision* 85)," "(*Age* 214–48)." If you include both the author's name and the title in the text, indicate only the pertinent page number or numbers in parentheses: "(85)," "(214–48)."

PRINT SOURCES

Dreiser's universe, according to E. L. Doctorow, "is
composed of merchants, workers, club-men, managers,
actors, salesmen, doormen, cops, derelicts--a Balzacian
population unified by the rules of commerce and the
ideals of property and social position" (Introduction
ix).

The brief but dramatic conclusion of chapter 13 of
Doctorow's <u>Welcome to Hard Times</u> constitutes the climax
of the novel (206-09).

In <u>The Age of Voltaire</u>, the Durants portray eighteenth-
century England as a minor force in the world of music
and art (214-48).

To Will and Ariel Durant, creative men and women make
"history forgivable by enriching our heritage and our
lives" (<u>Dual Autobiography</u> 406).

Shakespeare's <u>King Lear</u> has been called a "comedy of the
grotesque" (Frye, <u>Anatomy</u> 237).

For Northrop Frye, one's death is not a unique
experience, for "every moment we have lived through we
have also died out of into another order" (<u>Double Vision</u>
85).

ELECTRONIC SOURCES

Moulthrop sees the act of reading hypertext as
"struggle": "a chapter of chances, a chain of detours, a
series of revealing figures in commitment out of which
come the pleasures of the text" ("Traveling").

Hypertext, as one theorist puts it, is "all about
connection, linkage, and affiliation" (Moulthrop, "You
Say," par. 19).

Works Cited

Doctorow, E. L. Introduction. <u>Sister Carrie</u>. By Theodore
    Dreiser. New York: Bantam, 1982. v-xi.

---. <u>Welcome to Hard Times</u>. 1960. New York: Vintage-
    Random, 1988.

Durant, Will, and Ariel Durant. <u>The Age of Voltaire</u>. New
    York: Simon, 1965. Vol. 9 of <u>The Story of</u>
    <u>Civilization</u>. 11 vols. 1933-75.

---. <u>A Dual Autobiography</u>. New York: Simon, 1977.

Frye, Northrop. <u>Anatomy of Criticism: Four Essays</u>.
    Princeton: Princeton UP, 1957.
- - -. <u>The Double Vision: Language and Meaning in</u>
    <u>Religion</u>. Toronto: U of Toronto P, 1991.
Moulthrop, Stuart. "Traveling in the Breakdown Lane: A
    Principle of Resistance for Hypertext." 19 Apr.
    1995. 12 July 1998 <http://www.ubalt.edu/www/ygcla/
    sam/ESSAYS/BREAKDOWN.html>.
- - -. "You Say You Want a Revolution? Hypertext and the
    Laws of Media." <u>Postmodern Culture</u> 1.3 (1991): 53
    pars. 12 July 1998 <http://
    jefferson.village.virginia.edu/pmc/text-only/
    issue.591/moulthro.591>.

5.4.7. Citing Indirect Sources

Whenever you can, take material from the original source, not a secondhand one. Sometimes, however, only an indirect source is available—for example, someone's published account of another's spoken
remarks. If what you quote or paraphrase is itself a quotation, put the
abbreviation *qtd. in* ("quoted in") before the indirect source you cite in
your parenthetical reference. (You may document the original source
in a note; see 5.5.1.)

Samuel Johnson admitted that Edmund Burke was an
"extraordinary man" (qtd. in Boswell 2: 450).

The commentary of the sixteenth-century literary
scholars Bernardo Segni and Lionardo Salviati shows them
to be less-than-faithful followers of Aristotle (qtd. in
Weinberg 1: 405, 616-17).

Works Cited

Boswell, James. <u>The Life of Johnson</u>. Ed. George Birkbeck
    Hill and L. F. Powell. 6 vols. Oxford: Clarendon,
    1934-50.

Weinberg, Bernard. A History of Literary Criticism in
the Italian Renaissance. 2 vols. Chicago: U of
Chicago P, 1961.

5.4.8. Citing Literary and Religious Works

In a reference to a classic prose work, such as a novel or play, that is available in several editions, it is helpful to provide more information than just a page number from the edition used; a chapter number, for example, would help readers to locate a quotation in any copy of a novel. In such a reference, give the page number first, add a semicolon, and then give other identifying information, using appropriate abbreviations: "(130; ch. 9)," "(271; bk. 4, ch. 2)."

Raskolnikov first appears in Crime and Punishment as a
man contemplating a terrible act but frightened of
meeting his talkative landlady on the stairs (Dostoevsky
1; pt. 1, ch. 1).

In one version of the William Tell story, the son urges
the reluctant father to shoot the arrow (Sastre 315;
sc. 6).

In A Vindication of the Rights of Woman, Mary
Wollstonecraft recollects many "women who, not led by
degrees to proper studies, and not permitted to choose
for themselves, have indeed been overgrown children"
(185; ch. 13, sec. 2).

When you cite an unpaginated source, the chapter number or similar designation may be the only identifying information you can give.

Douglass notes that he had "no accurate knowledge" of
his date of birth, "never having had any authentic
record containing it" (ch. 1).

In citing classic verse plays and poems, omit page numbers altogether and cite by division (act, scene, canto, book, part) and line, with periods separating the various numbers—for example, "*Iliad* 9.19" refers to book 9, line 19, of Homer's *Iliad*. If you are citing only line numbers, do not use the abbreviation *l.* or *ll.*, which can be confused with numerals. Instead, initially use the word *line* or *lines* and then, having established that the numbers designate lines, give the numbers alone.

In general, use arabic numerals rather than roman numerals for division and page numbers. Although you must use roman numerals when citing pages of a preface or other section that are so numbered, designate volumes, parts, books, and chapters with arabic numerals even if your source does not. Some instructors prefer roman numerals, however, for citations of acts and scenes in plays (*King Lear* IV.i), but if your instructor does not require this practice, use arabic numerals (*King Lear* 4.1). On numbers, see 2.5.

When included in parenthetical references, the titles of the books of the Bible and of famous literary works are often abbreviated (1 Chron. 21.8, Rev. 21.3, *Oth.* 4.2.7–13, *FQ* 3.3.53.3). The most widely used and accepted abbreviations for such titles are listed in 6.7. Follow prevailing practices for other abbreviations (*Troilus* for Chaucer's *Troilus and Criseyde*, "Nightingale" for Keats's "Ode to a Nightingale," etc.).

In <u>Ballads and Lyrics of Socialism</u>, Nesbit declares, "Our arms and hearts are strong for all who suffer wrong" ("Marching Song" 11).

Like the bard who made the <u>Ballad of Sir Patrick Spence</u>, Coleridge sees the "new-moon winter bright" with the "old Moon in her lap, foretelling / The coming on of rain and squally blast" (1.9, 13-14).

The Dean and Chapter Library manuscript version of <u>Octovian</u>, as edited by Frances McSparran, has a more formal ending than other versions do: "And thus endis Octouean, / That in his tym was a doghety man [. . .]" (1629-30).

One Shakespearean protagonist seems resolute at first when he asserts, "Haste me to know't, that I, with wings as swift / As meditation [. . .] / May sweep to my revenge" (<u>Ham</u>. 1.5.35-37), but he soon has second thoughts; another tragic figure, initially described as

"too full o' th' milk of human kindness" (<u>Mac</u>. 1.5.17),
quickly descends into horrific slaughter.

In one of the most vivid prophetic visions in the Bible,
Ezekiel saw "what seemed to be four living creatures,"
each with the faces of a man, a lion, an ox, and an
eagle (<u>New Jerusalem Bible</u>, Ezek. 1.5-10). John of
Patmos echoes this passage when describing his vision
(Rev. 4.6-8).

Works Cited

Coleridge, Samuel Taylor. "Dejection: An Ode." <u>The
    Complete Works of Samuel Taylor Coleridge</u>. Ed.
    Ernest Hartley Coleridge. Vol. 1. Oxford:
    Clarendon, 1912. 362-68. <u>English Poetry Full-Text
    Database</u>. Rel. 2. CD-ROM. Cambridge, Eng.:
    Chadwyck-Healey, 1993.

Dostoevsky, Feodor. <u>Crime and Punishment</u>. Trans. Jessie
    Coulson. Ed. George Gibian. New York: Norton, 1964.

Douglass, Frederick. <u>Narrative of the Life of Frederick
    Douglass</u>. Boston, 1845. 30 Jan. 1997 <gopher://
    gopher.vt.edu:10010/02/73/1>.

Nesbit, E[dith]. <u>Ballads and Lyrics of Socialism</u>.
    London, 1908. <u>Victorian Women Writers Project</u>. Ed.
    Perry Willett. June 1998. Indiana U. 26 June 1998
    <http://www.indiana.edu/~letrs/vwwp/nesbit/
    ballsoc.html>.

The New Jerusalem Bible. Henry Wansbrough, gen. ed. New
    York: Doubleday, 1985.

Octovian. Ed. Frances McSparran. Early English Text Soc.
    289. London: Oxford UP, 1986. <u>The Electronic Text
    Center</u>. Ed. David Seaman. May 1995. Alderman Lib.,
    U of Virginia. 24 Feb. 1997 <ftp://
    etext.virginia.edu/pub/texts/AnoOctC>.

Sastre, Alfonso. <u>Sad Are the Eyes of William Tell</u>.
    Trans. Leonard Pronko. <u>The New Wave Spanish Drama</u>.

Ed. George Wellwarth. New York: New York UP, 1970.
165-321.

Shakespeare, William. <u>Hamlet</u>. Ed. Barbara A. Mowat and
Paul Werstine. New York: Washington Square-Pocket,
1992.

---. <u>Macbeth</u>. Ed. Barbara A. Mowat and Paul Werstine.
New York: Washington Square-Pocket, 1992.

Wollstonecraft, Mary. <u>A Vindication of the Rights of</u>
<u>Woman</u>. Ed. Carol H. Poston. New York: Norton, 1975.

5.4.9. Citing More Than One Work in a Single Parenthetical Reference

If you wish to include two or more works in a single parenthetical reference, cite each work as you normally would in a reference, and use semicolons to separate the citations.

(Kaku 42; McRae 101-33)

(National Research Council 25-35; Fitzgerald 330-43)

(Rabkin, Greenberg, and Olander vii; Boyle 96-125)

(Craner 308-11; Moulthrop, pars. 39-53)

(Gilbert and Gubar, <u>Madwoman</u> 1-25; Murphy 39-52)

(Gilbert and Gubar, <u>Norton</u>; Manning)

(<u>Guidelines</u>; Hallin 18-24)

(Lauter et al., vol. 1; Crane)

Keep in mind, however, that a long parenthetical reference such as the following example may prove intrusive and disconcerting to your reader:

(Taylor A1; Moulthrop, pars. 39-53; Armstrong, Yang, and
Cuneo 80-82; Craner 308-11; Kaku 42; Frank; Alston)

To avoid an excessive disruption, cite multiple sources in a note rather than in parentheses in the text (see 5.5.2).

Works Cited

Alston, Robin. "Bodley CD-ROM." Online posting. 15 June
     1994. ExLibris. 8 July 1998 <http://
     palimpsest.stanford.edu/byform/mailing-lists/
     exlibris/1994/06/msg00170.html>.

Armstrong, Larry, Dori Jones Yang, and Alice Cuneo. "The
     Learning Revolution: Technology Is Reshaping
     Education--at Home and at School." <u>Business Week</u> 28
     Feb. 1994: 80-88.

Boyle, Anthony T. "The Epistemological Evolution of
     Renaissance Utopian Literature, 1516-1657." Diss.
     New York U, 1983.

Crane, Stephen. <u>The Red Badge of Courage: An Episode of
     the American Civil War</u>. 1895. Ed. Fredson Bowers.
     Charlottesville: UP of Virginia, 1975.

Craner, Paul M. "New Tool for an Ancient Art: The
     Computer and Music." <u>Computers and the Humanities</u>
     25 (1991): 303-13.

Fitzgerald, John. "The Misconceived Revolution: State
     and Society in China's Nationalist Revolution,
     1923-26." <u>Journal of Asian Studies</u> 49 (1990):
     323-43.

Frank, Holly. <u>Negative Space: A Computerized Video
     Novel</u>. Vers. 1.0. Diskette, videocassette. Prairie
     Village: Diskotech, 1990.

Gilbert, Sandra M., and Susan Gubar. <u>The Madwoman in the
     Attic: The Woman Writer and the Nineteenth-Century
     Literary Imagination</u>. New Haven: Yale UP, 1979.

---, eds. <u>The Norton Anthology of Literature by Women:
     The Tradition in English</u>. 2nd ed. New York: Norton,
     1996.

<u>Guidelines for Family Television Viewing</u>. Urbana: ERIC
     Clearinghouse on Elementary and Early Childhood
     Educ., 1990. <u>ERIC</u>. CD-ROM. SilverPlatter. Oct.
     1993.

Hallin, Daniel C. "Sound Bite News: Television Coverage of Elections, 1968-1988." Journal of Communication 42.2 (1992): 5-24.

Kaku, Michio. Hyperspace: A Scientific Odyssey through Parallel Universes, Time Warps, and the Tenth Dimension. New York: Oxford UP, 1994.

Lauter, Paul, et al., eds. The Heath Anthology of American Literature. 2nd ed. 2 vols. Lexington: Heath, 1994.

Manning, Anita. "Curriculum Battles from Left and Right." USA Today 2 Mar. 1994: 5D.

McRae, Murdo William, ed. The Literature of Science: Perspectives on Popular Science Writing. Athens: U of Georgia P, 1993.

Moulthrop, Stuart. "You Say You Want a Revolution? Hypertext and the Laws of Media." Postmodern Culture 1.3 (1991): 53 pars. 12 July 1998 <http:// jefferson.village.virginia.edu/pmc/text-only/ issue.591/moulthro.591>.

Murphy, Cullen. "Women and the Bible." Atlantic Monthly Aug. 1993: 39-64.

National Research Council. China and Global Change: Opportunities for Collaboration. Washington: Natl. Acad., 1992.

Rabkin, Eric S., Martin H. Greenberg, and Joseph D. Olander. Preface. No Place Else: Explorations in Utopian and Dystopian Fiction. Ed. Rabkin, Greenberg, and Olander. Carbondale: Southern Illinois UP, 1983. vii-ix.

Taylor, Paul. "Keyboard Grief: Coping with Computer-Caused Injuries." Globe and Mail [Toronto] 27 Dec. 1993: A1+.

5.5. USING NOTES WITH PARENTHETICAL DOCUMENTATION

Two kinds of notes may be used with parenthetical documentation:

- Content notes offering the reader comment, explanation, or information that the text cannot accommodate
- Bibliographic notes containing either several sources or evaluative comments on sources

In providing this sort of supplementary information, place a superscript arabic numeral at the appropriate place in the text and write the note after a matching numeral either at the end of the text (as an endnote) or at the bottom of the page (as a footnote). See the examples in 5.5.1–2. For more information on using notes for documentation, see appendix B.

5.5.1. Content Notes

In your notes, avoid lengthy discussions that divert the reader's attention from the primary text. In general, comments that you cannot fit into the text should be omitted unless they provide essential justification or clarification of what you have written. You may use a note, for example, to give full publication facts for an original source for which you cite an indirect source and perhaps to explain why you worked from secondary material.

```
The commentary of the sixteenth-century literary
scholars Bernardo Segni and Lionardo Salviati shows them
to be less-than-faithful followers of Aristotle.[1]

                          Note
        [1] Examples are conveniently available in Weinberg.
See Segni, Rettorica et poetica d'Aristotile (Firenze,
1549) 281, qtd. in Weinberg 1: 405, and Salviati,
Poetica d'Aristotile parafrasata e comentata, 1586, ms.
2.2.11, Biblioteca Nazionale Centrale, Firenze, 140v,
qtd. in Weinberg 1: 616-17.
```

Work Cited

Weinberg, Bernard. <u>A History of Literary Criticism in
    the Italian Renaissance</u>. 2 vols. Chicago: U of
    Chicago P, 1961.

5.5.2. Bibliographic Notes

Use notes for evaluative comments on sources and for references containing numerous citations.

Many observers conclude that health care in the United
States is inadequate.[1]

Technological advancements have brought advantages as
well as unexpected problems.[2]

Notes

[1] For strong points of view on different aspects of
the issue, see Public Agenda Foundation 1-10 and Sakala
151-88.

[2] For a sampling of materials that reflect the
range of experiences related to recent technological
changes, see Taylor A1; Moulthrop, pars. 39-53;
Armstrong, Yang, and Cuneo 80-82; Craner 308-11; Kaku
42; Frank; and Alston.

Works Cited

Alston, Robin. "Bodley CD-ROM." Online posting. 15 June
    1994. ExLibris. 8 July 1998 <http://
    palimpsest.stanford.edu/byform/mailing-lists/
    exlibris/1994/06/msg00170.html>.

Armstrong, Larry, Dori Jones Yang, and Alice Cuneo. "The
    Learning Revolution: Technology Is Reshaping
    Education--at Home and at School." <u>Business Week</u> 28
    Feb. 1994: 80-88.

Craner, Paul M. "New Tool for an Ancient Art: The
    Computer and Music." <u>Computers and the Humanities</u>
    25 (1991): 303-13.

Frank, Holly. _Negative Space: A Computerized Video
    Novel_. Vers. 1.0. Diskette, videocassette. Prairie
    Village: Diskotech, 1990.

Kaku, Michio. _Hyperspace: A Scientific Odyssey through
    Parallel Universes, Time Warps, and the Tenth
    Dimension_. New York: Oxford UP, 1994.

Moulthrop, Stuart. "You Say You Want a Revolution?
    Hypertext and the Laws of Media." _Postmodern
    Culture_ 1.3 (1991): 53 pars. 12 July 1998 <http://
    jefferson.village.virginia.edu/pmc/text-only/
    issue.591/moulthro.591>.

Public Agenda Foundation. _The Health Care Crisis:
    Containing Costs, Expanding Coverage_. New York:
    McGraw, 1992.

Sakala, Carol. "Maternity Care Policy in the United
    States: Toward a More Rational and Effective
    System." Diss. Boston U, 1993.

Taylor, Paul. "Keyboard Grief: Coping with Computer-
    Caused Injuries." _Globe and Mail_ [Toronto] 27 Dec.
    1993: A1+.

6 Abbreviations

6.1. INTRODUCTION

Abbreviations are used regularly in the list of works cited and in tables but rarely in the text of a research paper (except within parentheses). In choosing abbreviations, keep your audience in mind. While economy of space is important, clarity is more so. Spell out a term if the abbreviation may puzzle your readers.

When abbreviating, always use accepted forms. In appropriate contexts, you may abbreviate the names of days, months, and other measurements of time (see 6.2); the names of states and countries (see 6.3); terms and reference words common in scholarship (see 6.4); publishers' names (see 6.5); and the titles of well-known literary and religious works (see 6.7).

The trend in abbreviation is to use neither periods after letters nor spaces between letters, especially for abbreviations made up of all capital letters.

BC	PhD	S
NJ	CD-ROM	US

The chief exception to this trend continues to be the initials used for personal names: a period and a space ordinarily follow each initial.

    J. R. R. Tolkien

Most abbreviations that end in lowercase letters are followed by periods.

assn.	fig.	Mex.
Eng.	introd.	prod.

In most abbreviations made up of lowercase letters that each represent a word, a period follows each letter, but no space intervenes between letters.

a.m.	i.e.
e.g.	n.p.

But there are numerous exceptions.

mph	os
ns	rpm

6.2. TIME DESIGNATIONS

Spell out the names of months in the text but abbreviate them in the
list of works cited, except for May, June, and July. Whereas words
denoting units of time are also spelled out in the text (*second, minute,
week, month, year, century*), some time designations are used only in
abbreviated form (*a.m., p.m., AD, BC, BCE, CE*).

AD	after the birth of Christ (from the Latin *anno Domini* 'in the year of the Lord'; used before numerals ["AD 14"] and after references to centuries ["twelfth century AD"])
a.m.	before noon (from the Latin *ante meridiem*)
Apr.	April
Aug.	August
BC	before Christ (used after numerals ["19 BC"] and references to centuries ["fifth century BC"])
BCE	before the common era (used after numerals and references to centuries)
CE	common era (used after numerals and references to centuries)
cent.	century
Dec.	December
Feb.	February
Fri.	Friday
hr.	hour
Jan.	January
Mar.	March
min.	minute
mo.	month
Mon.	Monday
Nov.	November
Oct.	October
p.m.	after noon (from the Latin *post meridiem*)
Sat.	Saturday
sec.	second
Sept.	September
Sun.	Sunday
Thurs.	Thursday
Tues.	Tuesday

Wed.	Wednesday
wk.	week
yr.	year

6.3. GEOGRAPHIC NAMES

Spell out the names of states, territories, and possessions of the United States in the text, except usually in addresses and sometimes in parentheses. Likewise, spell out in the text the names of countries, with a few exceptions (e.g., USSR). In documentation, however, abbreviate the names of states, provinces, and countries.

AB	Alberta
Afr.	Africa
AK	Alaska
AL	Alabama
Alb.	Albania
Ant.	Antarctica
AR	Arkansas
Arg.	Argentina
Arm.	Armenia
AS	American Samoa
Aus.	Austria
Austral.	Australia
AZ	Arizona
BC	British Columbia
Belg.	Belgium
Braz.	Brazil
Bulg.	Bulgaria
CA	California
Can.	Canada
CO	Colorado
CT	Connecticut
CZ	Canal Zone
DC	District of Columbia
DE	Delaware
Den.	Denmark
Ecua.	Ecuador
Eng.	England

Eur.	Europe
FL	Florida
Fr.	France
GA	Georgia
Ger.	Germany
Gr.	Greece
Gt. Brit.	Great Britain
GU	Guam
HI	Hawaii
Hung.	Hungary
IA	Iowa
ID	Idaho
IL	Illinois
IN	Indiana
Ire.	Ireland
Isr.	Israel
It.	Italy
Jap.	Japan
KS	Kansas
KY	Kentucky
LA	Louisiana
LB	Labrador
Leb.	Lebanon
MA	Massachusetts
MB	Manitoba
MD	Maryland
ME	Maine
Mex.	Mexico
MI	Michigan
MN	Minnesota
MO	Missouri
MS	Mississippi
MT	Montana
NB	New Brunswick
NC	North Carolina
ND	North Dakota
NE	Nebraska
Neth.	Netherlands
NF	Newfoundland
NH	New Hampshire
NJ	New Jersey

NM	New Mexico
No. Amer.	North America
Norw.	Norway
NS	Nova Scotia
NT	Northwest Territories
NV	Nevada
NY	New York
NZ	New Zealand
OH	Ohio
OK	Oklahoma
ON	Ontario
OR	Oregon
PA	Pennsylvania
Pan.	Panama
PE	Prince Edward Island
Pol.	Poland
Port.	Portugal
PQ	Quebec (Province de Québec)
PR	Puerto Rico
PRC	People's Republic of China
RI	Rhode Island
Russ.	Russia
SC	South Carolina
Scot.	Scotland
SD	South Dakota
SK	Saskatchewan
So. Amer.	South America
Sp.	Spain
Swed.	Sweden
Switz.	Switzerland
TN	Tennessee
Turk.	Turkey
TX	Texas
UK	United Kingdom
US, USA	United States, United States of America
USSR	Union of Soviet Socialist Republics
UT	Utah
VA	Virginia
VI	Virgin Islands
VT	Vermont
WA	Washington

WI	Wisconsin
WV	West Virginia
WY	Wyoming
YT	Yukon Territory

6.4. COMMON SCHOLARLY ABBREVIATIONS

The following list includes abbreviations commonly used in humanities research studies in English. Abbreviations within parentheses are alternative but not recommended forms. Most of the abbreviations listed would replace the spelled forms only in parentheses, tables, and documentation.

abbr.	abbreviation, abbreviated
abr.	abridgment, abridged
acad.	academy
adapt.	adapter, adaptation, adapted by
adj.	adjective
adv.	adverb
Amer.	America, American
anon.	anonymous
app.	appendix
arch.	archaic
art.	article
assn.	association
assoc.	associate, associated
attrib.	attributed to
aux.	auxiliary
b.	born
BA	bachelor of arts
bib.	biblical
bibliog.	bibliographer, bibliography, bibliographic
biog.	biographer, biography, biographical
bk.	book
BL	British Library, London
BM	British Museum, London (now British Library)
BS	bachelor of science
bull.	bulletin
©	copyright ("© 2001")

c. (ca.)	circa, *or* around (used with approximate dates: "c. 1796")
cap.	capital, capitalize
CD	compact disc
CD-ROM	compact disc read-only memory
cf.	compare (not "see"; from the Latin *confer*)
ch. (chap.)	chapter
chor.	choreographer, choreographed by
col.	column
coll.	college
colloq.	colloquial
com	commercial (used as a suffix in Internet domain names: "www.nytimes.com")
comp.	compiler, compiled by
compar.	comparative
cond.	conductor, conducted by
conf.	conference
Cong.	Congress
Cong. Rec.	*Congressional Record*
conj.	conjunction
Const.	Constitution
cont.	contents; continued
(contd.)	continued
d.	died
DA	doctor of arts
DA, DAI	*Dissertation Abstracts, Dissertation Abstracts International*
DAB	*Dictionary of American Biography*
def.	definition; definite
dept.	department
dev.	development, developed by
dict.	dictionary
dir.	director, directed by
diss.	dissertation
dist.	district
distr.	distributor, distributed by
div.	division
DNB	*Dictionary of National Biography*
doc.	document
DVD	originally *digital videodisc* but now used to describe discs containing a wide range of data

ed.	editor, edition, edited by
EdD	doctor of education
edu	educational (used as a suffix in Internet domain names: "www.indiana.edu")
educ.	education, educational
e.g.	for example (from the Latin *exempli gratia*; rarely capitalized; set off by commas, unless preceded by a different punctuation mark)
e-mail	electronic mail
encyc.	encyclopedia
enl.	enlarged (as in "rev. and enl. ed.")
esp.	especially
et al.	and others (from the Latin *et alii, et aliae*)
etc.	and so forth (from the Latin *et cetera*; like most abbreviations, not appropriate in text)
ex.	example
fac.	faculty
facsim.	facsimile
fig.	figure
fl.	flourished, *or* reached greatest development or influence (from the Latin *floruit*; used before dates of historical figures when birth and death dates are not known: "fl. 1200")
fr.	from
front.	frontispiece
FTP	File Transfer Protocol
fut.	future
fwd.	foreword, foreword by; forwarded (as in "fwd. by")
gen.	general (as in "gen. ed.")
gov	government (used as a suffix in Internet domain names: "www.census.gov")
govt.	government
GPO	Government Printing Office, Washington, DC
H. Doc.	House of Representatives Document
hist.	historian, history, historical
HMSO	Her (His) Majesty's Stationery Office, London
HR	House of Representatives
H. Rept.	House of Representatives Report
H. Res.	House of Representatives Resolution
HTML	Hypertext Markup Language
HTTP	Hypertext Transfer Protocol

i.e.	that is (from the Latin *id est*; rarely capitalized; set off by commas, unless preceded by a different punctuation mark)
illus.	illustrator, illustration, illustrated by
inc.	including; incorporated
infin.	infinitive
inst.	institute, institution
intl.	international
introd.	introduction, introduced by
ips	inches per second (used in reference to tape recordings)
irreg.	irregular
JD	doctor of law (from the Latin *juris doctor*)
jour.	journal
Jr.	Junior
KB	kilobyte
(l., ll.)	line, lines (avoided in favor of *line* and *lines* or, if clear, numbers only)
lang.	language
LC	Library of Congress
leg.	legal
legis.	legislator, legislation, legislature, legislative
lib.	library
lit.	literally; literature, literary
LLB	bachelor of laws (from the Latin *legum baccalaureus*)
LLD	doctor of laws (from the Latin *legum doctor*)
LLM	master of laws (from the Latin *legum magister*)
LP	long-playing phonograph record
ltd.	limited
MA	master of arts
mag.	magazine
MB	megabyte
MD	doctor of medicine (from the Latin *medicinae doctor*)
misc.	miscellaneous
mod.	modern
MOO	multiuser domain, object-oriented (cf. *MUD*)
MS	master of science
ms., mss.	manuscript, manuscripts (as in "Bodleian ms. Tanner 43"; cf. *ts., tss.*)

MUD	multiuser domain (cf. *MOO*)
n, nn	note, notes (used immediately after the number of the page containing the text of the note or notes: "56n," "56n3," "56nn3–5")
n.	noun
narr.	narrator, narrated by
natl.	national
NB	take notice (from the Latin *nota bene*; always capitalized)
n.d.	no date of publication
NED	*A New English Dictionary* (cf. *OED*)
no.	number (cf. *numb.*)
nonstand.	nonstandard
n.p.	no place of publication; no publisher
n. pag.	no pagination
ns	new series
NS	New Style (calendar designation)
numb.	numbered (cf. *no.*)
obj.	object, objective
obs.	obsolete
OCLC	Online Computer Library Center
OED	*The Oxford English Dictionary* (formerly *A New English Dictionary* [*NED*])
op.	opus (work)
orch.	orchestra (also Italian *orchestra*, French *orchestre*, etc.), orchestrated by
org	organization (used as a suffix in Internet domain names: "www.mla.org")
orig.	original, originally
os	old series; original series
OS	Old Style (calendar designation)
P	Press (used in documentation; cf. *UP*)
p., pp.	page, pages (omitted before page numbers unless necessary for clarity)
par.	paragraph
part.	participle
perf.	performer, performed by
PhD	doctor of philosophy (from the Latin *philosophiae doctor*)
philol.	philological
philos.	philosophical

pl.	plate; plural
poss.	possessive
pref.	preface, preface by
prep.	preposition
pres.	present
proc.	proceedings
prod.	producer, produced by
pron.	pronoun
pronunc.	pronunciation
PS	postscript
pseud.	pseudonym
pt.	part
pub. (publ.)	publisher, publication, published by
Pub. L.	Public Law
qtd.	quoted
r.	reigned
R	Reference (used to indicate the reference section in a library)
rec.	record, recorded
Ref	Reference (used to indicate the reference section in a library)
reg.	registered; regular
rel.	release
rept.	report, reported by
res.	resolution
resp.	respectively
rev.	review, reviewed by; revision, revised, revised by (spell out *review* where *rev.* might be ambiguous)
RLIN	Research Libraries Information Network
rpm	revolutions per minute (used in reference to phonograph recordings)
rpt.	reprint, reprinted by
S	Senate
sc.	scene (omitted when act and scene numbers are used together: "*King Lear* 4.1")
S. Doc.	Senate Document
sec. (sect.)	section
ser.	series
sess.	session

sic	thus in the source (in square brackets as an editorial interpolation, otherwise in parentheses; not followed by an exclamation point)
sing.	singular
soc.	society
spec.	special
Sr.	Senior
S. Rept.	Senate Report
S. Res.	Senate Resolution
st.	stanza
St., Sts. (S, SS)	Saint, Saints
Stat.	Statutes at Large
subj.	subject, subjective; subjunctive
substand.	substandard
supp.	supplement
syn.	synonym
trans. (tr.)	transitive; translator, translation, translated by
ts., tss.	typescript, typescripts (cf. *ms., mss.*)
U	University (also Spanish *Universidad*, Italian *Università*, German *Universität*, French *Université*, etc.; used in documentation; cf. *UP*)
univ.	university (used outside documentation—e.g., in parentheses and tables: "Montclair State Univ.")
UP	University Press (used in documentation: "Columbia UP")
URL	uniform resource locator
usu.	usually
var.	variant
vb.	verb
vers.	version
vol.	volume
vs. (v.)	versus (*v.* preferred in titles of legal cases)
writ.	writer, written by
www	World Wide Web (used in the names of servers, or computers, on the Web)

6.5. PUBLISHERS' NAMES

In the list of works cited, shortened forms of publishers' names immediately follow the cities of publication, enabling the reader to locate
books or to acquire more information about them. Since publications
like *Books in Print*, *Literary Market Place*, and *International Literary
Market Place* list publishers' addresses, you need give only enough
information so that your reader can look up the publishers in one of
these sources. It is usually sufficient, for example, to give "Harcourt"
as the publisher's name even if the title page shows "Harcourt Brace"
or one of the earlier names of that firm (Harcourt, Brace; Harcourt,
Brace, and World; Harcourt Brace Jovanovich). If you are preparing a
bibliographic study, however, or if publication history is important to
your paper, give the publisher's name in full.

In shortening publishers' names, keep in mind the following points:

- Omit articles (*A*, *An*, *The*), business abbreviations (*Co.*, *Corp.*, *Inc.*,
  Ltd.), and descriptive words (*Books*, *House*, *Press*, *Publishers*).
  When citing a university press, however, always add the abbrevia-
  tion *P* (Ohio State UP) because the university itself may publish
  independently of its press (Ohio State U).
- If the publisher's name includes the name of one person (Harry N.
  Abrams, W. W. Norton, John Wiley), cite the surname alone
  (Abrams, Norton, Wiley). If the publisher's name includes the
  names of more than one person, cite only the first of the surnames
  (Bobbs, Dodd, Faber, Farrar, Funk, Grosset, Harcourt, Harper,
  Houghton, McGraw, Prentice, Simon).
- Use standard abbreviations whenever possible (*Acad.*, *Assn.*,
  Soc., *UP*; see 6.4).
- If the publisher's name is commonly abbreviated with capital ini-
  tial letters and if the abbreviation is likely to be familiar to your
  audience, use the abbreviation as the publisher's name (GPO,
  MLA, UMI). If your readers are not likely to know the abbrevia-
  tion, shorten the name according to the general guidelines given
  above (Mod. Lang. Assn.).

Following are examples of how various types of publishers' names
are shortened:

Acad. for Educ. Dev.	Academy for Educational Development, Inc.
ALA	American Library Association
Basic	Basic Books

CAL	Center for Applied Linguistics
Cambridge UP	Cambridge University Press
Eastgate	Eastgate Systems
Einaudi	Giulio Einaudi Editore
ERIC	Educational Resources Information Center
Farrar	Farrar, Straus and Giroux, Inc.
Feminist	The Feminist Press at the City University of New York
Gale	Gale Research, Inc.
Gerig	Gerig Verlag
GPO	Government Printing Office
Harper	Harper and Row, Publishers, Inc.; HarperCollins Publishers, Inc.
Harvard Law Rev. Assn.	Harvard Law Review Association
HMSO	Her (His) Majesty's Stationery Office
Houghton	Houghton Mifflin Co.
Knopf	Alfred A. Knopf, Inc.
Larousse	Librairie Larousse
Little	Little, Brown and Company, Inc.
Macmillan	Macmillan Publishing Co., Inc.
McGraw	McGraw-Hill, Inc.
MIT P	The MIT Press
MLA	The Modern Language Association of America
NCTE	The National Council of Teachers of English
NEA	The National Education Association
Norton	W. W. Norton and Co., Inc.
PUF	Presses Universitaires de France
Random	Random House, Inc.
Scribner's	Charles Scribner's Sons
Simon	Simon and Schuster, Inc.
SIRS	Social Issues Resources Series
State U of New York P	State University of New York Press
St. Martin's	St. Martin's Press, Inc.
UMI	University Microfilms International
U of Chicago P	University of Chicago Press
UP of Mississippi	University Press of Mississippi

6.6. SYMBOLS AND ABBREVIATIONS USED IN PROOFREADING AND CORRECTION

6.6.1. Selected Proofreading Symbols

Proofreaders use the symbols below when correcting typeset material. Many instructors also use them in marking student papers.

✓	add an apostrophe or a single quotation mark
⌒	close up (basket ball)
⋀	add a comma
ℓ	delete
⋀	insert
¶	begin a new paragraph
No ¶	do not begin a new paragraph
⊙	add a period
✓✓	add double quotation marks
#	add space
∿	transpose elements (usually with *tr* in margin) (the*t*)

6.6.2. Common Correction Symbols and Abbreviations

‖	lack of parallelism
ab	faulty abbreviation
adj	improper use of adjective
adv	improper use of adverb
agr	faulty agreement
amb	ambiguous expression or construction
awk	awkward expression or construction
cap	faulty capitalization
d	faulty diction
dgl	dangling construction
frag	fragment
lc	use lowercase
num	error in use of numbers
p	faulty punctuation
ref	unclear pronoun reference
rep	unnecessary repetition
r-o	run-on sentence

sp	error in spelling
ss	faulty sentence structure
t	wrong tense of verb
tr	transpose elements
vb	wrong verb form
wdy	wordy writing

6.7. TITLES OF LITERARY AND RELIGIOUS WORKS

In documentation, you may abbreviate the titles of works and parts of works. It is usually best to introduce an abbreviation in parentheses immediately after the first use of the full title in the text: "In *All's Well That Ends Well* (*AWW*), Shakespeare [. . .]." Abbreviating titles is appropriate, for example, if you repeatedly cite a variety of works by the same author. In such a discussion, abbreviations make for more concise parenthetical documentation—"(*AWW* 3.2.100–29)," "(*MM* 4.3.93–101)"—than the usual shortened titles would: "(*All's Well* 3.2.100–29)," "(*Measure* 4.3.93–101)." For works not on the following lists, you may use the abbreviations you find in your sources, or you may devise simple, unambiguous abbreviations of your own.

6.7.1. Bible

The following abbreviations and spelled forms are commonly used for parts of the Bible (Bib.).

Old Testament (OT)

Gen.	Genesis
Exod.	Exodus
Lev.	Leviticus
Num.	Numbers
Deut.	Deuteronomy
Josh.	Joshua
Judg.	Judges
Ruth	Ruth
1 Sam.	1 Samuel

2 Sam.	2 Samuel
1 Kings	1 Kings
2 Kings	2 Kings
1 Chron.	1 Chronicles
2 Chron.	2 Chronicles
Ezra	Ezra
Neh.	Nehemiah
Esth.	Esther
Job	Job
Ps.	Psalms
Prov.	Proverbs
Eccles.	Ecclesiastes
Song Sol. (also Cant.)	Song of Solomon (also Canticles)
Isa.	Isaiah
Jer.	Jeremiah
Lam.	Lamentations
Ezek.	Ezekiel
Dan.	Daniel
Hos.	Hosea
Joel	Joel
Amos	Amos
Obad.	Obadiah
Jon.	Jonah
Mic.	Micah
Nah.	Nahum
Hab.	Habakkuk
Zeph.	Zephaniah
Hag.	Haggai
Zech.	Zechariah
Mal.	Malachi

Selected Apocryphal and Deuterocanonical Works

1 Esd.	1 Esdras
2 Esd.	2 Esdras
Tob.	Tobit
Jth.	Judith
Esth. (Apocr.)	Esther (Apocrypha)
Wisd. Sol. (also Wisd.)	Wisdom of Solomon (also Wisdom)
Ecclus. (also Sir.)	Ecclesiasticus (also Sirach)
Bar.	Baruch

Song 3 Childr.	Song of the Three Children
Sus.	Susanna
Bel and Dr.	Bel and the Dragon
Pr. Man.	Prayer of Manasseh
1 Macc.	1 Maccabees
2 Macc.	2 Maccabees

New Testament (NT)

Matt.	Matthew
Mark	Mark
Luke	Luke
John	John
Acts	Acts
Rom.	Romans
1 Cor.	1 Corinthians
2 Cor.	2 Corinthians
Gal.	Galatians
Eph.	Ephesians
Phil.	Philippians
Col.	Colossians
1 Thess.	1 Thessalonians
2 Thess.	2 Thessalonians
1 Tim.	1 Timothy
2 Tim.	2 Timothy
Tit.	Titus
Philem.	Philemon
Heb.	Hebrews
Jas.	James
1 Pet.	1 Peter
2 Pet.	2 Peter
1 John	1 John
2 John	2 John
3 John	3 John
Jude	Jude
Rev. (also Apoc.)	Revelation (also Apocalypse)

Selected Apocryphal Works

G. Thom.	Gospel of Thomas
G. Heb.	Gospel of the Hebrews
G. Pet.	Gospel of Peter

6.7.2. Shakespeare

Ado	*Much Ado about Nothing*
Ant.	*Antony and Cleopatra*
AWW	*All's Well That Ends Well*
AYL	*As You Like It*
Cor.	*Coriolanus*
Cym.	*Cymbeline*
Err.	*The Comedy of Errors*
F1	First Folio edition (1623)
F2	Second Folio edition (1632)
Ham.	*Hamlet*
1H4	*Henry IV, Part 1*
2H4	*Henry IV, Part 2*
H5	*Henry V*
1H6	*Henry VI, Part 1*
2H6	*Henry VI, Part 2*
3H6	*Henry VI, Part 3*
H8	*Henry VIII*
JC	*Julius Caesar*
Jn.	*King John*
LC	*A Lover's Complaint*
LLL	*Love's Labour's Lost*
Lr.	*King Lear*
Luc.	*The Rape of Lucrece*
Mac.	*Macbeth*
MM	*Measure for Measure*
MND	*A Midsummer Night's Dream*
MV	*The Merchant of Venice*
Oth.	*Othello*
Per.	*Pericles*
PhT	*The Phoenix and the Turtle*
PP	*The Passionate Pilgrim*
Q	Quarto edition
R2	*Richard II*
R3	*Richard III*
Rom.	*Romeo and Juliet*
Shr.	*The Taming of the Shrew*
Son.	*Sonnets*
TGV	*The Two Gentlemen of Verona*

Tim.	*Timon of Athens*
Tit.	*Titus Andronicus*
Tmp.	*The Tempest*
TN	*Twelfth Night*
TNK	*The Two Noble Kinsmen*
Tro.	*Troilus and Cressida*
Ven.	*Venus and Adonis*
Wiv.	*The Merry Wives of Windsor*
WT	*The Winter's Tale*

6.7.3. Chaucer

BD	*The Book of the Duchess*
CkT	The Cook's Tale
ClT	The Clerk's Tale
CT	*The Canterbury Tales*
CYT	The Canon's Yeoman's Tale
FranT	The Franklin's Tale
FrT	The Friar's Tale
GP	The General Prologue
HF	*The House of Fame*
KnT	The Knight's Tale
LGW	*The Legend of Good Women*
ManT	The Manciple's Tale
Mel	The Tale of Melibee
MerT	The Merchant's Tale
MilT	The Miller's Tale
MkT	The Monk's Tale
MLT	The Man of Law's Tale
NPT	The Nun's Priest's Tale
PardT	The Pardoner's Tale
ParsT	The Parson's Tale
PF	*The Parliament of Fowls*
PhyT	The Physician's Tale
PrT	The Prioress's Tale
Ret	Chaucer's Retraction
RvT	The Reeve's Tale
ShT	The Shipman's Tale
SNT	The Second Nun's Tale

SqT	The Squire's Tale
SumT	The Summoner's Tale
TC	*Troilus and Criseyde*
Th	The Tale of Sir Thopas
WBT	The Wife of Bath's Tale

6.7.4. Other Literary Works

Aen.	Vergil, *Aeneid*
Ag.	Aeschylus, *Agamemnon*
Ant.	Sophocles, *Antigone*
Bac.	Euripides, *Bacchae*
Beo.	*Beowulf*
Can.	Voltaire, *Candide*
Dec.	Boccaccio, *Decameron*
DJ	Byron, *Don Juan*
DQ	Cervantes, *Don Quixote*
Eum.	Aeschylus, *Eumenides*
FQ	Spenser, *The Faerie Queene*
Gil.	*Epic of Gilgamesh*
GT	Swift, *Gulliver's Travels*
Hept.	Marguerite de Navarre, *Heptaméron*
Hip.	Euripides, *Hippolytus*
Il.	Homer, *Iliad*
Inf.	Dante, *Inferno*
LB	Wordsworth, *Lyrical Ballads*
Lys.	Aristophanes, *Lysistrata*
MD	Melville, *Moby-Dick*
Med.	Euripides, *Medea*
Mis.	Molière, *Le misanthrope*
Nib.	*Nibelungenlied*
Od.	Homer, *Odyssey*
OR	Sophocles, *Oedipus Rex* (also called *Oedipus Tyrannus* [*OT*])
Or.	Aeschylus, *Oresteia*
OT	Sophocles, *Oedipus Tyrannus* (also called *Oedipus Rex* [*OR*])
Par.	Dante, *Paradiso*
PL	Milton, *Paradise Lost*
Prel.	Wordsworth, *The Prelude*
Purg.	Dante, *Purgatorio*

Rep.	Plato, *Republic*
SA	Milton, *Samson Agonistes*
SGGK	*Sir Gawain and the Green Knight*
Sym.	Plato, *Symposium*
Tar.	Molière, *Tartuffe*

Appendix A: Selected Reference Works by Field

A.1. Anthropology

A.2. Art

A.3. Biology

A.4. Business

A.5. Chemistry

A.6. Computer Science

A.7. Education

A.8. Environmental Sciences

A.9. Geography

A.10. Geology

A.11. History

A.12. Language and Literature

A.13. Law

A.14. Mathematics

A.15. Medicine

A.16. Music

A.17. Philosophy

A.18. Physics

A.19. Psychology

A.20. Religion

A.21. Science and Technology

A.22. Sociology

Each of the sections below is divided into two parts. The first contains titles of indexes, abstracts collections, annual bibliographies, and other such periodically published reference works; the availability of online and CD-ROM versions is indicated when relevant. The second part of each section contains titles of dictionaries, encyclopedias, and similar reference works.

A.1. ANTHROPOLOGY

Abstracts in Anthropology. Farmingdale: Baywood, 1970– .
Anthropological Literature. Pleasantville: Redgrave, 1979– . Available online and on CD-ROM.

Companion Encyclopedia of Anthropology. Ed. Tim Ingold. New York: Routledge, 1994.
The Dictionary of Anthropology. Ed. Thomas J. Barfield. New York: Blackwell, 1997.

A.2. ART

Art Index. New York: Wilson, 1929– . Available online and on CD-ROM.
Avery Index to Architectural Periodicals. 2nd ed. Boston: Hall, 1973– . Available online and on CD-ROM.
BHA: Bibliography of the History of Art / Bibliographie d'histoire de l'art. Vandoeuvre-lès-Nancy: Centre National de la Recherche Scientifique; Santa Monica: Getty Art History Information Program, 1991– . Available online and on CD-ROM.

The Dictionary of Art. Ed. Jane Turner. 34 vols. New York: Grove, 1996.
Encyclopedia of World Art. 17 vols. New York: McGraw, 1959–87.
McGraw-Hill Dictionary of Art. Ed. Bernard S. Myers. 5 vols. New York: McGraw, 1969.
The Oxford Dictionary of Art. Ed. Ian Chilvers and Harold Osborne. 2nd ed. New York: Oxford UP, 1997.

A.3. BIOLOGY

Biological Abstracts. Philadelphia: Biosis, 1926– . Available online (as part of *Biosis Previews*) and on CD-ROM.
Biological and Agricultural Index. New York: Wilson, 1964– . Available online and on CD-ROM.

Chambers Biology Dictionary. Ed. Peter Walker. 4th ed. New York: Cambridge UP, 1989.
Encyclopedia of Bioethics. Ed. Warren T. Reich. Rev. ed. 5 vols. New York: Macmillan-Simon, 1995.
Encyclopedia of Human Biology. Ed. Renato Dulbecco. 8 vols. San Diego: Harcourt, 1991.
Henderson's Dictionary of Biological Terms. Ed. Eleanor Lawrence. 11th ed. New York: Wiley, 1995.
The Penguin Dictionary of Biology. Ed. M. L. J. Abercrombie et al. 9th ed. New York: Viking, 1995.

A.4. BUSINESS

ABI/Inform. Ann Arbor: UMI, 1971– . Available online and on CD-ROM.
Business Periodicals Index. New York: Wilson, 1958– . Available online and on CD-ROM.
PAIS. New York: Public Affairs Information Service, 1972– . Available online and on CD-ROM.
Predicasts F and S Indexes. Cleveland: Predicasts, 1968– . Available online and on CD-ROM.

Dictionary of Business and Economics. Ed. Christine Ammer and Dean Ammer. Rev. ed. New York: Free, 1984.
Dictionary of Business and Management. Ed. Jerry M. Rosenberg. 3rd ed. New York: Wiley, 1992.
A Dictionary of Economics. Ed. John Black. New York: Oxford UP, 1997.
The HarperCollins Dictionary of Economics. Ed. Christopher Pass. New York: Harper, 1991.
McGraw-Hill Encyclopedia of Economics. Ed. Douglas Greenwald. 2nd ed. New York: McGraw, 1993.

The MIT Dictionary of Modern Economics. Ed. David Pearce. 4th ed. Cambridge: MIT P, 1992.

A.5. CHEMISTRY

Chemical Abstracts. Washington: Amer. Chemical Soc., 1907– . Available online and on CD-ROM.

Hawley's Condensed Chemical Dictionary. Ed. Richard J. Lewis. 13th ed. New York: Wiley, 1997.

Lange's Handbook of Chemistry. Ed. John A. Dean. 14th ed. New York: McGraw, 1992.

Macmillan Encyclopedia of Chemistry. Ed. Joseph J. Lagowski. 4 vols. New York: Macmillan, 1996.

Van Nostrand Reinhold Encyclopedia of Chemistry. Ed. Douglas M. Considine. 4th ed. New York: Van Nostrand, 1984.

A.6. COMPUTER SCIENCE

ACM Guide to Computing Literature. New York: Assn. for Computing Machinery, 1977– . Available online and on CD-ROM as part of *MathSciNet.*

Computer Abstracts. London: Technical Information, 1957– . Available online and on CD-ROM.

Computer Literature Index. Phoenix: Applied Computer Research, 1980– .

Dictionary of Computing. Ed. Valerie Illingsworth. 4th ed. Oxford: Oxford UP, 1997.

Encyclopedia of Computer Science. Ed. Anthony Ralston. 4th ed. New York: Wiley, 1997.

Macmillan Encyclopedia of Computers. Ed. Gary Bitter. 2 vols. New York: Macmillan, 1992.

A.7. EDUCATION

CIJE: Current Index to Journals in Education. Phoenix: Oryx, 1969– .
Available online and on CD-ROM as part of *ERIC.*
Education Index. New York: Wilson, 1929– . Available online and on
CD-ROM.
ERIC: Educational Resources Information Center. Washington: GPO,
1966- . Available online and on CD-ROM.
Resources in Education. Washington: GPO, 1967– . Available online
and on CD-ROM as part of *ERIC.*

Dictionary of Education. Ed. Fred Goodman. Phoenix: Oryx, 1998.
The Encyclopedia of Education. Ed. Lee C. Deighton. 10 vols. New
York: Free, 1971.
Encyclopedia of Educational Research. Ed. Marvin C. Alkin. 6th ed. 4
vols. New York: Macmillan, 1992.
World Education Encyclopedia. Ed. George T. Kurian. 3 vols. New
York: Facts on File, 1988.

A.8. ENVIRONMENTAL SCIENCES

Ecology Abstracts. Bethesda: Cambridge Scientific Abstracts, 1975– .
Available online.
Environment Abstracts. New York: Environment Information Center,
1971– . Available online and on CD-ROM.
Environmental Periodicals Bibliography. Santa Barbara: Environmen-
tal Studies Inst., 1972– . Available online and on CD-ROM.
Environment Index. New York: Environment Information Center,
1971– .
Pollution Abstracts. Bethesda: Cambridge Scientific Abstracts, 1970– .
Available online.

Dictionary of the Environment. Ed. Michael Allaby. 3rd ed. New York:
New York UP, 1989.
Encyclopedia of Ecology and Environmental Management. Ed. Peter
Calow. New York: Blackwell, 1997.
Environment Dictionary. Ed. David Kemp. New York: Routledge, 1998.

McGraw-Hill Encyclopedia of Environmental Science and Engineering. Ed. Sybil Parker. 3rd ed. New York: McGraw, 1993.

A.9. GEOGRAPHY

Geographical Abstracts. Norwich, Eng.: Geo Abstracts, 1972– . Available online and on CD-ROM as part of *Geobase.*

Companion Encyclopedia of Geography. Ed. Richard J. Huggett, M. E. Robinson, and Ian Douglas. New York: Routledge, 1996.
Encyclopedia of Geographic Information Sources. Ed. Jennifer Mossman. 4th ed. 2 vols. Detroit: Gale, 1986.
Longman Dictionary of Geography. Ed. Audrey N. Clark. London: Longman, 1986.
Modern Geography: An Encyclopedic Survey. Ed. Gary S. Dunbar. New York: Garland, 1991.

A.10. GEOLOGY

Bibliography and Index of Geology. Alexandria: Amer. Geological Inst., 1933– . Available online and on CD-ROM as part of *GeoRef.*

Challinor's Dictionary of Geology. 6th ed. New York: Oxford UP, 1986.
The Encyclopedia of Field and General Geology. Ed. Charles W. Finkl. New York: Van Nostrand, 1988.
McGraw-Hill Encyclopedia of the Geological Sciences. Ed. Sybil Parker. 2nd ed. New York: McGraw, 1988.
The New Penguin Dictionary of Geology. Ed. Philip Kearey. New York: Viking, 1996.

A.11. HISTORY

America: History and Life. Santa Barbara: ABC-Clio, 1964– . Available online and on CD-ROM.
Historical Abstracts. Santa Barbara: ABC-Clio, 1955– . Available online and on CD-ROM.

Dictionary of American History. Ed. James Adams. Rev. ed. 8 vols. New York: Scribner's, 1976.

Encyclopedia of American History. Ed. Richard B. Morris. 7th ed. New York: Harper, 1996.

An Encyclopedia of World History. Ed. William L. Langer. 5th ed. Boston: Houghton, 1972.

Larousse Dictionary of World History. Ed. Bruce Leman. New York: Larousse, 1995.

A.12. LANGUAGE AND LITERATURE

L'année philologique: Bibliographie critique et analytique de l'antiquité gréco-latine. Paris: Belles Lettres, 1924– . Available on CD-ROM as *DCB: Database of Classical Bibliography.*

Bibliographie linguistique / Linguistic Bibliography. Dordrecht: Kluwer, 1949– .

LLBA: Linguistics and Language Behavior Abstracts. San Diego: Sociological Abstracts, 1974– . Available online and on CD-ROM.

MLA International Bibliography. New York: MLA, 1921– . Available online and on CD-ROM.

The Cambridge Encyclopedia of Language. Ed. David Crystal. 2nd ed. New York: Cambridge UP, 1997.

The Cambridge Guide to Literature in English. Ed. Ian Ousby. 2nd ed. Cambridge: Cambridge UP, 1994.

The Cambridge Guide to World Theatre. Ed. Martin Banham. Cambridge: Cambridge UP, 1988.

An Encyclopaedia of Language. Ed. N. E. Collinge. New York: Routledge, 1990.

International Encyclopedia of Linguistics. Ed. William Bright. 4 vols. New York: Oxford UP, 1992.

Literary Research Guide. By James L. Harner. 3rd ed. New York: MLA, 1998.

The New Princeton Encyclopedia of Poetry and Poetics. Ed. Alex Preminger and T. V. F. Brogan. Princeton: Princeton UP, 1993.

The Oxford Classical Dictionary. Ed. Simon Hornblower and Antony Spawforth. 3rd ed. Oxford: Oxford UP, 1996.

The Oxford Companion to American Literature. Ed. James D. Hart and Phillip Leininger. 6th ed. New York: Oxford UP, 1995.

The Oxford Companion to Canadian Literature. Ed. Eugene Benson and William Toye. 2nd ed. New York: Oxford UP, 1998.

The Oxford Companion to Classical Literature. Ed. M. C. Howatson. 2nd ed. New York: Oxford UP, 1989.

The Oxford Companion to English Literature. Ed. Margaret Drabble. 5th ed. New York: Oxford UP, 1985.

A.13. LAW

Criminal Justice Abstracts. Monsey: Willow Tree, 1977– . Available online and on CD-ROM.

Criminal Justice Periodical Index. Ann Arbor: UMI, 1975– . Available online.

Index to Legal Periodicals and Books. New York: Wilson, 1908– . Available online and on CD-ROM.

Black's Law Dictionary. 6th ed. Saint Paul: West, 1990.

A Dictionary of Modern Legal Usage. Ed. Bryan A. Garner. 2nd ed. New York: Oxford UP, 1991.

Encyclopedia of Crime and Justice. Ed. Sanford H. Kadish. 4 vols. New York: Free, 1983.

A.14. MATHEMATICS

Mathematical Reviews. Providence: Amer. Mathematical Soc., 1940– . Available online and on CD-ROM as part of *MathSciNet.*

Companion Encyclopedia of the History and Philosophy of the Mathematical Sciences. Ed. Ivor Gratten-Guinness. New York: Routledge, 1993.

Encyclopedic Dictionary of Mathematics. Ed. Kiyosi Itô. 2nd ed. 4 vols. Cambridge: MIT P, 1987.

The HarperCollins Dictionary of Mathematics. Ed. E. J. Borowski and Jonathan M. Borwein. New York: Harper, 1991.

A.15. MEDICINE

Cumulative Index to Nursing and Allied Health Literature. Glendale: CINAHL Information Systems, 1977– . Available online and on CD-ROM as *Nursing and Allied Health Database.*
Index Medicus. Bethesda: US Natl. Lib. of Medicine, 1960– . Available online and on CD-ROM as part of *Medline.*

The American Medical Association Encyclopedia of Medicine. Ed. Charles B. Clayman. New York: Random, 1989.
Dorland's Illustrated Medical Dictionary. 28th ed. Philadelphia: Saunders, 1994.
Stedman's Medical Dictionary. 26th ed. Baltimore: Williams, 1995.

A.16. MUSIC

The Music Index. Detroit: Information Coordinators, 1949– . Available on CD-ROM.
RILM Abstracts of Musical Literature. New York: RILM, 1967– . Available online and on CD-ROM.

The HarperCollins Dictionary of Music. Ed. Christine Ammer. 3rd ed. New York: Harper, 1995.
The New Grove Dictionary of American Music. Ed. H. Wiley Hitchcock and Stanley Sadie. 4 vols. London: Macmillan, 1986.
The New Grove Dictionary of Music and Musicians. Ed. Stanley Sadie. 20 vols. New York: Macmillan, 1980.
The New Grove Dictionary of Opera. 4 vols. New York: Macmillan, 1992.
The New Harvard Dictionary of Music. Ed. Don M. Randel. Cambridge: Harvard UP, 1986.
The New Oxford Companion to Music. Ed. Denis Arnold. 2 vols. 1983. Oxford: Oxford UP, 1990.

A.17. PHILOSOPHY

The Philosopher's Index. Bowling Green: Bowling Green State U, 1967– . Available online and on CD-ROM.

Dictionary of Philosophy. Ed. Alan R. Lacey. 3rd ed. New York: Routledge, 1996.

Encyclopedia of Ethics. Ed. Lawrence C. Becker and Charlotte B. Becker. 2 vols. New York: Garland, 1992.

The Encyclopedia of Philosophy. Ed. Paul Edwards. 8 vols. New York: Free, 1967.

The HarperCollins Dictionary of Philosophy. Ed. Peter A. Angeles. 2nd ed. New York: Harper, 1992.

The Oxford Companion to Philosophy. Ed. Ted Honderich. New York: Oxford UP, 1995.

A.18. PHYSICS

Physics Abstracts. Surrey: Inst. of Electrical Engineers, 1898– . Available online and on CD-ROM as part of *Inspec.*

The Encyclopedia of Physics. Ed. Robert M. Besançon. 3rd ed. New York: Van Nostrand, 1985.

Encyclopedia of Physics. Ed. Rita G. Lerner and George L. Trigg. 2nd ed. New York: VCH, 1991.

McGraw-Hill Encyclopedia of Physics. Ed. Sybil Parker. 2nd ed. New York: McGraw, 1993.

A.19. PSYCHOLOGY

Psychological Abstracts. Washington: Amer. Psychological Assn., 1927– . Available online as *PsycINFO* and on CD-ROM as *PsycLIT.*

Companion Encyclopedia of Psychology. Ed. Andrew M. Colman. New York: Routledge, 1994.

Encyclopedia of Psychology. Ed. Raymond J. Corsini. 2nd ed. 4 vols. New York: Wiley, 1994.

The International Dictionary of Psychology. Ed. Stuart Sutherland. New York: Continuum, 1989.

A.20. RELIGION

Religion Index. Chicago: Amer. Theological Lib. Assn., 1977– . Available online and on CD-ROM.

The Anchor Bible Dictionary. Ed. David Noel Freedman et al. 6 vols. New York: Doubleday, 1992.

The Dictionary of Bible and Religion. Ed. William H. Gentz. Nashville: Abingdon, 1986.

The Encyclopedia of Religion. Ed. Mircea Eliade. 16 vols. New York: Macmillan, 1987.

The HarperCollins Dictionary of Religion. Ed. Jonathan Z. Smith et al. New York: Harper, 1995.

The International Standard Bible Encyclopedia. Ed. Geoffrey W. Bromiley et al. 4 vols. Grand Rapids: Eerdsmans, 1979–88.

A.21. SCIENCE AND TECHNOLOGY

Applied Science and Technology Index. New York: Wilson, 1958– . Available online and on CD-ROM.

Engineering Index. New York: Engineering Information, 1906– . Available online and on CD-ROM as part of *Compendex.*

General Science Index. New York: Wilson, 1978– . Available online and on CD-ROM.

Science Citation Index. Philadelphia: Inst. for Scientific Information, 1945– . Available online and on CD-ROM as part of *SciSearch.*

Hammond Barnhart Dictionary of Science. Ed. Robert Barnhart. Maplewood: Hammond, 1986.

McGraw-Hill Encyclopedia of Engineering. Ed. Sybil Parker. 2nd ed. New York: McGraw, 1993.

McGraw-Hill Encyclopedia of Science and Technology. Ed. Sybil Parker. 8th ed. 20 vols. New York: McGraw, 1997.

A.22. SOCIOLOGY

Sociological Abstracts. San Diego: Sociological Abstracts, 1953– . Available online and on CD-ROM as part of *Sociofile.*

Encyclopedia of Sociology. Ed. Edgar F. Borgatta and Marie L. Borgatta.
4 vols. New York: Macmillan, 1992.

The HarperCollins Dictionary of Sociology. Ed. David Jary and Julia
Jary. New York: Harper, 1991.

Appendix B:
Other Systems
of Documentation

This appendix describes three documentation systems other than the MLA system. The appendix ends with a selected list of specialized style manuals.

B.1. ENDNOTES AND FOOTNOTES

Some scholars in the fields of art, dance, history, music, religion, theater, and theology use endnotes or footnotes to document sources.

B.1.1. Documentation Notes versus the List of Works Cited and Parenthetical References

If you use notes for documentation, you may not need a list of works cited or a bibliography. (Check your instructor's preference.) The first note referring to a source includes the publication information found in a bibliographic entry—the author's name, the title, and the publication facts—as well as the page reference identifying the portion of the source you refer to at that point in the text. (Subsequent references to the work require less information; see B.1.9.) A bibliographic entry for a work published as part of a book or periodical usually ends with the inclusive page numbers for the entire work cited, but a documentation note, in contrast, ends with the page number or numbers only of the portion you refer to. Note form differs slightly from bibliographic form in other ways (see B.1.3), and note numbers replace parenthetical references at the points in the text where citations are necessary (see B.1.2). Documentation notes appear either at the end of the text, as endnotes, or at the bottoms of relevant pages, as footnotes (see B.1.4).

B.1.2. Note Numbers

Number notes consecutively, starting from 1, throughout a research paper, except for any notes accompanying special material, such as a figure or a table (see 3.7). Do not number them by page or designate them by asterisks or other symbols. Format note numbers as superior, or superscript, arabic numerals (i.e., raised slightly above the line, like this[1]), without periods, parentheses, or slashes. The numbers follow punctuation marks, except dashes. In general, to avoid interrupting the continuity of the text, place a note number, like a parenthetical reference, at the end of the sentence, clause, or phrase containing the material quoted or referred to.

B.1.3. Note Form versus Bibliographic Form

With some exceptions, documentation notes and bibliographic entries provide the same information but differ in form.

Bibliographic Form

A bibliographic entry has three main divisions, each followed by a period: the author's name reversed for alphabetizing, the title, and the publication data.

> Tannen, Deborah. <u>You Just Don't Understand: Women and Men in Conversation</u>. New York: Morrow, 1990.

Note Form

A documentation note has four main divisions: the author's name in normal order, followed by a comma; the title; the publication data in parentheses; and a page reference. There is a period only at the end.

> [1] Deborah Tannen, <u>You Just Don't Understand: Women and Men in Conversation</u> (New York: Morrow, 1990) 52.

B.1.4. Endnotes versus Footnotes

In research papers, make all notes endnotes, unless you are instructed otherwise. As their name implies, endnotes appear after the text, starting on a new page numbered in sequence with the preceding page. Center the title *Notes* one inch from the top, double-space, indent one-half inch (or five spaces, if you are using a typewriter) from the left margin, and add the note number, without punctuation, slightly above the line. Type a space and then the reference. If the note extends to two or more lines, begin subsequent lines at the left margin. Type the notes consecutively, double-spaced, and number all pages.

Footnotes appear at the bottoms of pages, beginning four lines (two double spaces) below the text. Single-space footnotes, but double-space between them. When a note continues on the following page, add a solid line across the new page two lines (one double space) below the last line of the text and continue the note two lines (one double space) below the solid line. Footnotes for the new page immediately follow the note continued from the previous page, after a double space.

B.1.5. Sample First Note References: Books and Other Nonperiodical Publications

For additional information on citing the following types of sources, consult the related sections on bibliographic entries, indicated in parentheses after the headings.

a. A Book by a Single Author (4.6.1)

[1] Frank R. Wilson, <u>The Hand: How Its Use Shapes the Brain, Language, and Human Culture</u> (New York: Pantheon, 1998) 32.

b. An Anthology or a Compilation (4.6.2)

[2] Paula R. Feldman, ed., <u>British Women Poets of the Romantic Era</u> (Baltimore: Johns Hopkins UP, 1997).

c. A Book by Two or More Authors (4.6.4)

[3] James W. Marquart, Sheldon Ekland Olson, and Jonathan R. Sorensen, <u>The Rope, the Chair, and the Needle: Capital Punishment in Texas, 1923-1990</u> (Austin: U of Texas P, 1994) 52-57.

d. A Book by a Corporate Author (4.6.6)

[4] Public Agenda Foundation, <u>The Health Care Crisis: Containing Costs, Expanding Coverage</u> (New York: McGraw, 1992) 69.

e. A Work in an Anthology (4.6.7)

[5] Isabel Allende, "Toad's Mouth," trans. Margaret Sayers Peden, <u>A Hammock beneath the Mangoes: Stories from Latin America</u>, ed. Thomas Colchie (New York: Plume, 1992) 83.

f. An Article in a Reference Book (4.6.8)

[6] "Mandarin," The Encyclopedia Americana, 1994 ed.

g. An Introduction, a Preface, a Foreword, or an Afterword (4.6.9)

[7] Emory Elliott, afterword, The Jungle, by Upton Sinclair (New York: Signet, 1990) 348-50.

h. An Anonymous Book (4.6.11)

[8] A Guide to Our Federal Lands (Washington: Natl. Geographic Soc., 1984) 241-47.

i. An Edition (4.6.12)

[9] Christina Rossetti, Selected Prose of Christina Rossetti, ed. David A. Kent and P. G. Stanwood (New York: St. Martin's, 1998) 121.

[10] Fredson Bowers, ed., The Red Badge of Courage: An Episode of the American Civil War, by Stephen Crane (1895; Charlottesville: UP of Virginia, 1975).

j. A Translation (4.6.13)

[11] Laura Esquivel, Like Water for Chocolate: A Novel in Monthly Installments, with Recipes, Romances, and Home Remedies, trans. Carol Christensen and Thomas Christensen (New York: Doubleday, 1992) 1-5.

k. A Book Published in a Second or Subsequent Edition (4.6.14)

[12] Geoffrey Chaucer, The Works of Geoffrey Chaucer, ed. F. W. Robinson, 2nd ed. (Boston: Houghton, 1957) 545.

l. A Multivolume Work (4.6.15)

[13] Paul Lauter et al., eds., The Heath Anthology of American Literature, 2nd ed., 2 vols. (Lexington: Heath, 1994).

[14] Arthur Conan Doyle, The Oxford Sherlock Holmes, ed. Owen Dudley Edwards, vol. 8 (New York: Oxford UP, 1993).

15 René Wellek, <u>A History of Modern Criticism, 1750-1950</u>, vol. 5 (New Haven: Yale UP, 1986) 322-26.

m. A Book in a Series (4.6.16)

16 Marshall R. Pihl, <u>The Korean Singer of Tales</u>, Harvard-Yenching Inst. Monograph Ser. 37 (Cambridge: Harvard UP, 1994) 62.

n. A Republished Book (4.6.17)

17 Margaret Atwood, <u>Surfacing</u> (1972; New York: Doubleday, 1998) 209-12.

o. A Publisher's Imprint (4.6.18)

18 Phillip Lopate, ed., <u>The Art of the Personal Essay: An Anthology from the Classical Era to the Present</u> (New York: Anchor-Doubleday, 1994).

p. A Book with Multiple Publishers (4.6.19)

19 J. Wight Duff, <u>A Literary History of Rome: From the Origins to the Close of the Golden Age</u>, ed. A. M. Duff, 3rd ed. (1953; London: Benn; New York: Barnes, 1967) 88.

q. A Pamphlet (4.6.20)

20 <u>London</u> (New York: Trip Builder, 1996).

r. A Government Publication (4.6.21)

21 United Nations, Centre on Transnational Corporations, <u>Foreign Direct Investment, the Service Sector, and International Banking</u> (New York: United Nations, 1987) 4-6.

s. The Published Proceedings of a Conference (4.6.22)

22 Kira Hall, Michael Meacham, and Richard Shapiro, eds., <u>Proceedings of the Fifteenth Annual Meeting of the Berkeley Linguistics Society, February 18-20, 1989: General Session and Parasession on Theoretical Issues in</u>

Language Reconstruction (Berkeley: Berkeley Linguistics
Soc., 1989).

t. A Book in a Language Other Than English (4.6.23)

[23] Emanuel Poche, Prazské Palace (Praha [Prague]:
Odeon, 1977) 1-5.

u. A Book Published before 1900 (4.6.24)

[24] John Dewey, The School and Society (Chicago,
1899) 104.

v. A Book without Stated Publication Information or Pagination (4.6.25)

[25] Zvi Malachi, ed., Proceedings of the
International Conference on Literary and Linguistic
Computing ([Tel Aviv]: [Fac. of Humanities, Tel Aviv U],
n.d.).

w. An Unpublished Dissertation (4.6.26)

[26] Carol Sakala, "Maternity Care Policy in the
United States: Toward a More Rational and Effective
System," diss., Boston U, 1993, 34.

x. A Published Dissertation (4.6.27)

[27] Rudolf F. Dietze, Ralph Ellison: The Genesis of
an Artist, diss., U Erlangen-Nürnberg, 1982, Erlanger
Beiträge zur Sprach- und Kunstwissenschaft 70 (Nürnberg:
Carl, 1982) 168.

B.1.6. Sample First Note References: Articles and Other Publications in Periodicals

For additional information on citing the following types of sources,
consult the related sections on bibliographic entries, indicated in
parentheses after the headings.

a. An Article in a Scholarly Journal with Continuous Pagination (4.7.1)

[1] Andrea Most, "'We Know We Belong to the Land': The Theatricality of Assimilation in Rodgers and Hammerstein's Oklahoma!," PMLA 113 (1998): 77.

b. An Article in a Scholarly Journal That Pages Each Issue Separately (4.7.2)

[2] Frederick Barthelme, "Architecture," Kansas Quarterly 13.3-4 (1981): 77-78.

c. An Article in a Scholarly Journal That Uses Only Issue Numbers (4.7.3)

[3] Marisa Lajolo, "The Female Reader on Trial," Brasil 14 (1995): 75-76.

d. An Article in a Scholarly Journal with More Than One Series (4.7.4)

[4] John Daniels, "Indian Population of North America in 1492," William and Mary Quarterly 3rd ser. 49 (1992): 300-02.

[5] Kathleen Spivack, "Between Two Cultures," Kenyon Review ns 17.3-4 (1995): 119-21.

e. An Article in a Newspaper (4.7.5)

[6] Trish Hall, "IQ Scores Are Up, and Psychologists Wonder Why," New York Times 24 Feb. 1998, late ed.: F1.

[7] Salem Alaton, "So, Did They Live Happily Ever After?," Globe and Mail [Toronto] 27 Dec. 1997: D2.

f. An Article in a Magazine (4.7.6)

[8] Mihaly Csikszentmihalyi, "The Creative Personality," Psychology Today July-Aug. 1996: 40.

g. A Review (4.7.7)

[9] John Updike, "Fine Points," rev. of The New Fowler's Modern English Usage, ed. R. W. Burchfield, New Yorker 23-30 Dec. 1996: 142-43.

[10] Thomas J. Socha, rev. of <u>Learning the Rules: The Anatomy of Children's Relationships</u>, by B. J. Bigelow, G. Tesson, and J. H. Lewko, <u>Communication Education</u> 47 (1998): 92.

[11] "The Cooling of an Admiration," rev. of <u>Pound/Joyce: The Letters of Ezra Pound to James Joyce, with Pound's Essays on Joyce</u>, ed. Forrest Read, <u>Times Literary Supplement</u> 6 Mar. 1969: 239-40.

[12] Rev. of <u>Anthology of Danish Literature</u>, ed. F. J. Billeskov Jansen and P. M. Mitchell, <u>Times Literary Supplement</u> 7 July 1972: 785.

h. An Abstract in an Abstracts Journal (4.7.8)

[13] Carol Sakala, "Maternity Care Policy in the United States: Toward a More Rational and Effective System," diss., Boston U, 1993, <u>DAI</u> 54 (1993): 1360B.

i. An Anonymous Article (4.7.9)

[14] "The Decade of the Spy," <u>Newsweek</u> 7 Mar. 1994: 26-27.

j. An Editorial (4.7.10)

[15] "Death of a Writer," editorial, <u>New York Times</u> 20 Apr. 1994, late ed.: A18.

k. A Letter to the Editor (4.7.11)

[16] Cynthia Ozick, letter, <u>Partisan Review</u> 57 (1990): 493-94.

l. A Serialized Article (4.7.12)

[17] Harrison T. Meserole and James M. Rambeau, "Articles on American Literature Appearing in Current Periodicals," <u>American Literature</u> 52 (1981): 704-05; 53 (1981): 164-66.

[18] Deborah Sontag, "A Mexican Town That Transcends All Borders," <u>New York Times</u> 21 July 1998, late ed.: A1;

pt. 3 of a series, Here and There: Immigration Now, begun 19 July 1998.

m. A Special Issue (4.7.13)

[19] Kwame Anthony Appiah and Henry Louis Gates, Jr., eds., <u>Identities</u>, spec. issue of <u>Critical Inquiry</u> 18.4 (1992): 625-884 (Chicago: U of Chicago P, 1995).

[20] <u>Science and Culture</u>, spec. issue of <u>Daedalus</u> 127.1 (1998): 1-236.

[21] Christiane Makward, "Reading Maryse Condé's Theater," <u>Maryse Condé</u>, ed. Delphine Perret and Marie-Denise Shelton, spec. issue of <u>Callaloo</u> 18.3 (1995): 681-82.

n. An Article in a Microform Collection of Articles (4.7.14)

[22] Dan Chapman, "Panel Could Help Protect Children," <u>Winston-Salem Journal</u> 14 Jan. 1990: 14, <u>NewsBank: Welfare and Social Problems</u> 12 (1990): fiche 1, grids A8-11.

o. An Article Reprinted in a Loose-Leaf Collection of Articles (4.7.15)

[23] Brad Edmondson, "AIDS and Aging," <u>American Demographics</u> Mar. 1990: 28+, <u>The AIDS Crisis</u>, ed. Eleanor Goldstein, vol. 2 (Boca Raton: SIRS, 1991) art. 24.

B.1.7. Sample First Note References: Miscellaneous Print and Nonprint Sources

For additional information on the following types of documentation, consult the related sections on bibliographic entries, indicated in parentheses after the headings.

a. A Television or Radio Program (4.8.1)

[1] "Frankenstein: The Making of the Monster," Great Books, narr. Donald Sutherland, writ. Eugenie Vink, dir. Jonathan Ward, Learning Channel, 8 Sept. 1993.

b. A Sound Recording (4.8.2)

[2] Roger Norrington, cond., Symphony no. 1 in C, op. 21, and Symphony no. 6 in F, op. 68, by Ludwig van Beethoven, London Classical Players, EMI, 1988.

[3] Billie Holiday, "God Bless the Child," rec. 9 May 1941, The Essence of Billie Holiday, Columbia, 1991.

[4] George C. Scott, narr., World War II, audiocassette, Carmichael, 1990.

[5] D. K. Wilgus, Southern Folk Tales, rec. 23-25 Mar. 1965, audiotape, U of California, Los Angeles, Archives of Folklore, B.76.82.

[6] David Lewiston, liner notes, The Balinese Gamelan: Music from the Morning of the World, LP, Nonesuch, n.d.

c. A Film or Video Recording (4.8.3)

[7] It's a Wonderful Life, dir. Frank Capra, perf. James Stewart, Donna Reed, Lionel Barrymore, and Thomas Mitchell, RKO, 1946.

[8] Rudolph Nureyev, chor., Swan Lake, by Pyotr Ilich Tchaikovsky, perf. Margot Fonteyn and Nureyev, Vienna State Opera Ballet, Vienna Symphony Orch., cond. John Lanchbery, 1966, DVD, Philips, 1997.

[9] Looking at Our Earth: A Visual Dictionary, sound filmstrip, Natl. Geographic Educ. Services, 1992.

d. A Performance (4.8.4)

[10] Diana Rigg, actor, Medea, by Euripides, trans. Alistair Elliot, dir. Jonathan Kent, Longacre Theatre, New York, 7 Apr. 1994.

[11] Scott Joplin, Treemonisha, dir. Frank Corsaro, cond. Gunther Schuller, perf. Carmen Balthrop, Betty

Allen, and Curtis Rayam, Houston Grand Opera, Miller
Theatre, Houston, 18 May 1975.

e. A Musical Composition (4.8.5)

[12] Ludwig van Beethoven, Symphony no. 8 in F,
op. 93.

f. A Painting, Sculpture, or Photograph (4.8.6)

[13] Rembrandt van Rijn, <u>Aristotle Contemplating the
Bust of Homer</u>, Metropolitan Museum of Art, New York.

[14] Mary Cassatt, <u>Mother and Child</u>, Wichita Art
Museum, <u>American Painting: 1560-1913</u>, by John Pearce
(New York: McGraw, 1964) slide 22.

g. An Interview (4.8.7)

[15] Federico Fellini, "The Long Interview," <u>Juliet of
the Spirits</u>, ed. Tullio Kezich, trans. Howard Greenfield
(New York: Ballantine, 1966) 56.

[16] Ralph Nader, interview with Ray Suarez, <u>Talk of
the Nation</u>, Natl. Public Radio, WBUR, Boston, 16 Apr.
1998.

[17] I. M. Pei, personal interview, 22 July 1993.

h. A Map or Chart (4.8.8)

[18] <u>Washington</u>, map (Chicago: Rand, 1995).

[19] <u>Japanese Fundamentals</u>, chart (Hauppauge: Barron,
1992).

i. A Cartoon (4.8.9)

[20] Roz Chast, cartoon, <u>New Yorker</u> 7 Apr. 1997: 72.

[21] Garry Trudeau, "Doonesbury," cartoon, <u>Star-Ledger</u>
[Newark] 17 June 1998: 23.

j. An Advertisement (4.8.10)

[22] The Fitness Fragrance by Ralph Lauren,
advertisement, <u>GQ</u> Apr. 1997: 111-12.

k. A Lecture, a Speech, an Address, or a Reading (4.8.11)

[23] Margaret Atwood, "Silencing the Scream," Boundaries of the Imagination Forum, MLA Convention, Royal York Hotel, Toronto, 29 Dec. 1993.

[24] Studs Terkel, address, Conf. on Coll. Composition and Communication Convention, Palmer House, Chicago, 22 Mar. 1990.

l. A Manuscript or Typescript (4.8.12)

[25] Mark Twain, notebook 32, ts., Mark Twain Papers, U of California, Berkeley, 50.

m. A Letter or Memo (4.8.13)

[26] Virginia Woolf, "To T. S. Eliot," 28 July 1920, letter 1138 of The Letters of Virginia Woolf, ed. Nigel Nicolson and Joanne Trautmann, vol. 2 (New York: Harcourt, 1976) 437-38.

[27] Thomas Hart Benton, letter to Charles Fremont, 22 June 1847, John Charles Fremont Papers, Southwest Museum Lib., Los Angeles.

[28] Toni Morrison, letter to the author, 17 May 1999.

[29] Daniel J. Cahill, memo to English dept. fac., Brooklyn Technical High School, New York, 1 June 1998.

n. A Legal Source (4.8.14)

[30] Stevens v. National Broadcasting Co., 148 USPQ 755, CA Super. Ct., 1966.

B.1.8. Sample First Note References: Electronic Publications

For additional information on citing the following types of sources, consult the related sections on bibliographic entries, indicated in parentheses after the headings.

a. An Online Scholarly Project, Information Database, or Professional or Personal Site (4.9.2)

[1] Britannica Online, vers. 98.2, Apr. 1998, Encyclopaedia Britannica, 8 May 1998 <http://www.eb.com/>.

[2] The Cinderella Project, ed. Michael N. Salda, vers. 1.1, Dec. 1997, De Grummond Children's Lit. Research Collection, U of Southern Mississippi, 15 Apr. 1998 <http://www-dept.usm.edu/~engdept/cinderella/cinderella.html>.

[3] "Catalán," Sí, España, ed. José Félix Barrio, vers. 2.0, Oct. 1996, Embassy of Spain, Ottawa, 3 Feb. 1998 <http://www.docuweb.ca/SiSpain/spanish/language/language/catalan.html>.

[4] "Selected Seventeenth-Century Events," Romantic Chronology, ed. Laura Mandell and Alan Liu, Oct. 1996, U of California, Santa Barbara, 22 June 1998 <http://humanitas.ucsb.edu/projects/pack/rom-chrono/chrono1a.htm>.

[5] Romance Languages and Literatures Home Page, 1 Jan. 1997, Dept. of Romance Langs. and Lits., U of Chicago, 8 July 1998 <http://humanities.uchicago.edu/romance/>.

b. An Online Book (4.9.3)

[6] Jane Austen, Pride and Prejudice, ed. Henry Churchyard, 1996, 10 Sept. 1998 <http://www.pemberley.com/janeinfo/pridprej.html>.

[7] Nathaniel Hawthorne, Twice-Told Tales, ed. George Parsons Lathrop (Boston: Houghton, 1883), 1 Mar. 1998 <http://eldred.ne.mediaone.net/nh/ttt.html>.

[8] E[dith] Nesbit, Ballads and Lyrics of Socialism (London, 1908), Victorian Women Writers Project, ed. Perry Willett, June 1998, Indiana U, 26 June 1998

⟨http://www.indiana.edu/~letrs/vwwp/nesbit/
ballsoc.html⟩.

[9] John Keats, "Ode on a Grecian Urn," <u>Poetical
Works</u>, 1884, <u>Project Bartleby</u>, ed. Steven van Leeuwen,
May 1998, Columbia U, 8 May 1998 ⟨http://
www.columbia.edu/acis/bartleby/keats/keats54.html⟩.

c. An Article in an Online Periodical (4.9.4)

[10] Michael Calabrese, "Between Despair and Ecstasy:
Marco Polo's Life of the Buddha," <u>Exemplaria</u> 9.1 (1997),
22 June 1998 ⟨http://web.english.ufl.edu/english/
exemplaria/calax.htm⟩.

[11] John Markoff, "The Voice on the Phone Is Not
Human, but It's Helpful," <u>New York Times on the Web</u> 21
June 1998, 25 June 1998 ⟨http://www.nytimes.com/
library/tech/98/06/biztech/articles/21voice.html⟩.

[12] Katherine Guckenberger, "A Convent with a View,"
<u>Atlantic Unbound</u> 22 Jan. 1998, 26 June 1998 ⟨http://
www.theAtlantic.com/atlantic/unbound/abroad/
kg980122.htm⟩.

[13] Gretchen V. Angelo, rev. of <u>The Book of the Body
Politic</u>, by Christine de Pizan, <u>Bryn Mawr Medieval
Review</u> 96.1.7 (1996), 26 Jan. 1997 ⟨gopher://
gopher.lib.virginia.edu:70/00/alpha/bmmr/v96/96-1-7⟩.

[14] Vern L. Bullough, "Medieval Concepts of
Adultery," <u>Arthuriana</u> 7.4 (1997): 5-15, abstract, 26
June 1998 ⟨http://dc.smu.edu/Arthuriana/Abstract/
Ab_list1.htm⟩.

[15] "Controlling Deadly Trade," editorial, <u>Christian
Science Monitor: Electronic Edition</u> 26 June 1998, 26
June 1998 ⟨http://www.csmonitor.com/durable/
1998/06/26/f-p16s1.htm⟩.

[16] Cleo Kung, letter, <u>New York Times on the Web</u> 28
June 1998, 28 June 1998 ⟨http://www.nytimes.com/
yr/mo/day/letters/1kung.html⟩.

d. A Publication on CD-ROM, Diskette, or Magnetic Tape (4.9.5)

[17] A. R. Braunmuller, ed., <u>Macbeth</u>, by William Shakespeare, CD-ROM (New York: Voyager, 1994).

[18] <u>English Poetry Full-Text Database</u>, magnetic tape, rel. 2 (Cambridge, Eng.: Chadwyck-Healey, 1993).

[19] Elaine C. Thiesmeyer and John E. Thiesmeyer, <u>Editor: A System for Checking Usage, Mechanics, Vocabulary, and Structure</u>, diskette, vers. 5.2 (New York: MLA, 1996).

[20] "Albatross," <u>The Oxford English Dictionary</u>, 2nd ed., CD-ROM (Oxford: Oxford UP, 1992).

[21] Steve Coates, "Et Tu, Cybernetica Machina User?," <u>New York Times</u> 28 Oct. 1996, late ed.: D4, <u>New York Times Ondisc</u>, CD-ROM, UMI-ProQuest, Dec. 1996.

[22] <u>Guidelines for Family Television Viewing</u> (Urbana: ERIC Clearinghouse on Elementary and Early Childhood Educ., 1990), <u>ERIC</u>, CD-ROM, SilverPlatter, June 1993.

[23] Leigh Ann Danzey, "The Price of Success: An Analysis of Funding Top Ten Men's and Women's Programs in Comparative Sports," <u>DAI</u> 58 (1997): 795A, Florida State U, 1997, <u>Dissertation Abstracts Ondisc</u>, CD-ROM, UMI-ProQuest, Mar. 1998.

[24] <u>Perseus 2.0: Interactive Sources and Studies on Ancient Greece</u>, CD-ROM, 4 discs (New Haven: Yale UP, 1996).

e. A Work in More Than One Publication Medium (4.9.6)

[25] <u>Perseus 1.0: Interactive Sources and Studies on Ancient Greece</u>, CD-ROM, laser disc (New Haven: Yale UP, 1992).

f. A Work from an Online Service (4.9.7)

[26] "Table Tennis," <u>Compton's Encyclopedia Online</u>, vers. 2.0, 1997, America Online, 4 July 1998, keyword: Compton's.

27 "Cloning," BioTech's Life and Science Dictionary,
30 June 1998, Indiana U, America Online, 4 July 1998,
path: Research and Learning; Science; Biology;
Biotechnology Dictionary.

28 Justin Fox, "What in the World Happened to
Economics?," Fortune 15 Mar. 1999: 90-102, ABI/INFORM
Global, ProQuest Direct, Regional Community Coll. Lib.,
Little Rock, 2 Mar. 1999 <http://www.umi.com/proquest/>.

g. A Work in an Indeterminate Medium (4.9.8)

29 John Bartlett, Familiar Quotations, 9th ed.
(Boston: Little, 1901), New York: Columbia U, Academic
Information Systems, 1995, electronic, ColumbiaNet,
Columbia U, 2 July 1998.

h. Other Electronic Sources (4.9.9)

30 "The Threat of Commercial Fishing," Earth
Matters, CNN, 18 Jan. 1998, transcript, Broadcast News,
CD-ROM, Primary Source Media, Jan. 1998, screen 10.

31 Franklin D. Roosevelt, "Americanism," 1920,
American Leaders Speak: Recordings from World War I and
the 1920 Election, 1996, American Memory, Lib. of
Congress, Washington, 19 Mar. 1997 <http://
lcweb2.loc.gov/mbrs/nforum/9000024.ram>.

32 F. W. Murnau, dir., Nosferatu, 1922, The Sync, 16
June 1998 <http://www.thesync.com/ram/nosferatu.ram>.

33 Hans Holbein, The Ambassadors, Microsoft Art
Gallery: The Collection of the National Gallery, London,
CD-ROM (Redmond: Microsoft, 1994).

34 Richard Price, interview with Larry Weissman,
Bold Type, June 1998, 25 June 1998 <http://
199.29.97.173/0698/price/interview.html>.

35 "Phoenix, Arizona," map, U.S. Gazetteer, US
Census Bureau, 30 June 1998 <http://www.census.gov/
cgi-bin/gazetteer>.

36 Al Cacicedo, "Private Parts: Preliminary Notes
for an Essay on Gender Identity in Shakespeare," working
paper, 12 Mar. 1997, 4 July 1998 <http://
www.arts.ubc.ca/english/iemls/shak/PRIVATE_PARTS.txt>.

37 James L. Harner, e-mail to the author, 20 Aug.
1998.

38 Wendell Piez, "Sustained Reading vs. Synchronic
Access," online posting, 23 Jan. 1997, Humanist
Discussion Group, 29 June 1998 <http://
lists.village.virginia.edu/lists_archive/Humanist/
v10/0238.html>.

39 Dene Grigar, online defense of dissertation
"Penelopeia: The Making of Penelope in Homer's Story
and Beyond," 25 July 1995, LinguaMOO, 1 July 1998
<http://wwwpub.utdallas.edu/~cynthiah/lingua_archive/
phd-defense.txt>.

40 TACT: Text-Analysis Computing Tools, vers.
2.1 gamma, 30 Apr. 1997 <gopher://
gopher.epas.utoronto.ca:70/11/cch/hum_comp/software/
TACT>.

B.1.9. Subsequent References

After fully documenting a work, use a shortened form in subsequent
notes. As in parenthetical references (see 5.2), include enough information to identify the work. The author's last name alone, followed by
the relevant page numbers, is usually adequate.

4 Frye 345-47.

If you cite two or more works by the same author — for example,
Northrop Frye's *Anatomy of Criticism* and his *The Double Vision*—
include a shortened form of the title following the author's last name
in each reference after the first.

8 Frye, Anatomy 278.

9 Frye, Double Vision 1-3.

Repeat the information even when two references in sequence refer to the same work. The abbreviations *ibid.* and *op. cit.* are not recommended.

B.2. AUTHOR-DATE SYSTEM

The author-date system, used in the social sciences and in many of the physical sciences, requires that a parenthetical reference include the author's last name, a comma, the work's year of publication, another comma, and the page reference, preceded by the abbreviation *p.* or *pp.*: "(Wilson, 1992, p. 73)." Information cited in the text is omitted from the parenthetical reference. The authoritative guide to this documentation system is the *Publication Manual of the American Psychological Association* (see the list of specialized style manuals in B.4), and the system is often called APA style.

APA and MLA bibliographic forms differ in a number of ways: in APA style, only the initials of the first and middle names are given; the year of publication, in parentheses, follows the author's name; for a book, only proper nouns and the first word of the title and of the subtitle are capitalized; the names of some publishers, such as university presses and associations, are spelled out; and the first line of the entry is indented, while the second and subsequent lines are flush with the left margin.

> Tannen, D. (1990). You just don't understand: Women and men in conversation. New York: Morrow.

If the book is edited, the abbreviation *Ed.* or *Eds.*, in parentheses, precedes the year of publication.

> Tannen, D. (Ed.). (1985). Gender and conversational interaction. New York: Oxford University Press.

If there are two or more authors, each name is reversed, and an ampersand (*&*), not the word *and*, precedes the final name.

> Durant, W., & Durant, A. (1977). A dual autobiography. New York: Simon and Schuster.

Titles of essays, book chapters, and articles in periodicals are capitalized like titles of books but are neither put in quotation marks nor underlined. Journal titles, however, are capitalized in a manner consistent with MLA capitalization style (see 2.6.1) and are underlined. The volume number, also underlined, follows the journal title and a comma; the issue number, if needed, appears in parentheses after the volume number; a comma and the inclusive page numbers for the article complete the entry.

```
        Craner, P. M. (1991). New tool for an ancient art:
    The computer and music. Computers and the Humanities,
    25, 303-13.
```

If the list of works cited includes more than one work by an author, the entries are arranged chronologically, and the author's name is repeated in each entry. If two or more works by the same author were published in a year, each is assigned a lowercase letter: "(1998a)," "(1998b)." For a multivolume work, the range of volume numbers is given in parentheses, preceded by the abbreviation *Vols.*: "(Vols. 1–4)."

The following parenthetical references and corresponding list of works cited demonstrate the author-date system.

```
Between 1968 and 1988, television coverage of
presidential elections changed dramatically (Hallin,
1992, p. 5).

Eighteenth-century England was a "humble satellite" in
the world of music and art (Durant & Durant, 1965, pp.
214-48).

Frye defined the alazon as a "self-deceiving or self-
deceived character in fiction" (1957a, p. 365).

Wellek admits in the middle of his multivolume history
of modern literary criticism, "An evolutionary history
of criticism must fail. I have come to this resigned
conclusion" (1955-92, Vol. 5, p. xxii).

There are several excellent essays in the book Sound and
Poetry (Frye, 1957b).
```

To Will and Ariel Durant, creative men and women make "history forgivable by enriching our heritage and our lives" (1977, p. 406).

Works Cited

Durant, W., & Durant, A. (1965). The age of Voltaire. New York: Simon and Schuster.

Durant, W., & Durant, A. (1977). A dual autobiography. New York: Simon and Schuster.

Frye, N. (1957a). Anatomy of criticism: Four essays. Princeton: Princeton University Press.

Frye, N. (Ed.). (1957b). Sound and poetry. New York: Columbia University Press.

Hallin, D. C. (1992). Sound bite news: Television coverage of elections, 1968-1988. Journal of Communication, 42 (2), 5-24.

Wellek, R. (1955-92). A history of modern criticism, 1750-1950. (Vols. 1-8). New Haven: Yale University Press.

B.3. NUMBER SYSTEM

Disciplines such as chemistry, mathematics, medicine, and physics use the number system, which varies from field to field (see the list of specialized style manuals by discipline in B.4). In the number system, arabic numerals designate entries in the list of works cited and appear in parenthetical documentation followed by commas and the relevant volume and page references, which are preceded by the appropriate abbreviations: "(13, Vol. 5, p. 259)." With this system, the year of publication remains at the end of the bibliographic entry, and the works are usually listed not in alphabetical order but in the order in which they are first cited in the text. Titles generally follow APA style (B.2).

But Peter Scotto has offered another view (1).

Frye defined the _alazon_ as a "self-deceiving or self-deceived character in fiction" (2, p. 365).

Wellek admits in the middle of his multivolume history of modern literary criticism, "An evolutionary history of criticism must fail. I have come to this resigned conclusion" (3, Vol. 5, p. xxii).

Eighteenth-century England was a "humble satellite" in the world of music and art (4, pp. 214-48).

To Will and Ariel Durant, creative men and women make "history forgivable by enriching our heritage and our lives" (5, p. 406).

Works Cited

1. Scotto, P. Censorship, reading, and interpretation: A case study from the Soviet Union. _PMLA_ 109 (1994): 61-70.

2. Frye, N. _Anatomy of criticism: Four essays_. Princeton: Princeton University Press, 1957.

3. Wellek, R. _A history of modern criticism, 1750-1950_. 8 vols. New Haven: Yale University Press, 1955-92.

4. Durant, W., and Durant, A. _The age of Voltaire_. New York: Simon and Schuster, 1965.

5. Durant, W., and Durant, A. _A dual autobiography_. New York: Simon and Schuster, 1977.

B.4. SPECIALIZED STYLE MANUALS

Every scholarly field has its preferred style, or set of guidelines for writing. MLA style, as presented in this manual, is widely accepted in humanities disciplines. The following manuals describe the styles of other disciplines.

Biology

Council of Biology Editors. *Scientific Style and Format: The CBE Manual for Authors, Editors, and Publishers*. By Edward J. Huth. 6th ed. Bethesda: Council of Biology Eds., 1994.

Chemistry

American Chemical Society. *The ACS Style Guide: A Manual for Authors and Editors*. By Janet S. Dodd. 2nd ed. Washington: Amer. Chemical Soc., 1997.

Geology

United States. Geological Survey. *Suggestions to Authors of the Reports of the United States Geological Survey*. 7th ed. Washington: GPO, 1991.

Linguistics

Linguistic Society of America. *LSA Bulletin*, Dec. issue, annually.

Mathematics

American Mathematical Society. *AMS Author Handbook*. Providence: Amer. Mathematical Soc., 1997.

Medicine

American Medical Association. *Manual of Style: A Guide for Authors and Editors*. By Cheryl Iverson. 9th ed. Chicago: Amer. Medical Assn., 1997.

Physics

American Institute of Physics. *Style Manual for Guidance in the Preparation of Papers*. 4th ed. New York: Amer. Inst. of Physics, 1990.

Psychology

American Psychological Association. *Publication Manual of the American Psychological Association*. 4th ed. Washington: Amer. Psychological Assn., 1994.

There are also style manuals that address primarily editors and concern procedures for preparing a manuscript for publication:

The Chicago Manual of Style. 14th ed. Chicago: U of Chicago P, 1993.

United States. Government Printing Office. *Style Manual.* Rev. ed. Washington: GPO, 1984.

Words into Type. By Marjorie E. Skillin, Robert M. Gay, et al. 3rd ed. Englewood Cliffs: Prentice, 1974. New ed. in preparation.

For other style manuals and authors' guides, see John Bruce Howell, *Style Manuals of the English-Speaking World* (Phoenix: Oryx, 1983).

SAMPLE PAGES OF
A RESEARCH PAPER
IN MLA STYLE

First Page of a Research Paper

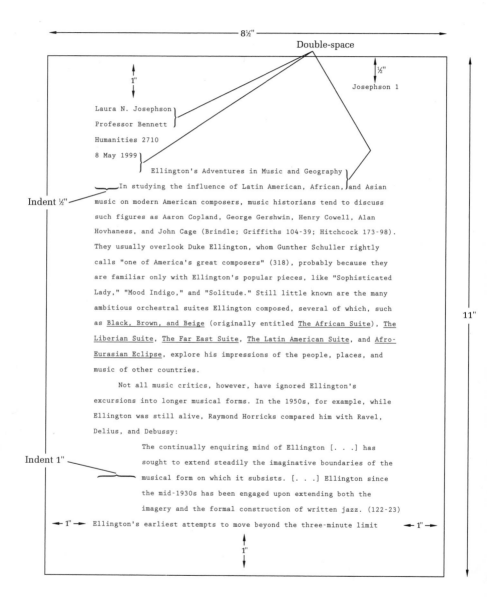

Double-space

8½"

1"

½"

Josephson 1

Laura N. Josephson

Professor Bennett

Humanities 2710

8 May 1999

Ellington's Adventures in Music and Geography

Indent ½"

In studying the influence of Latin American, African, and Asian music on modern American composers, music historians tend to discuss such figures as Aaron Copland, George Gershwin, Henry Cowell, Alan Hovhaness, and John Cage (Brindle; Griffiths 104-39; Hitchcock 173-98). They usually overlook Duke Ellington, whom Gunther Schuller rightly calls "one of America's great composers" (318), probably because they are familiar only with Ellington's popular pieces, like "Sophisticated Lady," "Mood Indigo," and "Solitude." Still little known are the many ambitious orchestral suites Ellington composed, several of which, such as <u>Black, Brown, and Beige</u> (originally entitled <u>The African Suite</u>), <u>The Liberian Suite</u>, <u>The Far East Suite</u>, <u>The Latin American Suite</u>, and <u>Afro-Eurasian Eclipse</u>, explore his impressions of the people, places, and music of other countries.

Not all music critics, however, have ignored Ellington's excursions into longer musical forms. In the 1950s, for example, while Ellington was still alive, Raymond Horricks compared him with Ravel, Delius, and Debussy:

Indent 1"

The continually enquiring mind of Ellington [. . .] has sought to extend steadily the imaginative boundaries of the musical form on which it subsists. [. . .] Ellington since the mid-1930s has been engaged upon extending both the imagery and the formal construction of written jazz. (122-23)

◄─1"─► Ellington's earliest attempts to move beyond the three-minute limit ◄─1"─►

1"

11"

First Page of a List of Works Cited

Double-space

1"

½"

Josephson 15

Works Cited

Brindle, Reginald Smith. "The Search Outwards: The Orient, Jazz,

Archaisms." The New Music: The Avant-Garde since 1945. New York:

Indent ½"

Oxford UP, 1975. 133-45.

Burnett, James. "Ellington's Place as a Composer." Gammond 141-55.

Ellington, Duke. Afro-Eurasian Eclipse. 1971. Fantasy, 1991.

---. Black, Brown, and Beige. 1945. RCA Bluebird, 1988.

---. The Far East Suite. LP. RCA, 1965.

---. The Latin American Suite. 1969. Fantasy, 1990.

---. The Liberian Suite. LP. Philips, 1947.

---. Music Is My Mistress. 1973. New York: Da Capo, 1976.

Gammond, Peter, ed. Duke Ellington: His Life and Music. 1958. New York:

Da Capo, 1977.

Griffiths, Paul. A Concise History of Avant-Garde Music: From Debussy

to Boulez. New York: Oxford UP, 1978.

Haase, John Edward. Beyond Category: The Life and Genius of Duke

Ellington. Fwd. Wynton Marsalis. New York: Simon, 1993.

Hitchcock, H. Wiley. Music in the United States: An Introduction. 2nd

ed. Englewood Cliffs: Prentice, 1974.

Horricks, Raymond. "The Orchestral Suites." Gammond 122-31.

Rattenbury, Ken. Duke Ellington, Jazz Composer. New Haven: Yale UP,

1990.

Schuller, Gunther. Early Jazz: Its Roots and Musical Development. New

York: Oxford UP, 1968.

Southern, Eileen. The Music of Black Americans: A History. 2nd ed. New

York: Norton, 1983.

Tucker, Mark, ed. The Duke Ellington Reader. New York: Oxford UP, 1993.

---. Ellington: The Early Years. Urbana: U of Illinois P, 1991.

1"

1"

11"

1"

1"

Index

dashes 2.2.5
databases, electronic
in list of works cited
on CD-ROM, diskette, mag-
netic tape 4.9.5
online 4.9.2a–b, 4.9.7
in note references B.1.8a, d, f
as research sources
access to 1.4.3b
and library catalogs 1.4.2
modem access to 1.4.2
printing or downloading from
1.4.3b–c
searching 1.4.3b–c, 1.4.4a
updating of 1.4.3b
See also CD-ROM, diskette, or
magnetic tape, publications
on; electronic publications;
online publications
dates, of access, for online sources
1.4.6b, 1.5, 4.9.1
dates, of publication
anthologies, works in 4.6.7
approximated 4.6.25
for books 4.6.1
c. (*circa*) with 4.6.25
for editions 4.6.12
for electronic publications 4.9.1
on CD-ROM, diskette, mag-
netic tape 4.9.5
online 4.9.2–4
updates 4.9.2a, 4.9.5
for multivolume works 4.6.15
not given
in list of works cited 4.6.25
in note references B.1.5v
for periodicals 4.7.1
placement of, in MLA style 4.2
pre-1900 4.6.24
for republished works 4.6.7,
4.6.17
to date 4.6.15
for works in progress 4.6.15
dates, writing of 2.5.5
abbreviations 6.2
with *AD, BC, BCE, CE* 2.5.5
as adjectives before nouns 2.5.5
capitalization
in French 2.8.1

dates, writing of, capitalization
(cont.)
in German 2.8.2
in Italian 2.8.3
in Spanish 2.8.4
centuries 2.5.5
in Italian 2.8.3
decades 2.5.5
format for 2.5.5
numerals 2.5.2
punctuation 2.2.2l–m, 2.5.5
ranges of years 2.5.6
seasons 2.2.2l
days
abbreviations for 6.2
capitalization of
in French 2.8.1
in German 2.8.2
in Italian 2.8.3
in Spanish 2.8.3
decades, writing of 2.5.5
Decameron, abbreviation for 6.7.4
decimal fractions, numerals in
2.5.2
Declaration of Independence 4.8.14
See also historical documents
deductive arguments 1.9.3
definitions, dictionary *See*
dictionary entries
degrees, academic
abbreviations for 6.4
in list of works cited 4.6.1
deuterocanonical works, abbreviations for 6.7.1
Dewey decimal classification system 1.4.4d
diagonals (/) *See* slashes
dialogue, quotations of 2.7.4
dictionaries, as reference sources
1.4.3a, 1.12
dictionary entries
in list of works cited 4.6.8
electronic sources 4.9.2a–b,
4.9.5a
in note references B.1.5f
electronic sources B.1.8a, d
in parenthetical references
5.4.4

302

medicine
documentation style in B.3
reference works for A.15
style manual for B.4
Melville, *Moby-Dick*, abbreviation
for 6.7.4
memos
in list of works cited 4.8.13
in note references B.1.7m
metapages, on Internet 1.4.6b
microcards 1.4.5 *See also* microform, publications in
microfiche 1.4.5, 4.7.14 *See also*
microform, publications in
microfilms 1.4.5 *See also* microform, publications in
microform, publications in
definition of 1.4.5
in list of works cited 4.7.14
in note references B.1.6n
style manual for citing 4.8.8
Milton, abbreviations for works of
6.7.4
misanthrope, Le, abbreviation for
6.7.4
Miss 2.4.2
mistakes, in research paper, correcting
abbreviations and symbols for
6.6
on final draft 3.8
with word processor 1.10
MLA International Bibliography
1.4.3c
MLA style 4.2, 5.1
*MLA Style Manual and Guide to
Scholarly Publishing* 2.4.1,
2.8
Moby-Dick, abbreviation for 6.7.4
models, in list of works cited 4.8.8
modifiers, restrictive vs. nonrestrictive 2.2.2e *See also* adjectives
Molière, abbreviations for works of
6.7.4
money, numerals for 2.5.2, 2.5.4
months
abbreviations of 6.2

months *(cont.)*
capitalization of
in French 2.8.1
in Italian 2.8.3
in Spanish 2.8.4
monuments, names of 2.6.5
MOOs, postings in
in list of works cited 4.9.9l
in note references B.1.8h
movies *See* films
Mr. 2.4.2
Mrs. 2.4.2
Ms. 2.4.2
MUDs, postings in
in list of works cited 4.9.9l
in note references B.1.8h
multi-, hyphen with 2.2.6h
multidisc publications
in list of works cited 4.9.5c
in note references B.1.8h
multimedia publications *See* multiple publication media,
works in
multiple authors *See under*
authors, names of
multiple publication media, works
in
in list of works cited 4.9.6
in note references B.1.8e
multiple publishers, works with
in list of works cited 4.6.19
in note references B.1.5p
multivolume works
in list of works cited 4.6.15
in note references B.1.5l
in parenthetical references
5.4.3
museums
dioramas in 4.8.8
in list of works cited 4.8.6
in note references B.1.7f
music
documentation style in field of
B.1
reference works for A.16
musical compositions
divisions of, mentioned in text
2.6.5

note references *(cont.)*
  page numbers cited in B.1.1,
    B.1.3
  books with no page numbers
    B.1.5v
  pamphlets in B.1.5q
  paperbacks in B.1.5n
  vs. parenthetical documentation
    B.1.1
  performances in B.1.7d
  periodical articles in B.1.6
    from anthologies B.1.5e
    electronic sources B.1.8c–d, f
    from reference books B.1.5f
  personal sites, online, in B.1.8a
  photographs in B.1.7f
  plays in B.1.7d
    electronic sources B.1.8a–b, d
  poetry in B.1.5e
    electronic sources B.1.8a–b, d
  postings, online, in B.1.8h
  prefaces in B.1.5g
  pre-1900 publications in B.1.5u
  proceedings of conferences in
    B.1.5s
  professional sites, online, in
    B.1.8a
  publication information, missing
    B.1.5v
  publishers, multiple, works with,
    in B.1.5p
  publishers' imprints in B.1.5o
  punctuation of B.1.3–4
  radio programs in B.1.7a
    interviews B.1.7g
  readings (oral presentations) in
    B.1.7k
    online B.1.8h
    sound recordings of B.1.7b
  recordings in
    sound B.1.7b, B.1.8h
    video B.1.7c
  reference works in B.1.5f
    electronic sources B.1.8a, d
  reprints of articles in
    anthologies B.1.5e
    on CD-ROM B.1.8d
    loose-leaf collections B.1.6o

note references, reprints of articles
  in *(cont.)*
    microform collections B.1.6n
    online databases B.1.8f
  republished books in B.1.5n
  reviews in B.1.6g
    online B.1.8c
  serialized articles in B.1.6l
    online B.1.8c
  series in
    books B.1.5m
    journals B.1.6d
    television and radio B.1.7a
  short stories in B.1.5e
    electronic sources B.1.8a–b, d
  software in B.1.8d, h
  songs in B.1.7b
  sound recordings in B.1.7b
    online B.1.8h
  special issues of journals in
    B.1.6m
  speeches in B.1.7k
    online B.1.8h
    sound recordings of B.1.7b
  subsequent references in B.1.9
  television programs in B.1.7a
    electronic sources B.1.8h
    interviews B.1.7g
    transcripts B.1.8h
  translated works in B.1.5j
  two or more works by same
    author in B.1.9
  typescripts in B.1.7l
  video recordings in B.1.7c
  volume numbers in
    journals B.1.6a–d
    multivolume books B.1.5l
  Web sites in B.1.8a–c, h
  See also endnotes and footnotes
notes
  editors' explanatory
    in list of works cited 4.6.12
    in note references B.1.5i
  with parenthetical references
    5.5
    bibliographic 5.5.2
    content 5.5.1
  for tables and illustrations 3.7

outlines, of research paper *(cont.)*
    revisions of 1.9.1, 1.10
    thesis statement in 1.9.2
    working 1.9.1
over-, hyphen with 2.2.6h

page numbers, in documentation
    commas in 2.5.3
    in list of works cited 4.6.1, 4.6.7,
        B.1.1
        abbreviations with, avoiding
            4.6.7
        anthologies, works in 4.6.7
        books with no page numbers
            4.6.25
        consecutive 4.7.6
        cross-references 4.6.10
        dictionaries 4.6.8
        encyclopedia articles 4.6.8
        interrupted page numbering
            4.7.1, 4.7.5–6
        journals 4.7.1–2
        magazines 4.7.6
        missing 4.6.25
        multivolume works 4.6.15
        newspapers 4.7.5
        nonconsecutive 4.7.6
        periodicals 4.7.1, 4.7.5–6
        placement of 4.6.1
        plus signs (+) with 4.7.1, 4.7.5
        serialized articles 4.7.12
    in note references B.1.1, B.1.3
        books with no page numbers
            B.1.5v
    numerals for
        commas in 2.5.3
        instead of words 2.5.2
        roman 2.5.7, 5.4.8
    in parenthetical references 5.1–2
        literary works 5.4.8
        multivolume works 5.4.3
        no page numbers 5.2, 5.4.2,
            5.4.8
        omitting 5.2
        parts of works 5.4.2
    in subsequent note references
        B.1.9
page numbers, of research paper
    abbreviations with, avoiding 3.6

page numbers, of research paper
    (cont.)
    for endnotes section B.1.4
    in list of works cited 4.4
    placement of 3.6, 4.4
pages, World Wide Web *See* World
    Wide Web, publications on
paintings *See* artworks
pamphlets
    in list of works cited 4.6.20
    in note references B.1.5q
    titles of 2.6.1–2
paper, for research paper 3.2
paperbacks, as republished works
    in list of works cited 4.6.17
    in note references B.1.5n
Paradise Lost, abbreviation for
    6.7.4
Paradiso, abbreviation for 6.7.4
paragraph numbers, in electronic
    publications *See* reference
    markers
paragraphs, indentation of first
    word of 3.3
paraphrasing 2.7.1
    parenthetical references for 5.4.2
parentheses 2.2.5
    abbreviations in 6.4, 6.7
    within parentheses 2.2.9
    square brackets with 2.2.9
parenthetical documentation 5
    authors' names in 5.2–3
        corporate authors 5.4.5
        initials with 5.2
        more than three authors 5.2
        multiple authors with same
            name 5.2
        one author with multiple
            works 5.4.6
        shortened names 5.2
        two or three authors 5.2
        when to include 5.3
    of Bible 5.4.8
    with ellipses 2.7.5
    of entire works 5.4.1
    guidelines for 5.1–4
    of indirect sources 5.4.7
    information required in 5.2
    of literary works 5.4.8

parenthetical documentation *(cont.)*
    of multiple works in single refer-
        ence 5.4.9
    of multivolume works 5.4.3
    notes with 5.5
    page numbers in 5.1–2
    of parts of works 5.4.2
    placement of 5.3
    of poetry 2.7.3, 5.4.8
    and punctuation 2.7.7, 5.3
        with ellipses 2.7.5
    with quotations 2.7.7, 5.3
        drama 2.7.4
        ellipses 2.7.5
        poetry 2.7.3, 5.3
        prose 2.7.2, 5.3
    readability and 5.3
    of reference works 5.2
    of religious works 5.4.8
    of sources listed by title 5.2,
        5.4.4
    volumes in 5.4.3
parts of works
    arabic numerals for 5.4.8
    mentioned in text 2.6.5
    in note references 5.4.2
path, in list of works cited 4.9.7
peer review 1.6
pen names   *See* pseudonyms
percentages, numerals vs. words for
    2.5.2, 2.5.4
performances
    in list of works cited 4.8.4
        reviews 4.7.7
    in note references B.1.7d
        reviews B.1.6g
    in parenthetical references 5.4.1,
        5.4.4
periodicals
    definition of 4.7.1
    evaluating 1.6
    finding 1.4.2–5
    in list of works cited 4.7
        a, an, the in titles 4.7.1
        on CD-ROM 4.9.5b
        microform collections 4.7.14
        online 4.9.4
        page numbering 4.7.1–2, 4.7.5
        publication dates 4.7.1

periodicals, in list of works cited
    (cont.)
        reprints 4.6.7, 4.7.14–15
        in series 4.7.4
        special issues of 4.7.13
    in note references B.1.6
    in parenthetical references
        5.4.1–2, 5.4.4
    titles of 2.6.1–2
    See also articles, periodical
periods 2.2.11
    with abbreviations 6.1
    in ellipses 2.7.5
    ending a sentence 2.2.11
    parenthetical references and
        2.7.2, 2.7.5, 2.7.7
    after quotations 2.7.5, 2.7.7
    after titles ending in quotation
        marks 2.6.4
personal sites, online
    in list of works cited 4.9.2c
    in note references B.1.8a
persons   *See* names, of persons;
        titles, of persons
philosophy, reference works for
        A.17
photocopies, of research paper 3.2
photographs
    as illustrations in research paper
        3.7
    in list of works cited
        of artworks 4.8.6
        electronic sources 4.9.9d
        personal 4.8.6
        slide programs 4.8.3
    in note references B.1.7f
phrases, punctuation of
    alternative or contrasting 2.2.2g
    introductory 2.2.2f
    restrictive vs. nonrestrictive
        2.2.2e
    in series 2.2.2b
physical sciences, documentation
        in B.2
physics
    documentation style in B.3
    reference works for A.18
    style manual for B.4
place-names   *See* names, of places

running heads, in research paper 3.6

Russian, names of persons and capitalization in 2.8

sacred writings *See* Bible; religious works

Samson Agonistes, abbreviation for 6.7.4

sayings, familiar, omitting documentation for 1.8

scenes, in plays
mentioned in text 2.6.5
numerals for 2.5.7, 5.4.8

science
documentation style in 4.2, B.3
reference works for A.21
style manuals for B.4
See also individual fields

scores, musical, in list of works cited 4.8.5

screen numbers, in list of works cited 4.9.5a

sculpture *See* artworks

searches, computer
of Internet 1.4.6b
of library catalogs 1.4.4a
of reference databases 1.4.3b–c
using Boolean logic 1.4.3c, 1.4.4a

seasons, punctuation with 2.2.2m

sections of works, mentioned in text 2.6.5

semi-, hyphen with 2.2.6h

semicolons 2.2.3
between independent clauses 2.2.3a
in online topic sequence 4.9.7
in parenthetical references 5.4.9
with quotation marks 2.7.7
in series with commas 2.2.2b, 2.2.3b

seminars, titles of 2.6.5

serialized articles
in list of works cited 4.7.12
online 4.9.4i
in note references B.1.6l
online B.1.8c

series
in list of works cited
books 4.6.1, 4.6.16
journals 4.7.4
television and radio 4.8.1
in note references
books B.1.5m
journals B.1.6d
television and radio B.1.7a
titles of 2.6.5

services, online subscription, works from
in list of works cited 4.9.7
in note references B.1.8f

sexist language, avoiding 1.11–12

Shakespeare, abbreviations for works of 6.7.2

ships, names of 2.6.2

short stories
in list of works cited 4.6.7
electronic sources 4.9.2a–b, 4.9.3a–c, 4.9.5a
in note references B.1.5e
electronic sources B.1.8a–b, d
in parenthetical references 5.4.2–3
titles of 2.6.1, 2.6.3
within titles 2.6.4

sic 2.7.6, 6.4

Sir Gawain and the Green Knight, abbreviation for 6.7.4

sites, World Wide Web *See* World Wide Web, publications on

slashes (/)
in network addresses (URLs) 4.9.1
for paired alternatives 2.2.10
in poetry quotations 2.7.3

slide programs
in list of works cited 4.8.3
in note references B.1.7c

so, comma before 2.2.2a

so-called, omitting quotation marks after 2.2.8a

social sciences
documentation style in B.2
reference works for A.22
See also individual fields